BASIC PROGRAMMING PRIMER

by
Mitchell Waite
and
Michael Pardee

Illustrated by Robert Gumpertz
Photography by John Werner

Formerly Titled
BASIC PRIMER
by Mitchell Waite and Michael Pardee

Howard W. Sams & Co., Inc.
4300 WEST 62ND ST. INDIANAPOLIS, INDIANA 46268 USA

Copyright © 1978 by Mitchell Waite and
Michael Pardee

FIRST EDITION
THIRD PRINTING—1980

All rights reserved. No part of this book shall be
reproduced, stored in a retrieval system, or
transmitted by any means, electronic, mechanical,
photocopying, recording, or otherwise, without
written permission from the publisher. No patent
liability is assumed with respect to the use of the
information contained herein. While every precaution
has been taken in the preparation of this book,
the publisher assumes no responsibility for errors
or omissions. Neither is any liability assumed for
damages resulting from the use of the information
contained herein.

International Standard Book Number: 0-672-21586-1
Library of Congress Catalog Card Number: 78-64987

Printed in the United States of America.

Preface

Less than two years ago, there was talk of a "computer revolution" that would unfold as a direct result of great strides in microelectronic technology. The philosophy, "a computer in every home," projected by some experts would spur manufacturers to produce better equipment and better products at a lower cost to the consumer.

The keyword here is "products." These are most frequently found to be specialized uses of a particular computer. This means that there is more to the product than only some electronic equipment. There is also an ever so elusive abstract, the "program." Often considered to be as costly or even more costly than the computer itself, "program products" are becoming a most sought-after commodity. It has been estimated that in two years, the demand for computer programmers will be twice that which the supply can meet. If the computer revolution does indeed reach these proportions, there will be limitless new markets created for the most diverse kinds of computer program products imaginable.

Many, if not most, of these new program products will be designed and developed using a programming language known as BASIC (used as an acronym for *B*eginners *A*ll-purpose *S*ymbolic *I*nstruction *C*ode). Originally developed at Dartmouth College and used by the students there, BASIC is the easiest programming language to learn and to apply. While considered a "high-level language" because of the powerful commands and statements it executes, it is also a "gentle language" in the way that it relates to the programmer. It does *not* require a PhD in computer science to be able to write a BASIC program. Children, in fact, probably use it better than PhD's, and are often quick to learn how to make the computer perform for them.

This book is written in such a way that readers at many different levels of computer involvement can learn BASIC in a few hours. In order to concentrate on the language we will consider the computer as a "black box" which responds to commands that we issue using BASIC. The black box has a keyboard like a typewriter, and a screen like a tv with which it can "communicate" with the "real world." Sound like a space drama? Well it can be if you program it that way. Or, what if business programs are what you are looking for? Add a simple hard-copy printer to the black box, and print mountains of reports. That is how versatile the BASIC language really is.

Through the use of many example programs, and our own recipe for presentation, we hope to arouse your interest, sharpen your wit, and hopefully open your eyes to how to write a BASIC program. (If we can put a smile on your face while you read, we'll consider it a bonus.) If you think there are things that we have left out, you're right. It was hard, but we did manage to deliberately omit several of the more advanced attributes of BASIC. We considered these areas to be outside of the intended scope of this book, and have filed them away under "good ideas for future books maybe." However we think that we have covered all of the important bases, and that you will be quite pleased when you discover that you can learn to program a computer just by reading a book.

If you happen to have a computer around, that would be nice too. We were lucky enough to have one to make sure that the programs we included in the book would really work. It happened to be one which uses a particular version of BASIC (called Microsoft basic) that may work differently from some other versions available on the market today. However, we have compared different versions for you where we thought there might be some hazy areas, but for the sake of simplicity, we have ignored the more trivial differences.

Once you have read the book, you will only need to refer back to it occasionally to make sure how some of the commands work. Realizing this, we have included a removable reference card which has condensed examples of all of the BASIC language. It is a lot easier to carry around than the book, and the reference card was actually created using a computer-based "word processing" system.

So, carry on then, and enjoy your trip into BASIC. We have enjoyed writing it, and hope that you are able to benefit from it.

MITCHELL WAITE
MICHAEL PARDEE

Contents

CHAPTER 1

BASIC BASIC 9
    What is BASIC? 9
        Many BASIC Dialects
    What Can Be Done?—BASIC Applications 11
        Business Applications—Entertainment Applications—Educational Applications—Scientific Applications
    Getting Started 17
    Your First Program 20
    Line Numbers 21
    RUN Line Number 24
    STOP and END 25
    Numbers 27
    PRINT With Commas 29
        Double Commas
    PRINT With Semicolons 32
    The Direct Mode 34
    Figuring in BASIC 35
    Exponentiation 36
    Little Variable Boxes 37
    Variable Names 41
    String Variables 42
        Concatenation
    INPUT 44
    TAB 48
    BASIC NO-NOs 50
        Reserved Words
    Putting it all Together—the Loan Program 52
    Expanding a Program 56
    Documenting Your Programs (REM) 57

CHAPTER 2

PROGRAM CONTROL 61
    The Decision Making Statements 61
        FOR...NEXT, the Programmed Loop—IF...THEN, Conditional Branches—GOTO Unconditional Branch—The Endless Loop—ON...GOTO, Indexed Branching

Enhancing the Loan Program 71
Metric Conversion Program and the Menu Concept 76
Simple Function Statements 81
    ABS, Absolute Value Function—INT, Integerize Function
    —RND, Randomize Function—Combining Functions
The Subroutine Concept 87
    ON...GOSUB, Indexed Subroutine Branching
Numeric "Round-Off" Subroutine 91
Error-Checking Subroutine 97

CHAPTER 3

GETTING ORGANIZED 103
Arrays and Subscripted Variables 103
Dimension With DIM 106
Game BASIC: TIC-TAC-TOE 110
    Remember the Rules?—Representing the Board—Representing the Men—Overall Flow of the Game—Displaying the Board—Check for a Tie—Check for a Winner—Input Players Move—Computer Move Algorithm—Finishing the Program

CHAPTER 4

ADDING MORE POWER 131
DATA and READ Statements 131
Metric Conversion Program Enhanced 135
Numeric Functions 138
    AND, OR, and NOT—SIN, COS, and ATN—EXP and LOG—SQR Function—SGN Function—MOD Function
String Functions 150
    ASC and CHR$—LEFT$, MID$ and RIGHT$—STR$ and VAL—LEN Function

CHAPTER 5

VARIATIONS 159
PEEK and POKE 159
    Controlling the External World With PEEK and POKE—Manipulating Screen Data With PEEK and POKE—Setting Controls and Options With PEEK and POKE
INP and OUT 167
CALL or USR 169
    What CALL Can Do
CSAVE and CLOAD 175
BASIC Command Aids 179
    NEW or SCRATCH—AUTO—CLEAR—CONT—DELETE—EDIT—RENUM or REN—DEBUG COMMANDS—TRACE and NOTRACE (TRON and TROFF)—DSP
Video Plotting With TAB 187
    What Is Your SIN?

APPENDIX A

NUMBERING SYSTEMS 193
    The Binary System 194
        Counting—Binary Addition and Subtraction—Binary Multiplication and Division—Representing Binary Numbers—Pulse Representation of Binary Numbers—Serial and Parallel Transmission—Negative Numbers—The Use of Complements—Two's Complement—Binary—Coded Number Representation
    Octal Number System 205
        Addition in Octal—Octal Subtraction—Octal Multiplication—Octal Division
    The Hexadecimal Systems 208
        Hexadecimal Addition—Subtraction in Hexadecimal—Hexadecimal Multiplication

APPENDIX B

ASCII CHARACTER CODES 211

APPENDIX C

WHEN PROGRAMS GET TOO BIG—SPACE-SAVING HINTS . . . 213
    Storage Allocation in Microsoft BASIC 221

APPENDIX D

WHEN PROGRAMS GET TOO SLOW—SPEED HINTS 217

APPENDIX E

BASIC LANGUAGE REFERENCE 219

APPENDIX F

BASIC GRAPHIC STATEMENTS 213

INDEX 235

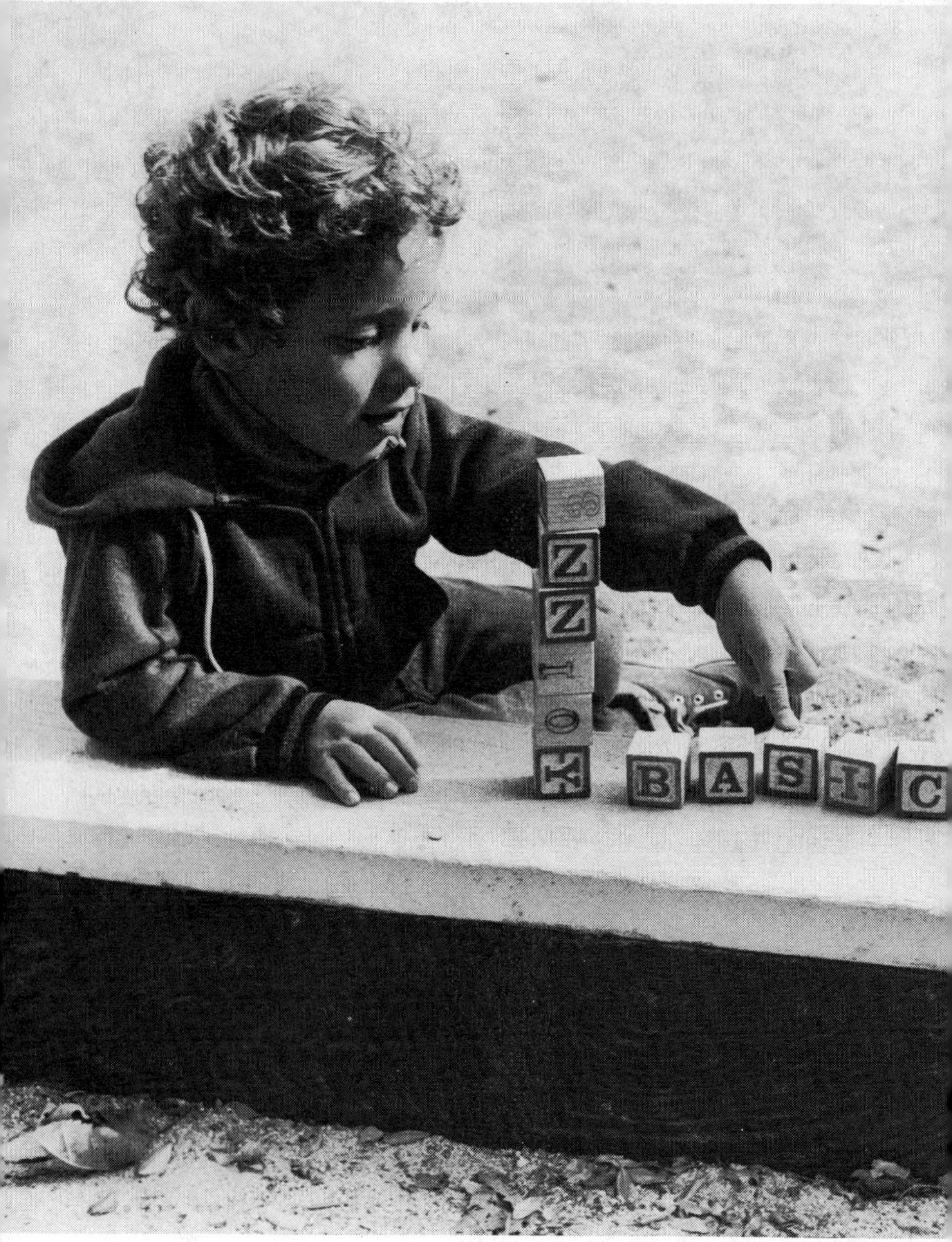
B A S I C

CHAPTER

1

Basic BASIC

WHAT IS BASIC?

BASIC is a programming language for computers. It is especially easy to learn and has quickly become the most popular language among computer users in the world today. The reason for the popularity of BASIC has to do with its origins. The language was developed at Dartmouth College so students with no background in programming could learn to use a computer. You don't need to become a computer scientist to learn how to use a computer. The BASIC language is designed for students and professionals alike. It has all the power of a computer language but is inherently simple to learn and to use.

BASIC has been called the "all purpose" computer language. This is because it can be applied in hundreds of areas ranging from the sciences to the arts to industrial control. Unlike other computer languages, BASIC can be learned outside normal teaching environments. With the recent appearance of "home" computers people have begun to learn BASIC in their homes, or at computer learning centers across the country.

BASIC is not the only language for computers being used today. Many other languages exist and each has its own particular merits and shortcomings. FORTRAN, for example, is a scientific language, used to perform advanced calculations and laboratory work. COBOL is used best in business data processing applications. And then there is SNOBOL, FOCAL, RPG, APL, PILOT, PL/M, LISP, and even versions called SUPER BASIC which are nothing more than enhanced implementations of the standard BASIC language.

Don't let the exotic abbreviations confuse you. They each mean something special about the language, but it is not necessary to know them to learn BASIC. And furthermore, none of these other languages can offer the simplicity and gentleness that makes BASIC so easy to learn.

Many BASIC Dialects

Just as there are variations of a language when spoken in different areas of a country there are several variations in the structure and content of the BASIC language. We call these differences "dialect" variations. Most of the differences are minor, and mainly due to the fact that there is no fixed "standard" for the elements of the BASIC language. Most other computer languages have been created around a government standard called the ANSI standard (American National Standards Institute) but BASIC somehow missed the boat in this area, and only a minimum report has been suggested.

Since its creation at Dartmouth College, BASIC has undergone several modifications but it still maintains its overall structure. What this means to the user of BASIC is that each manufacturer will add features to its BASIC that are not necessarily found in another version of the language. For example, manufacturer A may include commands that make it possible to use graphics with BASIC, while manufacturer B may include complex mathematical functions and leave graphics out. Or manufacturer A may allow variable names to be up to 31 characters in length while manufacturer B may only allow two-character variable names. On top of this are the differences caused by the particular computer the BASIC language is designed for. A BASIC language designed for an 8080 based microcomputer may not work on a 6502 based computer and vice-versa. And it is not usually possible to take a program written on machine A and get it to work immediately on machine B. We call this characteristic "portability." BASIC is *not* portable, like a standardized language such as FORTRAN. Another way to look at this is to say that BASIC is almost always a "machine-dependent" language.

But for the most part the differences between the various BASICs are such that they can be easily identified and worked around. To make learning BASIC as simple as possible we have set aside Chapter 5, called Variations, to explore these differences in detail. The bulk of the first four chapters deals with those features of BASIC which are most common to all those on the market today.

WHAT CAN BE DONE?—BASIC APPLICATIONS

The list of things we can program in BASIC is almost endless, but for clarity we can lump applications into four broad categories: Business, Entertainment, Education, and Science. In this section we will examine some of the types of programs we can create in each of these areas. Later in the book we will explore some of these in more detail.

Business Applications

Although BASIC was never specifically intended to be a business data processing language, it has nonetheless become a popular language for creating business solutions with the computer. Some business program applications include:

> General Ledger
> Order Processing
> Inventory Control
> Customer Billing
> Mailing Label Preparation

A *General Ledger* (or G/L for short) is a program or a group of programs that automates all the accounting needs of a company on the computer. A G/L replaces the error-prone manual method of bookkeeping. Business transactions are entered into the computer just as they would be entered into a book. They are "posted" to certain accounts, and then summarized into meaningful financial statements or reports. Financial transactions can be entered from data on check stubs, invoices, deposit slips, or may be noncash entries such as depreciation. A G/L in BASIC helps a company keep track of where its money is being spent and how to make the best use of its financial resources. It also helps to prepare income tax

11

forms at the end of the year. These G/Ls are often sold by independent software vendors in a form that can be adapted to a particular type of business.

Order Processing programs allow the user to enter customer orders into the computer and to make up shipping and billing invoices for certain products or services. A computerized Order Entry program can check inventory stock almost instantly and shipments can be made on a "same day" basis.

Inventory Control programs keep track of the number of items a company has in stock, and allow specific information about the movement of stock items to be displayed. The programs help a business maintain tight control over the volume of merchandise stored in the company warehouses. This in turn helps to increase the inventory turnover rate and save the company money.

Customer Billing programs are used to generate invoices and billing forms for a product or service. They maintain a list of customers and produce bills for these accounts on a periodic basis.

Mailing Label Preparation programs are used to produce mailing addresses for sending bills, invoices, and other data to customers or clients. A mailing label program usually involves some sorting of addresses according to ZIP code, and so on. Enormous amounts of time are saved by having the computer print the mailing labels instead of having employees do it manually.

Entertainment Applications

This is perhaps where most of the action is today in BASIC programming. Because BASIC is a relatively new language (and for a while the only language available to home and hobby computer users) literally hundreds of entertaining diversions have been created in the BASIC language. Things like General Ledgers are rather large and complex programs and thus take a longer time to appear on the market. When they do, there is usually a high cost involved. Games on the other hand are usually free and listings of BASIC game programs are available in numerous books and magazines today. All you have to do is copy the program into your computer to use it (usually with a few minor modifications).

Among the entertainment programs on the scene today are intelligent games like chess, checkers, and TIC-TAC-TOE which pit your skills against the computer. Word puzzles, mazes, and games of manual dexterity such as PONG and BREAKOUT are available. Simulation games like STARTREK allow you to command the starship Enterprise, and (with the aid of the "Ship's Computer), rid the Galaxy of evil Klingons. There are also games of chance, such as Poker, Blackjack, Backgammon. And there are "cybernetic" games like LUNAR LANDER where you use Newton's Laws of falling bodies to safely land a rocket on the surface of the moon.

Why are these computer games programmed in BASIC? Take the game of Poker. When played against a modern computer programmed in BASIC using graphics, the computer will "draw" the entire card hand so they look like real playing cards on the screen of a video terminal. In a game like Chess, a colored game board is drawn on the computer screen or television and individual pieces appear in their proper places on the board. HANGMAN word-spelling games draw a gallows and a picture of a man being "hung" as the game proceeds. STARTREK shows Klingon battle cruisers moving through a simulated star space. Phasers cause the entire screen to flash on and off.

Another use of BASIC programs that falls under entertainment are those applications that can create special sound effects and even music. Many of the home computers contain a built-in speaker. With some special BASIC instructions your programs can make an incredible array of squeaks, bonks, pops, squeals, honks, screams, and even voice synthesis. With the proper program you can "play" melodies ranging from Beethoven to the Beatles. Musicians can turn the computer into a musical "dream machine" by using it to process the sounds coming out of an instrument like a guitar or piano. (The computer serves as a super synthesizer/modifier to alter the sound structure of an instrument or to create any form of sound desired. Before you write off computers as only sophisticated toys for playing games consider the possible uses of computers and BASIC programs in the area of education.

Educational Applications

In the area of education the computer is having an overwhelming influence on the way our children learn. Computers with color graphics and music ability create educational and interactive experiences of a kind never before possible. For example, there are learning programs like COLORMATH where the computer randomly draws big colored number problems for the student to figure out, like 5 + 2 = ??. The student types in the answer to the math problem at the keyboard of the computer. If the student is correct the computer rewards him by drawing a big colored "happy face" smiling on the screen while at the same time a chorus of bright happy tones pours forth. If the student is wrong, a deep sounding "bonk" is played out and the student must try again. Sometimes the correct answer shoots darts on a video target. The closer your answer is to the real answer, the closer your dart comes to hitting center on the target. Teaching programs such as this one are valuable because they allow the student to learn while playing and keep up a large degree of interest throughout the session.

There are also BASIC educational programs that take the student through a special world where adventures are created according to how well they answer questions, riddles, or problems in history, science, and the arts. Each answer causes a specific turn of events in the adventure. These are called "Epic" computer games, and may one day play an important role in education.

BASIC programs can also be used by teachers or administrators to grade tests and make up quizzes. A BASIC computer program can dip into a special "library" of built-in problems for a course, and produce a unique test for each class or for each student. The computer can process and grade individual test scores to determine the average score, the standard deviation, and so on.

Lastly, in the area of education are those applications that teach programming itself. The experience of creating your own custom program on the computer in BASIC is an exciting one. Programming requires the skills of logic coupled with the freedom of imagination. Programming is for people who like to make things work in a logical and smooth fashion.

Scientific Applications

Computers programmed in the BASIC language have been used in scientific and laboratory environments for quite some time. Traditionally, BASIC programs are used in scientific and lab applications to perform complicated mathematical functions in a specific logical sequence to produce solutions to equations that would take years to solve by hand. BASIC programs can model the natural laws of hundreds of physical processes, and the model can be changed and studied by simply changing the program.

In what are called "real time" applications, computers programmed in BASIC can monitor, sense, and control external events such as the regulating of temperatures, the weighing of materials, or the movement of mechanical devices. Such applications usually involve some sort of "hardware interface," a device that converts signals from the "real world" to a form that the computer can deal with. You don't really need to understand the interface device to use it. As an example, a BASIC program can be designed to measure and keep track of the rotational velocity of a wind anemometer (a spinning device that measures wind speed) if a hardware interface is attached to it that produces pulses of electricity each time the anemometer turns. The computer program can count these pulses at predetermined intervals throughout the day, it can scale them to represent wind speed in miles per hour, or feet per second, and store the values inside the memory of the computer for later analysis. What is more, the program can be made to work in such a way that each time the measurement is made it takes only a few seconds of computer time and leaves the computer free to do other things.

On the other hand, a BASIC program can be made to control external events rather than simply to monitor them. Lamps can be turned on and off at predefined intervals throughout the day. Valves can be opened and closed based on some internal or external event. Motors can be turned in particular directions for specific periods of time. In fact, just about anything you can imagine that contains some kind of switch or electric power source can be controlled by

the computer. Again a hardware interface device is needed but in some cases the device may be extremely simple, such as a single relay or a single lamp. You can see that the computer is a universal kind of "programmed regulator." You can use it to regulate the flow of water to your house plants, or to regulate the flow of chemicals to an industrial process cycle.

We have seen that these four BASIC applications span an enormous range of possibilities, and BASICally the sky's the limit. In the next sections we will begin to explore how to program in BASIC.

GETTING STARTED

Let us assume that you are sitting down in front of the computer. In front of you is the computer keyboard. It looks very much like a standard typewriter keyboard. Above the keyboard is the screen of the computer. The screen is called a cathode ray tube, or crt for short. The crt is where all the information appears. A crt takes the place of typewriter paper.

If you are new to this game of computers you'll have to make sure that a couple of things are in order before you start:

1. Is the computer turned on (or, as they say, is the computer "up and running")?
2. Is BASIC ready to go and inside your computer? In some computers you have to "call" or "load" or somehow "initialize" BASIC. The instructions for doing this can usually be found inside the manual that comes with the computer.

Let us say your computer is up and running some version of BASIC. Now to get the feel of the way a computer works we can simply type in something to the computer and see what happens. Remember, BASIC is in the computer now. Suppose you type:

```
HI COMPUTER
```

When you finish typing, press the Carriage Return key. Sometimes this key is labeled RETURN, CR, or ENTER.

What happens now is that the computer will type out an error message in response to what you typed. It might look like this:

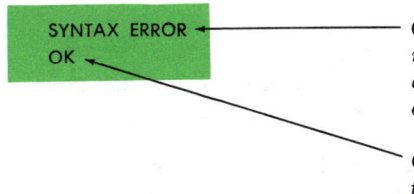

SYNTAX ERROR ◄──────── Computer types this and tells you you
OK ◄   made an error. Anything the computer
                       doesn't understand is considered an
                       error.

                       OK is also printed. It means every-
                       thing is fine with the computer and
                       it is ready to continue.

The computer typed SYNTAX ERROR because it didn't understand what we wanted it to do. The point is that computers have not yet been designed that understand plain English. So to make the computer do something we use a computer "language," like BASIC, to enter our instructions to the computer. The word OK means just that everything is all right, and the computer is ready for more work.

Understand that a SYNTAX ERROR doesn't mean you have done any harm to the computer. The computer simply ignores you until you type in something it understands, something in the vocabulary of the BASIC language.

Now let us get serious. Usually we start a session in BASIC by typing in the word:

19

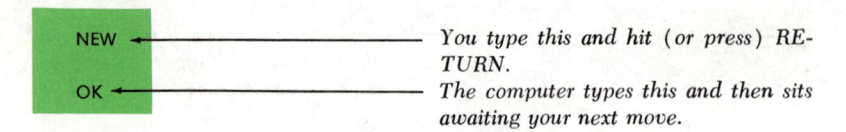

| NEW ← | ———— *You type this and hit (or press) RE-TURN.* |
| OK ← | ———— *The computer types this and then sits awaiting your next move.* |

Now any previous instructions that were in the computer memory have been "cleared" or "scratched" and the computer is ready to accept NEW instructions. The memory is the place where all the work in the computer occurs. It is where the BASIC program is kept. The memory can be erased by typing NEW so do not type NEW unless you wish to erase your program. Some computers use SCR or READY to clear out programs.

YOUR FIRST PROGRAM

Let us begin by typing in something the computer language can understand. Suppose we typed:

```
10 PRINT "ISN'T THIS NEAT"
```

When you are done, hit the RETURN key.

Now type in the word RUN and then press the RETURN key again. Here is what happens:

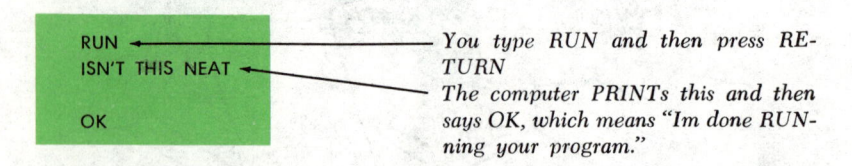

RUN ←	———— *You type RUN and then press RE-TURN*
ISN'T THIS NEAT ←	
OK	———— *The computer PRINTs this and then says OK, which means "Im done RUNning your program."*

Congratulations are now in order. You have just "entered" or typed in a "computer program" and caused the computer to RUN or "execute" your program. The program is kind of small and doesn't do anything great, but nonetheless, it is a program.

What we have done here is tell the computer to PRINT what was inside the quotation marks. Our program was the statement 10 PRINT "ISN'T THIS NEAT." We caused the program to execute once by typing RUN. The computer responded by typing ISN'T THIS NEAT and then OK to tell us it was done. The word OK is printed out after every normal execution of a BASIC program. Abnormal programs caused SYNTAX ERROR to be printed.

LINE NUMBERS

Line numbers are used so the computer can tell the order in which it is supposed to execute "statements." When you tell the computer to RUN a program, it starts by following or executing the statement or instruction with the smallest "line number." The instruction you gave to the computer is called a PRINT statement. When you typed RUN and hit RETURN, the computer responded by printing the information between the quotation marks. The information between the quotation marks is called a "string."

Here is what the pieces of the print statement are called:

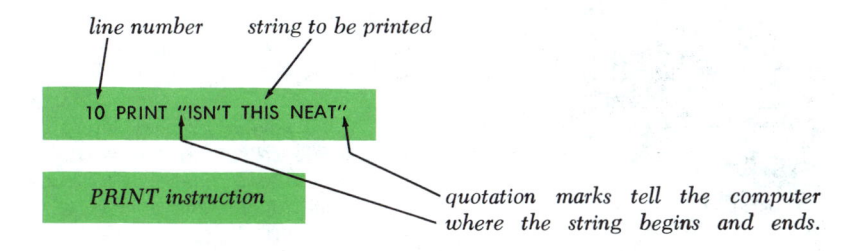

line number   *string to be printed*

10 PRINT "ISN'T THIS NEAT"

PRINT instruction

quotation marks tell the computer where the string begins and ends.

In a BASIC program, an "indirect" statement such as

10 PRINT "ISN'T THIS NEAT"

always begins with a line number. A line number may be any positive number between 0 and 65529 although on some computers line numbers are limited to between 1 and 9999 or 0 and 32767. Thus to make it possible for your program to run on many different versions of BASIC use line numbers between 1 and 9999. In our example we used 10 as the line number.

In BASIC, "direct" statements such as

NEW or RUN

are not part of the "program" and therefore do not require line numbers. Most of the statements we will learn about are "indirect" statements, the kind with line numbers. Direct statements are more in the area of programming "aids" and so we will save the bulk of them for the last chapter. Sometimes direct statements are called BASIC "commands" because they immediately command the computer to do something for us, whereas with indirect statements we must wait for the computer to RUN them.

A program is made up of several statements, each with its own unique line number. The statement with the lowest line number gets executed first. When it is finished doing or executing the first statement, it goes on to the next statement in numerical order.

For an example of how line numbers work type in this program (remember to type NEW since this is a new program) and then RUN it:

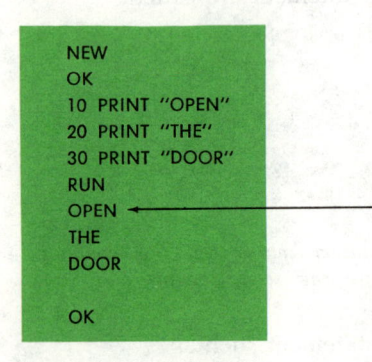

```
NEW
OK
10 PRINT "OPEN"
20 PRINT "THE"
30 PRINT "DOOR"
RUN
OPEN
THE
DOOR

OK
```

Hit RETURN after the end of each statement in the program, and also after you type RUN

First the computer executes line 10 and PRINTs OPEN. Next it goes to statement 20 and prints THE and then to the highest line number 30, and prints DOOR.

Now let us examine line numbers. First of all, to type in a program you don't have to enter in line number order. That is, you can enter line numbers in any order you want, say 30 first then 20 then 10, and the computer will put them in the proper "line number order" for you. This means we can easily insert more statements in a program already stored in the computer's memory.

Note how we numbered the statements by 10s. This clever idea makes it easy for us to add more statements between existing line numbers, i.e., up to nine more statements can be added between lines 10 and 20 and so on.

For an example of this, type in this new program. Notice how the line numbers are not entered in order:

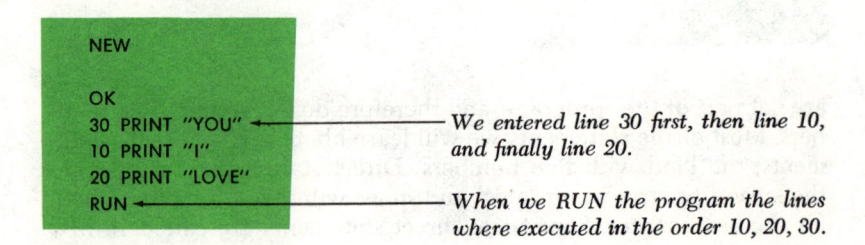

```
NEW

OK
30 PRINT "YOU"
10 PRINT "I"
20 PRINT "LOVE"
RUN
```

We entered line 30 first, then line 10, and finally line 20.

When we RUN the program the lines where executed in the order 10, 20, 30.

```
I
LOVE
YOU

OK
```

As you can see, the computer ran the program in the order dictated by the line numbers, not the order we entered them. To see how BASIC has rearranged the program statements we can use the direct statement:

```
LIST
```

What LIST does, is just what it says—it causes the program in the memory of the computer to be displayed on the screen. Try it:

```
LIST

10 PRINT "I"
20 PRINT "LOVE"
30 PRINT "YOU"
```

Note that LIST listed each statement in the program in line number order. You can LIST a program anytime the computer is not running a program. Don't forget to hit return after typing LIST.

To see how easy it is to add statements, type in the following (don't type NEW this time because we are adding to our current program):

```
15 PRINT "DON'T"
```

Now list the program to see what happens to statement 15:

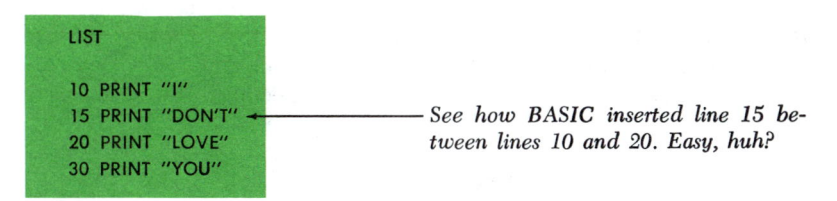

```
LIST

10 PRINT "I"
15 PRINT "DON'T"  ◄─────── See how BASIC inserted line 15 be-
20 PRINT "LOVE"              tween lines 10 and 20. Easy, huh?
30 PRINT "YOU"
```

23

```
RUN
I
DON'T
LOVE
YOU

OK
```

See how easy it is? Removing statements from your program is just as simple. To remove a statement type the line number of that statement and then press RETURN. This removes that line from the program. For example, to remove line 30 (PRINT "YOU") from our program type:

```
30 (CR)
```

The CR stands for CARRIAGE RETURN and is just to remind you to press the key. Don't type CR!

Now if we list the program with LIST, look what has happened:

```
LIST

10 PRINT "I"
15 PRINT "DON'T"
20 PRINT "LOVE"

OK
```

RUN LINE NUMBER

Sometimes we would like to RUN the program so it starts somewhere other than at the beginning line number. This comes up when you are "debugging" or testing a program. (A "bug" is a term left over from the days of World War II and secret codes. It means that something is wrong with the way the program works. Debugging is removing bugs. No DDT is required!)

In order to make a program RUN at a specific line number we would type:

    RUN line number

Where "line number" appears is the line where we want the program to start. For example, in our last program we could make it start at line 15 by typing:

    RUN 15
    DON'T
    LOVE
    OK

As you can see, the program started with line 15, then executed line 20. You can RUN at any line that actually exists in the program. But if you type RUN 50 and the line 50 does not exist, this will happen:

    RUN 50
    UNDEFINED LINE NUMBER
    OK

Since there is no line 50 in our current program in memory the computer told us so and stopped.

STOP and END

So far we've seen how to start a program, but what about stopping the program? In all our previous examples the program stopped after it executed the last statement in the last line number. Most BASICs require that you end all programs with the statement called END. In Microsoft BASIC the END statement is not mandatory, but is still useful.

END causes the computer to stop and return to the command level. (Remember, the command level is when the computer has printed out OK, and is ready for you to command it.) The END statement should usually be at the end of your program, but it can be used elsewhere in the program.

No matter where the END statement is located, as soon as it is executed the computer stops dead in its tracks. To see how END works, first LIST the current program in memory (or reenter it if it is not still in memory):

```
LIST
10 PRINT "I"
15 PRINT "DON'T"
20 PRINT "LOVE"
OK
```

Now add this statement (remember you simply type in the new line number followed by the new statement):

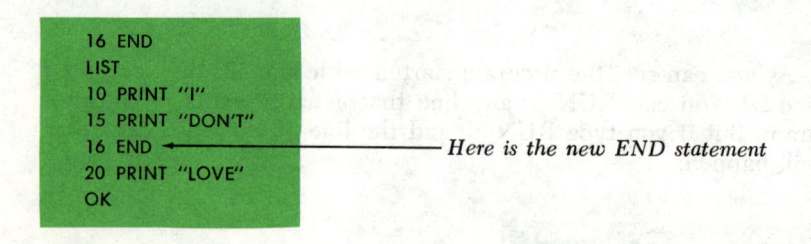

```
16 END
LIST
10 PRINT "I"
15 PRINT "DON'T"
16 END         ◄─────────── Here is the new END statement
20 PRINT "LOVE"
OK
```

```
RUN
I
DON'T
OK
```

The computer PRINTed out lines 10, 15, and then ended at line 16. LOVE never got executed.

Notice what happened here. The computer executed line 10 and PRINTed "I," executed line 15 and PRINTed "DON'T," and then found line 16 which said "END" and so the computer ended the program. This is evident by the "OK" that was printed. In general, if you come upon a program that has been running and the last thing printed on the screen was OK, then the computer is probably done and in the command mode. In fact, some computers return to the command mode and print the words READY, or DONE, or just show some kind of character like > or [. Whatever, the point is that END may appear anywhere in the program and it will cause the computer to end the program when it is executed. Normally END is at the end of the program.

There is another useful statement for terminating program execution. Enter this in place of the END statement and then RUN the program:

```
16 STOP
RUN
I
DON'T
BREAK IN 16
OK
```

What happened here is the computer found the STOP statement and, like the END statement, it stopped the computer program. However, STOP also made the computer print out "where" it stopped. BREAK IN 16 means "I stopped running your program at line 16," or in other words, the computer took a "break."

Use STOP whenever you wish the program to end prematurely. For example, during debugging you may wish the computer to stop somewhere in the middle of the program so you can isolate the part that is not working right. STOP will help you here. Or as we will see later, you can make the computer execute a STOP statement "only" if it gets into trouble.

For now keep STOP in mind as another form of END.

NUMBERS

Now we have learned that PRINT "message" causes the string enclosed by the quote marks to be printed on the screen. BASIC can also handle numbers with considerable ease. Enter this program and RUN it:

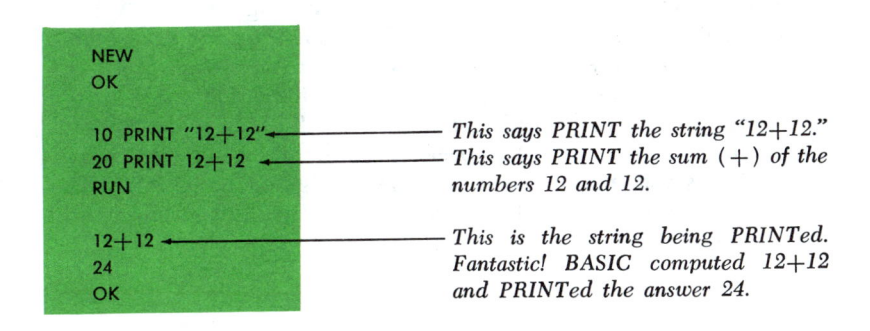

```
NEW
OK

10 PRINT "12+12"          ← This says PRINT the string "12+12."
20 PRINT 12+12            ← This says PRINT the sum (+) of the
RUN                          numbers 12 and 12.

12+12                     ← This is the string being PRINTed.
24                           Fantastic! BASIC computed 12+12
OK                           and PRINTed the answer 24.
```

Note in this program we have done something new. The statement PRINT 12+12 has NO quote marks around it. When the statement was executed it calculated 12+12 and printed out 24. Or as is said in computer talk, the computer "evaluated the expression" and PRINTed the results.

BASIC can perform the kind of arithmetic found on a standard pocket calculator. Here are some rules about BASIC arithmetic:

- Too ADD on the computer use +
- To SUBTRACT on the computer use −
- To MULTIPLY on the computer use *
- To DIVIDE on the computer use /

In programming we call these four symbols (+ − * /) the BASIC "arithmetic operators." The operators operate on numbers. Try typing in this program:

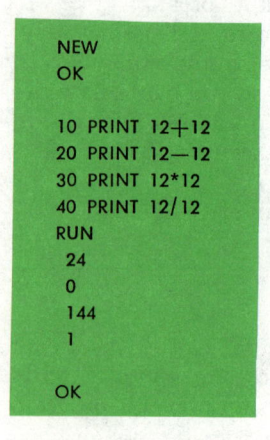

```
NEW
OK

10 PRINT 12+12
20 PRINT 12—12
30 PRINT 12*12
40 PRINT 12/12
RUN
 24
 0
 144
 1

OK
```

There are several things to notice about this program. First BASIC printed out the results of four expressions, one after the other. Note that the numbers are printed with a space in front of each. This can be seen by the fact that the answers are shifted one space to the right of the RUN command and the word OK. This space contains the "sign" of the number, but because the numbers are all positive, the + sign is not printed. The only time the sign of the number actually gets printed is when the number is negative. For example, add this statement and RUN the program:

```
50 PRINT 12—13
RUN

 24
 0
```

```
144
1
−1
```

Here the answer to PRINT 12−13 is −1 and the − sign got printed. The rule is: if the number is positive (greater than one) then a space is made for an "invisible" plus (+) sign. On the other hand if the number is negative (less than one) then a minus (−) sign is printed in front of the number.

PRINT WITH COMMAS

Let us take our knowledge a little further with PRINT and calculations. Try typing in this program and RUN it:

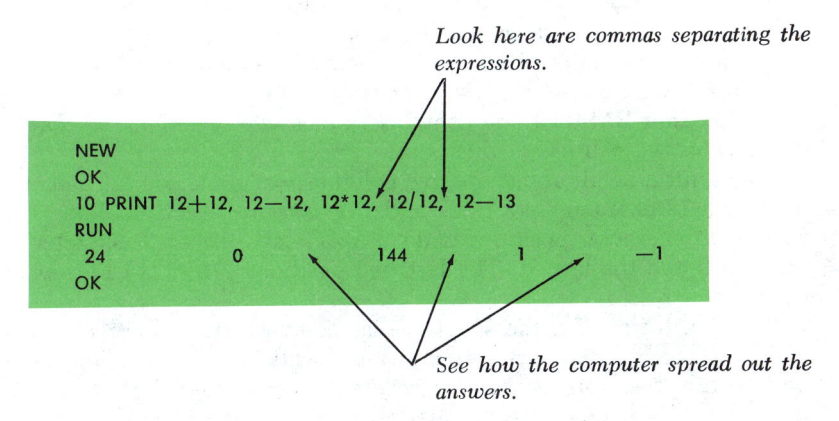

Look here are commas separating the expressions.

```
NEW
OK
10 PRINT 12+12, 12−12, 12*12, 12/12, 12−13
RUN
 24        0         144        1        −1
OK
```

See how the computer spread out the answers.

This time we entered five expressions all in a single PRINT statement, using "commas" to separate them. You can see from the RUN of the program that the commas caused the results to be spread across the screen with lots of space being inserted between the answers.

Commas make our answers look pretty by spreading them across the page neatly and precisely. The computer takes care of the spacing for us. Take a whack at this program, type it in, and RUN it.

```
NEW

OK
10 PRINT
20 PRINT "TIMES SEVEN TABLE"
30 PRINT 7*1, 7*2, 7*3, 7*4, 7*5, 7*6, 7*7, 7*8, 7*9
```

```
RUN
TIMES SEVEN TABLE
 7             14            21            28            35
 42            49            56            63
OK
```

There are several new things to notice about this program and the results that were printed. As you can see, using commas to separate items of expressions in a single PRINT statement gives you five "columns," "places," or "print zones" across the line.

Also when we exceed the number of columns in a line, the computer simply overflows the additional information onto the columns on the next line.

On most computers a "line" is defined as having 72 "character positions," where a character is any number, letter, symbol, or single space. Some computer terminals have 80 character lines, some have 64, some 40, and so on. In any case, you can consult your manual to find out what is true for your computer.

In Microsoft BASIC a line contains 72 character positions, so that is the value we will use in this book.

Now a little detail about the five columns, or "print zones." Since there are 72 character positions and five columns, each column is exactly 14 character positions wide. BASIC calls the first character position 0 and the last 71. The last two positions (70 & 71) are not used.

To get a feeling for the spacing that commas cause, here is the output of our previous program printed with a row of numbers underneath it so you can see where the commas cause the answers to be PRINTed. Read the numbers we printed up and down, like this: 2 means 20, 5 means 56, and so on.

    0   6
Here is the output of the program:

```
 7             14            21            28            35
 42            49            56            63
01234567891111111111222222222233333333334444444444555555555566666666667 7
          01234567890123456789012345678901234567890123456789012345678901
          ↑             ↑             ↑             ↑             ↑
Col one       Col two       Col three     Col four      Col five
```

As you can see by the numbers below the output, the columns start in positions 0, 14, 28, 42, and 56. When you look at how the actual numbers get printed you can see that the number always has a leading blank space in front of it. The blank is the space for the assumed plus sign.

Note how numbers start in the left hand edge of the column, and expand to the right as the number of digits increase. In computer talk we say the numbers are "left justified."

Now we know a little about making our numeric answers look pretty. But guess what . . . commas work with strings as well as numbers.

Type in this new program:

```
NEW

OK
10 PRINT "JOHN", "HARRY", "JOE", "FRANK", "BILL"
RUN
JOHN          HARRY         JOE           FRANK         BILL

OK
```

See how the computer spread out the strings. Like numbers, the strings begin in successive columns. The first word starts in print position 0, the next at 14, and so on.

Does this ability to columnize suggest anything to you? How about using strings with commas to label the columns and then use expressions in a PRINT statement with commas so the values come out under the desired string labels. Try this program:

```
NEW
OK
10 PRINT
20 PRINT "RATE=$11 PER HOUR"
30 PRINT "$/HR", "$ PER DAY", "$ PER WEEK", "$ PER MONTH", "$ PER YEAR"
40 PRINT 11, 11*8, 11*40, 11*40*4, 11*40*52
RUN

RATE=$11 PER HOUR
 $/HR          $ PER DAY    $ PER WEEK    $ PER MONTH  $ PER YEAR
 11            88           440           1760         22880
OK
```

Pretty neat but not very useful yet. This does give us an idea of how we can "columnize" the results of our programs. Notice statement 10 (10 PRINT). This makes the computer move down one line and puts space between the word RUN and the beginning of

31

the program output. If you wish more spacing simply add more PRINT statements, like this:

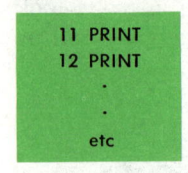

```
11 PRINT
12 PRINT
    .
    .
    .
   etc
```

Line 20 (20 PRINT "RATE=$11 PER HOUR") causes the computer to print out the message about the amount of the hourly rate used in the rest of the program. Line 30 prints out the titles or labels for the columns. Line 40 evaluates the five expressions based on the $11 hourly rate and prints out the results under the proper columns. That's it!

Double Commas

You can use all the commas you want in a PRINT statement and each will simply cause the computer to move a column to the right before displaying. Try this:

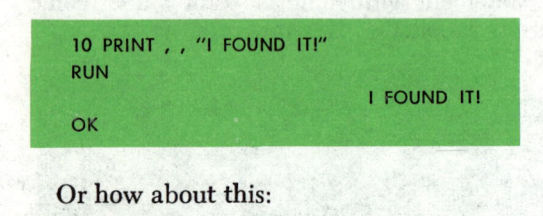

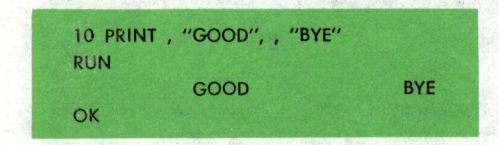

```
10 PRINT , , "I FOUND IT!"
RUN
                        I FOUND IT!
OK
```

Or how about this:

```
10 PRINT , "GOOD", , "BYE"
RUN
            GOOD            BYE
OK
```

PRINT WITH SEMICOLONS

Commas are used to put our output in precise predefined columns. The semicolon has a different but similar use. Type in and RUN this new program:

```
NEW

OK
10 PRINT "LARRY"; "MOE"; "CURLY JOE"
RUN
LARRYMOECURLY JOE
OK
```

Here we typed in three famous names with semicolons between them instead of commas.
The results show the computer simply printed them with no intervening spaces.

As you can see in our program, the semicolon was used instead of the comma. Instead of printing the results in columns, the computer PRINTed the three names as one string of characters. Try changing the program like this:

```
10 PRINT "   LARRY"; "   MOE"; "   CURLY JOE"
RUN
   LARRY   MOE   CURLY JOE
OK
```

In this example we change line 10 so that each name contains three blank spaces before the name. Since the semicolon forces the output to be squeezed together, the blank spaces are counted as characters and separate the individual names so we can read them more easily now.

We can mix strings with numbers. Try typing in and RUNning this program:

```
NEW

OK
10 PRINT "10 + 10 = "; 10+10
RUN
10 + 10 = 20
OK
```

Can you figure out how this works? Here is a diagram of the statement:

33

This is a string enclosed by quotation marks. The computer doesn't evaluate arithmetic inside of strings.

The computer does evaluate this (10 +10) because it isn't enclosed by quotation marks and is therefore not a string.

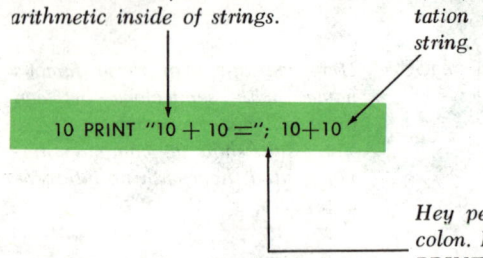

```
10 PRINT "10 + 10 ="; 10+10
```

Hey people, this is the famous semicolon. It says to print the parts of the PRINT statement close together.

That is enough about semicolons for now. Throughout the book we will see how they can come to the rescue to make our programming life "more better."

PRETTY PRINT

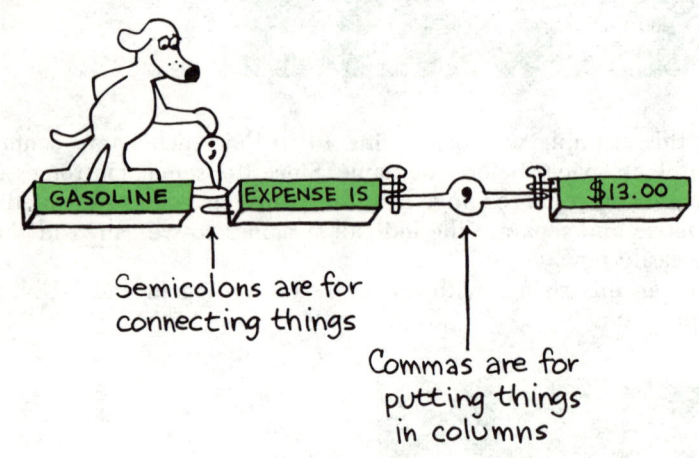

Semicolons are for connecting things

Commas are for putting things in columns

THE DIRECT MODE

So far we have been using BASIC in the indirect or program mode. That is, we enter a statement with a line number, then type RUN to execute the program statement. Another way to make statements work is to just type the statement in without a line number. Then it will do what you typed immediately after you hit the RETURN key. We call this the immediate or direct mode. Try this example:

```
PRINT "HI IM A COMPUTER"
HI IM A COMPUTER
OK
```

Notice there is no line number. When we hit RETURN the string HI IM A COMPUTER printed immediately; Note we didn't type RUN.

Now try this:

```
PRINT 2*2*2*2
16
OK
```

Again we entered the statement without a line number. BASIC understood this to mean "execute the expression 2*2*2*2 immediately and display the result."

We can use the direct mode often in our programming. A good example of its use is to see how the BASIC arithmetic operators work together in figuring out an expression.

FIGURING IN BASIC

Try this program in the "direct mode":

```
PRINT 3+3*4
15
OK
```
— *Direct mode has no line number.*

Now try this slightly different version of the same expression:

```
PRINT (3+3)*4
24
OK
```

There are a few things to note here. In the first statement, the computer multiplied before it added, even though the + sign came before the * sign. In the second statement we used left and right parentheses to make the addition happen before we multiply. We say multiplication has precedence over addition and subtraction. Parentheses override these precedences of BASIC. Try this:

```
PRINT 3+3/2—1
3.5
OK
```

and then this:

```
PRINT (3+3)/2—1
2
OK
```

Like multiplication, division (/) occurs before addition or subtraction. Here is a final example:

```
PRINT 4*4/2/2
4
OK
```

Here the operators are * and /. These operators have "equal" precedence, and in this case BASIC evaluates the expression from left to right. In our example BASIC multiplies 4*4, divides by 2 to get 8 and divides by 2 again to get 4. That's it!

EXPONENTIATION

There is a special arithmetic operator in BASIC for raising a number to a power. Try these two programs in the direct mode:

```
PRINT 2*2*2*2*2
32
OK

PRINT 2^5
32
OK
```

The two statements do the same thing. The symbol is called the circumflex character. On some computers it is an "up-arrow" symbol. As you can see in the second example, it means multiply a number by itself as many times as specified by the number after the symbol. Now try this:

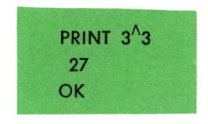

```
PRINT 3^3
27
OK
```

Obviously this is the same as 3*3*3, or 27. We call the operation caused by the ^ operator "exponentiation," or raising a number to a power. In this last example we say 3 raised to the third power. Here is 4 raised to the second power:

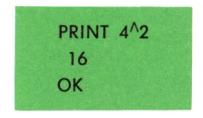

```
PRINT 4^2
16
OK
```

We will see more of the exponentiation operator later.

LITTLE VARIABLE BOXES

Imagine for a moment that way down inside the computer are stacks of tiny boxes. Each box has two compartments. The left side of the box can hold a number called the "value of the variable." Things look like this:

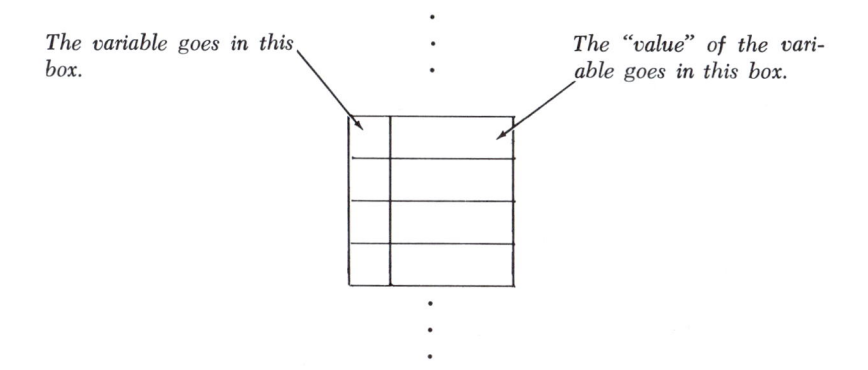

The variable goes in this box.

The "value" of the variable goes in this box.

The dots here and above mean the memory continues, and this is just four of many compartments.

37

Take a look at the little boxes below. Some of the boxes have the variable labels filled in, and with values "assigned" to the variables. We have LET variable B have the value 12. That means the value 12 is placed in the box called B, or in simple terms B=12. Variable X is assigned the value of −4.5, or X=−4.5. And similarly the variable Q is assigned the value of 102 in the last box.

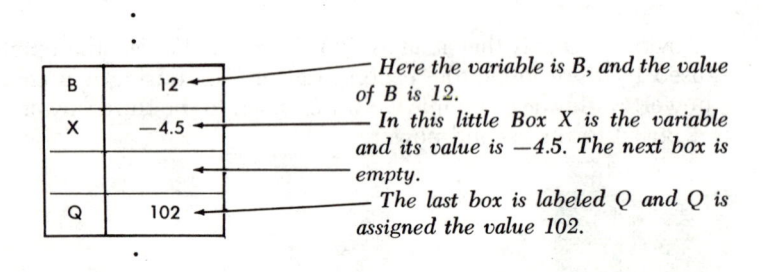

B	12
X	−4.5
Q	102

Here the variable is B, and the value of B is 12.
In this little Box X is the variable and its value is −4.5. The next box is empty.
The last box is labeled Q and Q is assigned the value 102.

Now we will learn a way to get the computer to fill in the little boxes; that is, to assign values to variables.
Try this program:

```
10 LET A=64
20 PRINT A
RUN
 64
OK
```

When we ran the program a little box was set up by the LET statement (line 10) and the statement assigned, or "Let," the variable A have the value 64.
Now the box looks like this:

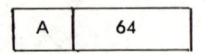

| A | 64 |

Change statement 10 to this:

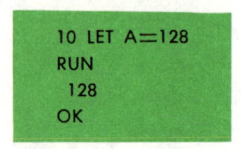

```
10 LET A=128
RUN
 128
OK
```

Now see by changing the value assigned to the variable A to 128 we also changed the value in the little box and when we went PRINT A the new value of 128 got printed. The box looks like this now:

| A | 128 |

You can have one value in the box at a time. The new value replaces the old value.

Let us try a little program that shows off how LET is used. Enter and RUN this program:

```
NEW

OK
10 LET A=5
20 Let B=10
30 LET C=15
40 LET D=(A+B+C)/3
50 PRINT "THE AVERAGE IS"; D
RUN
THE AVERAGE IS 10
OK
```

Here we used three LET statements to assign values to the three variables A, B, and C. Statement 40 added them together and divided the sum by 3 to obtain the average and then the LET statement assigned the result to the variable D. Statement 50 printed out the message THE AVERAGE IS and printed the value assigned to D. The boxes look like this before line 40 is executed:

A	5
B	10
C	15

Remember these are just four of the many boxes we can use for storing variables and values.

After we calculate the average and a value for the variable D, things look like the example at the top of the next page:

39

A	5
B	10
C	15
D	10

Hey, look at this, here is our new variable D and its calculated value 10!

As you can see D has its own little box now and the value we calculated and assigned to D is in the box (10).

Here is another practice using LET:

```
10 LET X=2
20 LET Y=10
30 LET Z=X^Y
40 PRINT "X", "Y", "X^Y"
50 PRINT X, Y, Z
RUN
X          Y          X^Y
2          10         1024
OK
```

Here we used the LET statement to create and assign values to the variables X and Y. Statement 30 (LET Z=X^Y) multiplies X by itself Y times. In this example since X equals 2 and Y equals 10, the value of X^Y is:

$$2*2*2*2*2*2*2*2*2*2 \text{ or } 1024$$

Can you see why LET Z=X^Y makes things easier for us?

Here is another fact to know about variables. Sometimes in our programs we wish to assign several variables a special value. We can do it like this:

```
10 LET P1=3.14159
20 LET C=P1
30 LET D=P1
40 LET E=P1
50 PRINT C, D, E
RUN
   3.14159          3.14159          3.14159
OK
```

Here we are assigning the same value to three variables, and the value we are assigning is itself a variable. In this the value is 3.14159 (which is pi).

VARIABLE NAMES

Thus far we used single letters to stand for variables. BASIC "lets" you use more than a single letter. Most BASICs allow a single letter and a single number for the numeric variable. (We say numeric because, as you may have wondered, there are variables for words too called string variables—which will be discussed later.) For example, these are legal numeric variables:

    A   A1   Q   Z9   I5   B0

Other BASICs, including the Microsoft BASIC we are using here, allow any length variable up to 255 characters, although only the first two characters have any significance to the computer. The first letter must always be a letter and the second can be a letter or a number. The rest of the characters in the name can be letters or numbers, but the BASIC doesn't use them at all. Here are some legal numeric variables in Microsoft BASIC:

Variable ⟶	X	X9	ALPHA	B5555	ZERO
Name					
Only this part ⟶	X	X9	AL	B5	ZE
of the variable					
name is recognized					
by Microsoft					
BASIC.					

To be sure about what is allowed in your version of BASIC, consult your BASIC manual. If you want your programs to work on all versions of BASIC, stick with single characters, or, at most, a letter and a number for variable names. Longer names will help you tell what the program does and how it works but not all BASICs allow them.

Compare the two programs. Which is easier to understand?

Version #1   Single letter variables

```
10 LET A=25
20 LET B=78
30 LET C=55
40 LET D=(A+B+C)/3
50 PRINT "THE CLASS AVERAGE IS"; D
```

41

Version #2   Multiple letter variables

```
10 LET AL=25
20 LET BILL=78
30 LET CATHY=55
40 LET AVERAGE=(AL+BILL+CATHY)/3
50 PRINT "THE CLASS AVERAGE IS"; AVERAGE
```

STRING VARIABLES

As you may have already suspected there is more to variables than just putting numbers in boxes. Instead of a number, a variable box can contain a string of letters or characters. This type of variable is called a string variable. In order for BASIC to know we are dealing with a string variable and not a numeric variable, the label or variable name ends with a $; for example, X$ or A1$. The string that is being assigned to the string variable is enclosed by quotes, just as in the PRINT statement. Remember our program that printed out the names of three famous comedians? Here is how we could do it with string variables:

```
10 LET A$="LARRY"
20 LET B$="MOE"
30 LET C$="CURLY JOE"
40 PRINT A$; B$; C$
RUN
LARRYMOECURLY JOE
OK
```

Just as in the case of numeric variables, string variables can be imagined as being held in little boxes like this:

A$	LARRY
B$	MOE
C$	CURLY JOE

The only thing wrong with our program is that there is no separation between the three names. Can you think of a remedy? Here are two answers:

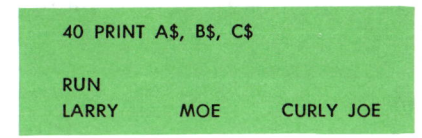

```
40 PRINT A$, B$, C$
RUN
LARRY      MOE       CURLY JOE
```

Simple, huh? Just changed the semicolons to commas.

This works better:

```
40 PRINT A$; " "; B$; " AND "; C$
RUN
LARRY MOE AND CURLY JOE
```

In this trick we printed out A$ followed by two spaces, followed by B$, followed by two spaces, the word AND, two more spaces, and then C$. Whew! In computer talk you are imbedding your variables within strings—a creative approach to displaying results.

Concatenation

Believe it or not, strings can be joined together as one happy unit with the plus (+) symbol. No, this doesn't mean addition; it is just another way of saying join two things together. Probably the inventors of BASIC could think of no better symbol than +. In computer talk we call joining of two strings concatenation (pronounced con-cat-ten-a-shon). Here's an example:

```
10 LET A$="EVERYBODY"
20 LET B$="NEEDS "
30 LET C$="SOMEBODY "
40 LET D$=A$+B$+C$
50 PRINT D$
RUN
EVERYBODY NEEDS SOMEBODY
OK
```

What happened is that we defined three separate strings to three separate string variables and then in line 40 we "concatenated" them with A$+B$+C$ and called this D$ and PRINTed it out. Neat, huh!

INPUT

There is another way of putting labels in little boxes and assigning them values. The INPUT statement allows us a way to get values and variables into the computer after the program is started by RUN. Try this example:

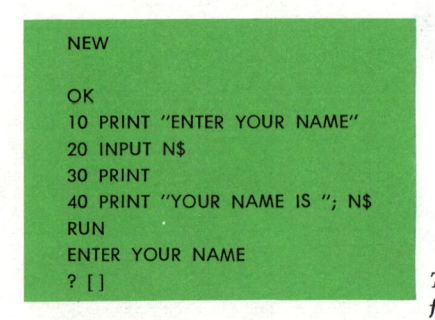

```
NEW

OK
10 PRINT "ENTER YOUR NAME"
20 INPUT N$
30 PRINT
40 PRINT "YOUR NAME IS "; N$
RUN
ENTER YOUR NAME
? [ ]
```

The computer is sitting and waiting for some input from you.

(*The* [ ] *shows where the cursor is.*)

Notice the question mark. This was caused by the INPUT statement which says "INPUT something." In this case that something is a string of characters because the variable after the INPUT is a string variable. (Some BASICs require a semicolon after the INPUT, like this: INPUT ;N$.)

The computer is waiting for you to INPUT so it can put something in the little box inside the computer marked N$. You must respond by typing in a name (or any string) and then hitting the RETURN key, like this:

```
ENTER YOUR NAME
? GYRO GEARLOOSE

YOUR NAME IS GYRO GEARLOOSE
OK
```

Here the computer made N$="GYRO GEARLOOSE" and we didn't even need quote marks like most strings do. Our little box looks like this:

| N$ | GYRO GEARLOOSE |

The only time we need quotes around our string INPUTs is when there is a comma in the string, or when we want to have spaces at the end of a string, like this:

```
RUN
ENTER YOUR NAME
? "HUN WING SING CHOY "

YOUR NAME IS HUN WING SING CHOY
OK
```

This last space made the use of quotes necessary

or

```
RUN
ENTER YOUR NAME
? "EINSTEIN, ALBERT"

YOUR NAME IS EINSTEIN, ALBERT
OK
```

Note in our program we used a PRINT statement to tell us what the INPUT statement wanted, in this case a string name. The question mark by itself doesn't tell us much. We can eliminate the PRINT statement in the program by putting it inside the INPUT statement like this:

```
10 INPUT "ENTER YOUR NAME"; N$
20 PRINT
30 PRINT "YOUR NAME IS "; N$

RUN
ENTER YOUR NAME? HARCOMB MUD

YOUR NAME IS HARCOMB MUD
OK
```

Note the space and the semicolon. Not all BASICs require the semicolon.

We call this an INPUT statement with a "Prompt" string. It makes our programming simpler and eliminates an extra PRINT statement. You can also INPUT numbers into little boxes with INPUT, like this enhancement of our previous program:

45

```
10 INPUT "ENTER YOUR NAME"; N$
20 INPUT "ENTER YOUR AGE IN YEARS"; Y
30 LET D=Y*364.25
40 PRINT "YOU'RE"; D; " DAYS OLD "; N$
RUN
ENTER YOUR NAME? MITCH
ENTER YOUR AGE IN YEARS? 32
YOU'RE 11656 DAYS OLD MITCH
OK
```

Here we used INPUT in line 20 to ask the user to enter their age in years. This number is then assigned to the variable Y. Next in line 30 we multiply Y times the number of days in a year (364.25) and assign this value to D. In line 40 we PRINT out the value of D, a short string and the name of the person (N$). Here is how the boxes look:

N$	MITCH	←	—— *This is the string name.*
Y	32	←	—— *This is the age in years.*
D	11656	←	—— *This is the age in days.*

Sometimes you may wish to input several variables at once. As it is right now, we must use separate INPUT statements to do this. Here's another way:

```
10 INPUT "ENTER YOUR NAME, A COMMA, AND YOUR AGE IN YEARS"; N$, Y
20 LET D=Y*364.25
30 PRINT "YOU'RE"; D; " DAYS OLD "; N$
RUN
ENTER YOUR NAME, A COMMA, AND YOUR AGE IN YEARS; PLUTO,4
YOU'RE 1457 DAYS OLD PLUTO
OK
```

Notice the comma that separates the two inputs (PLUTO and 4).

In this example you can see that BASIC allows several variables to be defined and assigned values in a single INPUT statement. We use commas to separate them in the INPUT statement itself, and in the answer we give to the computer. You can also use the carriage return key instead of the comma to separate the information:

```
10 INPUT "ENTER YOUR NAME AND AGE" N$, A
RUN
ENTER YOUR NAME AND AGE? BRUCE(CR)
? 1
YOU'RE 364.25 DAYS OLD BRUCE
OK
```

CR means we pressed RETURN

Here we typed in a name (BRUCE) and when we hit carriage return the next ? appeared to tell us BASIC is ready for the next variable (Y). This approach may be used better for an application like this:

```
NEW

OK
10 PRINT "ENTER FIVE NUMBERS"
20 INPUT A, B, C, D, E
30 LET F=(A+B+C+D+E)/5
40 PRINT "THE AVERAGE OF THE NUMBERS IS"; F
RUN
ENTER FIVE NUMBERS
? 10
?? 20
?? 30
?? 40
?? 50
THE AVERAGE OF THE NUMBERS IS 30
OK
```

Notice the two ?? are printed after we enter the first value of the INPUT statement. This is how BASIC tells us that an INPUT statement is requesting more input.

What about making mistakes using INPUT, what happens? Try running the previous program but answer the questions as shown below.

```
RUN
ENTER FIVE NUMBERS
? HI
? REDO FROM START
? 1
?? "#$%&
?? REDO FROM START
?? 2
?? 3
?? 4
?? 5
```

Here we entered a string for a numeric variable and the computer barfed and said REDO FROM START which means type the number in again.

47

Sometimes when BASIC is requesting input for an INPUT statement you may not wish to answer the question. To abort the INPUT and return BASIC to the command mode (direct mode) type CONTROL C (C). This will terminate the INPUT and BASIC will print BREAK and then OK, like this:

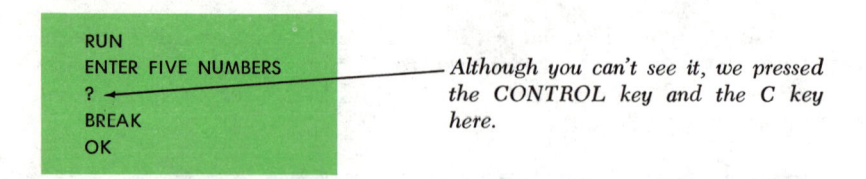

```
RUN
ENTER FIVE NUMBERS
?
BREAK
OK
```

— *Although you can't see it, we pressed the CONTROL key and the C key here.*

A simple way to remember the rule for input is: you can enter numbers into a string variable but you can't enter letters into a numeric variable. This is because a string variable will accept any character. An example would be a phone number or street address ... you would not want to add these numbers together so you would use a string variable.

TAB

TAB is a keyword always used with PRINT. Its purpose is to cause the "cursor" to move horizontally a specific number of positions before printing the information in the PRINT statement. The form of TAB is:

```
PRINT TAB(var) var,var, . . .
```

You are already familiar with the PRINT statement. When TAB appears in a PRINT statement the variables (var,var,...) after TAB are printed out on the terminal starting at the horizontal column position specified by the value of variable *var* in the TAB parentheses. It is assumed that the variable *var* is greater than zero and less than the width of your terminal. In some BASICs if the value of *var* exceeds the terminal width, the information is printed on the next line until the number of column positions specified by *var* has been reached. In essence TAB is like the TAB on a typewriter, it moves the print head to the right by so many spaces. In the case of the computer, we have a special control of the movement of the cursor (which is analogous to the print head on the typewriter) through the variable *var*. It is also assumed that *var* is an "integer" variable because there is no such thing as a fractional cursor position.

As an example, consider that you wish to print out a heading for a program so that it is centered on the terminal or screen page. There are two ways to do this. One way is to simply place the correct number of blanks inside the quote marks around the string you wish to display. The blanks precede the message and cause the message to be printed to the right of the first column position, like this:

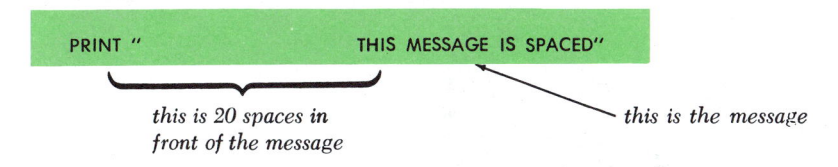

```
PRINT "                    THIS MESSAGE IS SPACED"
```

        this is 20 spaces in   *this is the message*
        front of the message

When the PRINT statement is executed in BASIC the message appears like this:

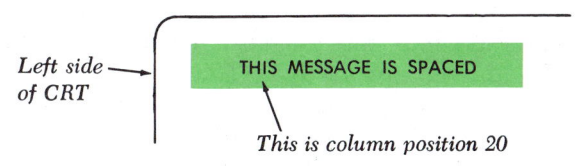

Left side of CRT | THIS MESSAGE IS SPACED

This is column position 20

We can accomplish the same thing and shorten our statement by using TAB and making the value of the variable *var* 20, like this:

```
PRINT TAB(20) "THIS MESSAGE IS SPACED"
```

This statement makes the message begin at column position 20. If we wanted to move the message frequently or test its spacing at various positions, we could do this:

```
10 INPUT I
20 PRINT TAB(I) "THIS MESSAGE IS SPACED"
RUN
?10
          THIS MESSAGE IS SPACED
RUN
?5
     THIS MESSAGE IS SPACED
RUN
?1
 THIS MESSAGE IS SPACED
```

The program allows us to INPUT a TAB value and see how the string THIS MESSAGE IS SPACED gets printed out. Note that when we entered a TAB value of 1, the string began one space over from the left side of the screen. This shows us that there is a column position "0," and the first column is column zero.

The use of TAB is not restricted to string messages only. We can force a TAB on any item in a PRINT statement. For example, consider the case where you wish to print out several numbers in column positions that are different than the ones set by the comma:

```
100 A=10
101 B=20
102 C=30
110 PRINT TAB(5) A;" ";B;" ";C
RUN
       10   20   30
```

Note that the entire group of three numbers (A, B, and C) was shifted five spaces to the right by TAB(5). The semicolon and the string " " was used to place two spaces between each number. TAB affects the group of characters A, B, and C, but the spacing relationship between the values of A, B, and C remain fixed.

Let us step back for a moment and take a look at what we've learned. Computers operate using three main functions:

1. They INPUT information.
2. They PROCESS the information.
3. They OUTPUT the results of the process.

All three of these functions have their own variations which provide you with a huge variety of program techniques.

BASIC NO-NOs

As we mentioned earlier, some BASICs allow variables to be given names longer than one or two characters. For example, we can call a variable XVALUE in some BASICs and only X in others. This longer name option is really nice except for a subtle danger. The danger is that you cannot name a variable with a name that is already used in your version of the BASIC language for some statement command or function.

For example, if you call a variable RUN5, the computer will think you mean to "run" or execute line 5. Or if you have a statement: FORMAT=10 when BASIC executes it, it will think that this

INPUT   PROCESS   OUTPUT

is a FOR...NEXT loop because it sees the letters FOR and you will get an error of some kind.

In order to avoid these problems, your BASIC manual should come with a list of "reserved words." These are all the words that BASIC reserves for its own purposes. You may not use any of these words in your variable names. They may not appear anywhere *inside* a variable name either.

Reserved Words

Here is a list of reserved words for the industrial standard Microsoft Altair BASIC version 4.51. Since Microsoft BASIC is available in 4K, 8K and Disk versions (17K) the reserved words are listed below in order of the version for which they are reserved, starting with those reserved in all versions and ending with those reserved only in Disk Altair BASIC. Words reserved in larger versions may be used in smaller versions, although one may want to avoid all reserved words in the interest of compatibility. In addition to the words listed below, intrinsic function names are reserved words in all versions in which they are available.

Words reserved in all versions:

CLEAR	INPUT	RETURN
DATA	LET	RUN
DIM	LIST	STOP
END	NEW	TO
FOR	NEXT	TAB
GOSUB	PRINT	THEN
GOTO	READ	USR
IF	REM	

Words reserved in 8K and Disk Versions. All the previous plus:

AND	NOT	OUT
CONT	NULL	POKE
DEF	ON	SPC
FN	OR	WAIT

Words reserved in Disk Version. All the previous plus:

AUTO	DELETE	MOD
CONSOLE	EDIT	NAME
DEFDBL	ELSE	RENUM
DEFINT	LINE	RESET
DEFSNG	LLIST	RESUME
DEFSTR	LOAD	SPACE$
	LPRINT	STRING$
		SWAP
		SYSTEM

PUTTING IT ALL TOGETHER—THE LOAN PROGRAM

We now have, with just three simple keywords of the BASIC language, INPUT, LET, and PRINT and five arithmetic operators (+ − * / ^), the ability to perform complicated and useful programs by simply combining them in some logical order, according to a predetermined plan we devise.

Although there are literally hundreds of things you could think up to program in BASIC, the ones that BASIC is most suited for involve things that would be difficult to do with a calculator and almost impossible to do by hand.

As an example of a practical program you could use the computer for, consider the everyday problem of borrowing money. Everyone at one time or another has had to take out a loan from a bank, credit union, or other lending institution. Have you ever wondered how the bank figures your monthly payment? Or did you ever wish you could check to see if the figure was right, or if you could determine the payment on your own without having to call the bank? The program we are about to introduce polls everything we have learned so far to calculate the total monthly payment of a loan. The program illustrates the three laws of computing, and the way that a complex formula can be simplified into a LET statement.

The way banks figure out your monthly payment for a loan is to use special tables of figures that chart out the various payment schedules for certain loan amounts, spread over a specified number of years or months, and at a certain interest rate. There is also a special formula that can be used to compute the loan payment for any combination of loan amount, term or length, and interest.

The special formula is called an *amortization loan* formula. Amortization refers to the fact that the monthly payment is based on interest computed each month on the unpaid balance. A *simple loan* formula on the other hand would just take a percentage of the total borrowed amount, add it to the amount borrowed, and divide the total by the number of months of the loan, called the term.

The amortization formula looks like this when written down on paper:

$$\text{Mon. Payment} = \frac{\text{Loan Amount} \times \text{Interest}}{1 - (1 + \text{Interest})^{-\text{months}}}$$

What the formula says is take the total amount borrowed, and the interest rate and the number of months the loan is spread over, and perform the calculations to obtain the monthly payment. The interest rate is the monthly interest, not the yearly, and is obtained by dividing the yearly interest rate (called annual rate) by the number of months in a year (12). Months is the total number of months of payments, and is found by multiplying the number of years of the term by the number of months in a year (12).

Now we can see that the program must require three steps to work. We must INPUT three parameters to the program, PROCESS them to compute a result called the monthly payment, and OUTPUT the result for us to read.

Thus, to start the program requires we INPUT three parameters and assign them variable names that sort of explain what each stands for in the formula:

The amount of the loan (L)
The annual interest rate (R)
The term of the loan in years (Y)

This can be accomplished quite easily with the INPUT statement:

```
1000 INPUT "ENTER THE AMOUNT OF THE LOAN"; L
1100 INPUT "ENTER THE ANNUAL INTEREST RATE"; R
1120 INPUT "ENTER THE TERM IN YEARS"; Y
```

We now must convert the annual interest rate (R) to a monthly interest rate which we will call I, like this:

```
1210 LET I = R/12
```

Next we must convert the term of the loan in years (Y) to the number of months this represents which we will call M, like this:

```
1230 LET M = Y*12
```

Now we are ready to convert the loan formula into a BASIC statement using LET. Notice the formula uses exponentiation, raising the product of interest times loan amount to a power determined by the length of the loan in months. This is how it is done:

```
1310 LET A = (I*L)/((1−(I+1)^−M))
```

And finally we must print out the result (A) like this:

```
1320 PRINT "THE MONTHLY PAYMENT IS"
1330 PRINT A
```

54

Do not let the formula scare you. You do not really have to understand why it works, but you do have to make sure it is entered into the LET statement properly so the program executes it just like it should. The parentheses are used to make the formula operations occur in the proper order. Notice for a moment that the values in the formula cause a small number (I) to be raised to a large power (M). Doing this on the calculator would be quite a complex process, but in BASIC it is easy.

Now we are ready to list the entire program and RUN it.

```
1010 INPUT "ENTER THE AMOUNT OF THE LOAN"; L
1110 INPUT "ENTER THE ANNUAL INTEREST RATE"; R
1120 INPUT "ENTER THE TERM IN YEARS"; Y
1210 LET I = R/12
1230 LET M = Y*12
1310 LET A = (I*L)/((1—(I+1)^—M))
1320 PRINT "THE MONTHLY PAYMENT IS"
1330 PRINT A
1400 END
```

```
RUN
ENTER THE AMOUNT OF THE LOAN? 5000.00
ENTER THE ANNUAL INTEREST RATE? .09
ENTER THE TERM IN YEARS? 4
THE MONTHLY PAYMENT IS
124.43
```

In this first case we entered the amount we wanted to borrow for an automobile loan ($5000.00), the interest rate annually was 9% (.09), and the term of the loan was 4 years. The program quickly figured out that the loan monthly payment was 124 dollars and 43 cents.

We could use the program to figure the monthly payment on a home we want to borrow for. For example, if you want to buy a house that costs $100,000 and the bank will finance 80% of this ($80,000) for 30 years at 11% then the user would type in the following:

```
ENTER THE AMOUNT OF THE LOAN? 80000.00
ENTER THE ANNUAL INTEREST RATE? .11
ENTER THE TERM IN YEARS? 30
THE MONTHLY PAYMENT IS
761.86
```

EXPANDING A PROGRAM

There is an old saying that the closer a program is to being done, the more things you will discover to add to it. Adding more functions to a BASIC program is actually quite a simple task, because BASIC was made to be expandable. All we have to do is figure out where the new statements go and type them in. For example, consider an enhancement of the Loan program that computes the actual total interest we are paying on the amount borrowed. In order to arrive at this figure we must first find the total amount we are to pay by multiplying the monthly payment (A) times the number of months of payments (M). Then we subtract the actual principal we borrowed (L) from this, and the result is the amount of the loan going toward the interest. In the form of a LET statement we can compute the interest total like this (calling the total interest (T)):

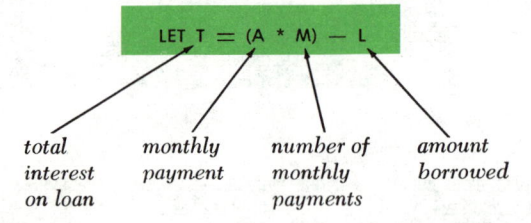

$$\text{LET } T = (A * M) - L$$

- total interest on loan
- monthly payment
- number of monthly payments
- amount borrowed

Once the amount of interest (T) is computed we can print it out with:

```
1420 PRINT "TOTAL INTEREST ON LOAN IS"
1430 PRINT T
```

Now our program looks like this:

```
1010 INPUT "ENTER THE AMOUNT OF THE LOAN"; L
1110 INPUT "ENTER THE ANNUAL INTEREST RATE"; R
1120 INPUT "ENTER THE TERM IN YEARS"; Y
1210 LET I = R/12
1230 LET M = Y*12
1310 LET A = (I*L)/((1—(I+1)^—M))
1320 PRINT "THE MONTHLY PAYMENT IS"
1330 PRINT A
1410 LET T = (A*M)—L
1420 PRINT "TOTAL INTEREST ON LOAN IS"
1430 PRINT T
1500 END
```

```
RUN
ENTER THE AMOUNT OF THE LOAN? 5000.00
ENTER THE ANNUAL INTEREST RATE? .09
ENTER THE TERM IN YEARS? 4
THE MONTHLY PAYMENT IS
124.43
TOTAL INTEREST ON LOAN IS
972.51
```

See how easy it was to expand the program? Later in the book we will learn how to even further enhance the program but for now what is important is that you see that a program can be added to by simply inserting new logical statements in the proper locations.

Notice that $972.51 in interest represents almost 20% of the $5000 we originally borrowed. This clearly shows how an 11% amortized loan actually means the interest is much more than 11% of $5000, and a larger amount is paid in interest than it would seem necessary. This shows how loan companies make their profits. The longer the term of the loan and the larger the amount borrowed, for a fixed interest the larger the interest payment will be.

On the practical side, the interest total can be used as a number to subtract from your income tax (if you itemize on the long form). Without the program you couldn't easily figure out ahead of time how much of the loan was going towards the interest.

DOCUMENTING YOUR PROGRAMS (REM)

Suppose you wrote a program in 1978 and then in 1981 came back to it and attempted to modify its design. Because few of us have photographic memories what we have to do is "re-learn" how the program works. Although BASIC is a simple language, one cannot just look at a program listing and immediately tell how it works. Furthermore the program lacks information which points out what it actually accomplishes when it is run, and unless you are really sharp, deciding what statements perform what functions can be very difficult.

In order to alleviate this problem, BASIC provides a special statement, called REM, which stands for REMark. What REM does is allows us to add program "documentation" information which appears in the program listing but has no effect on the way the program works. REMs are called nonexecutable statements because when the computer encounters one in the program flow it simply ignores it and goes to the next line.

The form of the REM statement is like this:

> line#   REM   a message goes here about the program. . .

For example in our loan program we can use a REM statement right away to tell us the name of the program, like this:

> 1000 REM   LOAN AMORTIZATION PROGRAM

Now when we come back to the program at a later date and read the listing, the first REM statement will tell us the name and purpose of the program. The REM statement is therefore used throughout the program to explain to you, or to an outsider, what the statements in the program actually do to complete the total job.

Keep in mind that the REM statements do not get executed by the computer. When one is encountered the computer knows that it is to ignore the statement and execute the next statement after the REM. But when we list the program with the LIST command the information in the REM statement will be displayed for us.

One thing you will certainly discover as your programming experience grows is that "the other guy" never seems to document his program good enough for you to understand. In fact the secret of good programming is super documentation, but most programmers are weak in these areas. A program without adequate REM statements is like a machine with no operator's manual. If you get stuck, or if you want to change something, you must reinvent what the original maker had in mind when it was designed.

So to be an especially accomplished programmer, strive to keep your programs as full of REMs as you can. The only negative thing about REMs is that they consume extra memory without adding any computing power to the program. In the case of excessively long programs the additional memory consumption by the REMs can be a problem. So at worst you should at least place REMs in the critical parts of the body of the program.

As an example of good documentation, here is our loan program rewritten to include REM statements. See if you think it is easier to understand now:

As you can see we added several REM statements and to make them easy to find with the eye, three preceding dashes (---) were added to the message in the REM to flag that this is a nonexecutable statement that is for the purpose of documentation only.

```
   0 REM   PROGRAM BY MITCHELL WAITE AND MICHAEL PARDEE
   1 REM   WRITTEN: JULY 1978
   2 REM   USED AS EXAMPLE IN THE BOOK: BASIC PRIMER
   3 REM   ALL RIGHTS RESERVED WORLDWIDE
1000 REM   ---LOAN AMORTIZATION PROGRAM
1010 REM   ---INPUT SECTION
1100 INPUT "ENTER THE AMOUNT OF THE LOAN"; L
1110 INPUT "ENTER THE ANNUAL INTEREST RATE"; R
1120 INPUT "ENTER THE TERM IN YEARS"; Y
1200 REM   ---CHANGE ANNUAL RATE TO MONTHLY RATE
1210 LET I = R/12
1220 REM   ---CHANGE YEARS TO MONTHS
1230 LET M = Y*12
1300 REM   ---COMPUTE THE MONTHLY PAYMENT AND PRINT
1310 LET A = (I*L)/((1—(I+1)^—M))
1230 PRINT "THE MONTHLY PAYMENT IS $"; A
1400 REM   ---COMPUTE THE TOTAL INTEREST AND PRINT
1410 LET T = (A*M)—L
1420 PRINT "THE TOTAL INTEREST IS $"; T
1500 END
```

Now we have a good idea of the three most simple BASIC keywords INPUT, LET, and PRINT as well as some special purpose characters for formatting our output (semicolons and commas). We also know a little about numbers and variables. Now we are ready to take a bigger step into BASIC and learn how programs can be increased greatly in power and flexibility by some new BASIC keywords called program control statements.

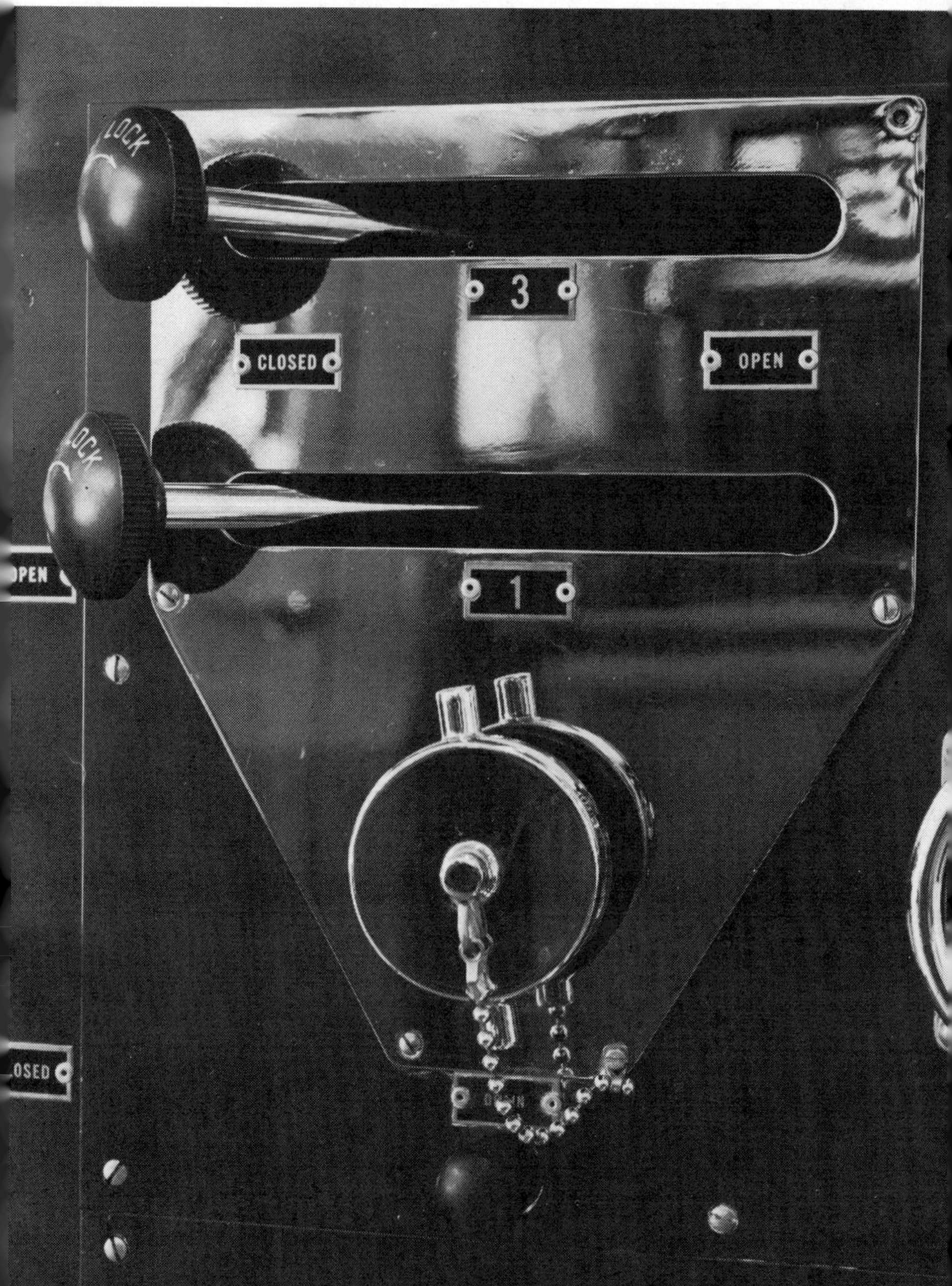
LOCK
3
CLOSED
OPEN
LOCK
OPEN
1
CLOSED

CHAPTER 2

Program Control

Very often, we are confronted with certain situations which require us to make a decision of some sort. We have to take a good look at all of the information which we have available, consider all of the alternatives, and then most likely go right ahead and make an emotional decision. Yes, objectivity is a very difficult quality to maintain during any decision-making process that affects us personally. We are involved in decision making during a good part of our daily lives. With the great degree of "free will" which we humans have, and the tremendous variety of choices, we are almost constantly making decisions of one sort or another.

The computer differs from man in this area in that it is never emotionally involved in any decision. As long as sufficient information is available to the computer, it can evaluate it and make a completely unbiased decision. This decision-making power allows the computer to follow alternate instructions based upon the value of a number, or the sequence of letters that are entered. In this section we will discuss the BASIC statements which provide the program with a means of doing a variety of different things, all based upon the evaluation of some information. This concept is what really makes the computer a powerful tool. It is not "locked in" to doing only one thing over and over again. Rather, it can change its processing according to the nature of the information.

THE DECISION MAKING STATEMENTS

There are several BASIC statements that come under the category of decision making statements. Each has a specific use and function. In many cases these statements can be combined in such a way as to offer even greater decision making power to the computer.

FOR...NEXT, the Programmed Loop

In most programming applications there will arise a need to do the same steps over and over again. This process is known in computer talk as "iteration." It is also referred to quite often as "looping," since it usually involves setting up the program so that it will loop back and repeat itself. If a program is written in such a way, it might easily get stuck in the loop and keep on repeating itself forever. For this reason, there is usually some means of keeping track of just how many times the program is supposed to repeat itself. In BASIC language, all of these considerations are taken care of by the FOR and NEXT statements.

The FOR statement sets up the beginning of the loop and determines how many times it will be repeated. The NEXT statement marks the end of the loop, and causes the program to go back and repeat itself if necessary. To use a simple example: Let us suppose that what we want our program to do is to INPUT four numbers from the keyboard, add them together and PRINT the total on the screen. Now, the four numbers could easily be entered through the use of just one INPUT statement, but for the sake of the example, let us say that the numbers are to be entered separately. The program looks like this:

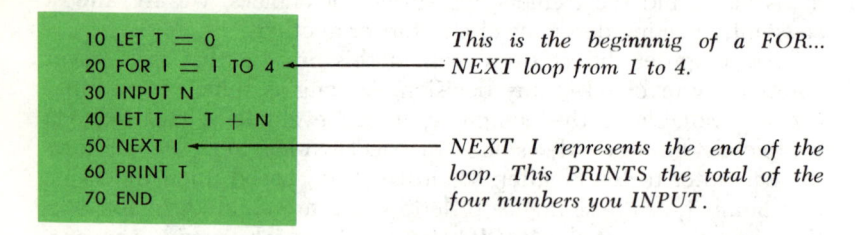

```
10 LET T = 0
20 FOR I = 1 TO 4
30 INPUT N
40 LET T = T + N
50 NEXT I
60 PRINT T
70 END
```

This is the beginnnig of a FOR...NEXT loop from 1 to 4.

NEXT I represents the end of the loop. This PRINTS the total of the four numbers you INPUT.

Now, let us take a closer look at this program, statement by statement. First of all, at statement 10 we begin by setting the variable T equal to zero. This is the variable that we will use to accumulate the total of the four numbers to be INPUT. At statement 20 we see the FOR statement. It controls how many times the following statements will be performed. It specifies that the "index" I will be initialized to the value of 1, and the loop will continue until I has reached a value of 4. Statement 30 lets us INPUT a number into the variable called N. At statement 40, another LETstatement is used to replace the current value of T (the running total), with the sum of T and the number N. Now, at statement 50, the NEXT I statement defines the end of the loop, and causes the value of I to be increased by 1. At this point, if I is greater than 4, the next statement in the program will be performed. That would be the PRINT statement at 60 which causes the total of the four numbers stored in the variable T to be PRINTed on the screen. If however, I is less than or equal to 4 after the NEXT I statement has increased I by one, the program will return to the first statement following the FOR statement where the loop begins. Another number will be read from the keyboard into the varible N. It will then be added to the current value of the total stored in the variable T, and so on.

FOR ... NEXT

There is a more powerful version of the FOR statement which allows the increment that is added to the "index" I to be some value other than one. This advanced FOR statement looks like this:

```
FOR I = 1 TO 50 STEP 3
```

Notice the addition of the word STEP to the statement. This statement would begin by initializing the index I to one. Then when the NEXT I statement was encountered later in the program, the value of three would be added to I instead of one. Then, as before, the value of I would be checked to see if it had exceeded the termination value of the loop, 50.

Let us suppose that we want to write a program that will add up all of the odd numbers between 0 and 100, and print the answer. The program could be done like this:

```
10 LET T = 0
20 FOR I = 1 TO 100 STEP 2     ———  "STEP 2" makes I go 1, 3, 5 . . .
30 LET T = T + I
40 NEXT I
50 PRINT T
```

Quite a simple program really. First, at line 10, we set up a variable called T and initialize it to zero. The next line is the beginning of the FOR...NEXT loop which starts at 1, and goes to 100 by 2s. Each time through the loop, the value of I is added to the total being accumulated in T. Finally, when the value of I exceeds 100, the answer is printed.

If you think about it, you will see that I will never be equal to 100. It goes, 1, 3, 5, . . . 95, 97, 99. When 2 is added to the value 99, the result is 101 which is greater than 100, and therefore causes the termination of the loop.

IF...THEN, Conditional Branches

These keywords are used to provide the BASIC language with its real decision making powers. There are many forms of the IF...THEN statement, ranging from very simple data evaluation, to quite complex combinations of conditions.

To get a quick idea of what this statement is like, let us use a simple analogy.

IF today is Wednesday THEN take out the garbage

Here we have set up a conditional decision. If the premise is true (that it is Wednesday), then the result of the decision causes the action of taking out the garbage. Of course, the converse situation (that it is NOT Wednesday) would cause no action to be taken. It is only when the premise is true that the part following the word THEN is carried out.

In BASIC, things work the same way. A sample of a BASIC statement using IF...THEN is the following:

```
IF A = 5 THEN PRINT "END OF JOB"
```

Here, the current value of the variable A is tested to see if it is equal to five. If it is, the program will output the message "END OF JOB." Again, if A is not equal to five, the message will not be printed. Notice that the condition being tested in this statement is the value of the variable A. This is done by using one of the arithmetic operators (=) to indicate that it is equality that is being tested. The variety of different expressions that may be included as part of the premise is quite great. For example, the following are some other forms of the IF...THEN statement.

```
IF A+3 = B THEN LET C = 0
IF 2*B—5 = C+2 THEN PRINT "MATCH"
```

Other relational operators that may be used in the IF...THEN statement are

> < less than
> \> greater than
> <= less than or equal to
> \>= greater than or equal to
> <> not equal to (sometimes the # symbol)

The following are some examples of these relational IF...THEN statements:

```
IF A<3 THEN GOTO 100
IF 2*B+4>20 THEN LET A = 1
IF B+C+6<>0 THEN PRINT "NOT EQUAL"
```

There are variations on the "THEN" side of the IF...THEN statement as well. We have already seen that we may cause something to be printed if the premise of the IF statement is true. We may also cause other things to happen as the following examples so readily illustrate.

```
IF ..... THEN LET A = 125
IF ..... THEN LET B = A + C
IF ..... THEN INPUT N
```

So there are many things that the program can do based upon the premise of the IF statement being true. Once again, if the premise is NOT true, the object of the statement (that part which follows the word THEN) will not be performed. Instead, the program will just proceed to the next statement in sequence.

To make this statement even more powerful, there are variations which use what are known as "logical operators" to form compound IF...THEN statements. Some examples include:

```
IF A=3 AND B<4 THEN LET C=10
IF B>2 OR C<2 THEN PRINT "INVALID"
```

In the first example, the object of the IF statement will only be executed if both conditions are true. That is, "A must be equal to 3," and "B must be less than 4." If either of these premises is not true, then the object will not be performed. In the second example, if either one of the two premises is true, then the message "INVALID" will be printed. That is, if either "B is greater than 2," or "C is less than 2," the message will be printed. We can see that by using this type of IF...THEN statement, many conditions may be tested at once, and at the same time very complex logical decisions can be made.

GOTO, Unconditional Branch

The GOTO statement is not really a decision making statement. It is used to force the program to go to some other statement and perform the program there. It is however used most commonly in conjunction with the decision making statements and so has been included in this section. By itself, the GOTO statement will simply cause the program to "branch" to another statement. For example:

```
GOTO 1200
```

This statement would cause the program to branch to the statement bearing the number 1200 and to execute it and then continue on with the next statement after 1200. This is known as an "unconditional branch," that is, it occurs no matter what.

The GOTO statement is often used as the object of an IF...THEN statement to allow the program to be controlled by the condition of some data. For example,

```
IF A = 5 THEN GOTO 100
```

GOTO Indianapolis

This is known as a "conditional branch" since it only occurs if the premise of the IF...THEN statement is true. If the current value of the variable A is equal to 5, the branch to statement 100 will occur; otherwise, the next statement after the IF...THEN statement will be executed. Let us use a simple example program to illustrate the use of both the IF...THEN statement and the GOTO statement. This program will INPUT two numbers, and a single character string variable that will direct the program to either "A" add the two numbers together and print out the result, or "D" divide the first number by the second number and print out the result.

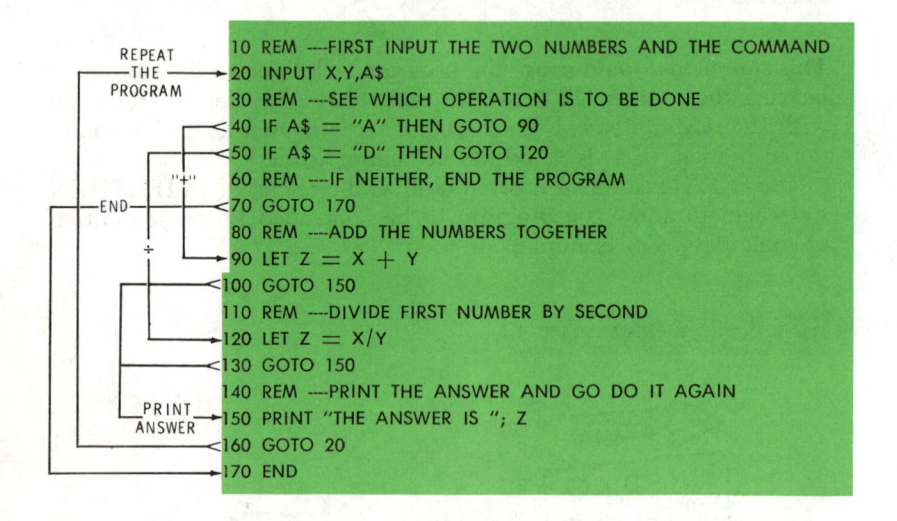

```
10  REM ----FIRST INPUT THE TWO NUMBERS AND THE COMMAND
20  INPUT X,Y,A$
30  REM ----SEE WHICH OPERATION IS TO BE DONE
40  IF A$ = "A" THEN GOTO 90
50  IF A$ = "D" THEN GOTO 120
60  REM ----IF NEITHER, END THE PROGRAM
70  GOTO 170
80  REM ----ADD THE NUMBERS TOGETHER
90  LET Z = X + Y
100 GOTO 150
110 REM ----DIVIDE FIRST NUMBER BY SECOND
120 LET Z = X/Y
130 GOTO 150
140 REM ----PRINT THE ANSWER AND GO DO IT AGAIN
150 PRINT "THE ANSWER IS "; Z
160 GOTO 20
170 END
```

From the above example, we can see how the IF...THEN and GOTO statements can be used in conjunction to provide extensive program control.

The Endless Loop

There will be times when you are testing your new program and things just don't seem to operate properly. There are many reasons why programs don't work properly, and one of them is an "endless loop." The endless loop can be brought about in a number of ways, the simplest of which is a GOTO statement that inevitably causes the program to repeat a sequence of statements indefinitely. Something like:

```
10 LET X=1
20 GOTO 10
30 PRINT X
```

No doubt about it, this program is going to get caught up in an endless loop. The PRINT statement at line 30 will never be executed. When you tell your computer to RUN this program, it will appear to "fall asleep." The prompting "OK" will never be seen again in the program.

To provide the programmer with some alternative in these situations, most BASICs will respond to the entry on the keyboard of a "control-C sequence." This is done by holding down the key labeled "CNTL," and pressing the "C" key at the same time. This will cause the BASIC program to be interrupted, and the "OK" prompt returned to the screen. Also, the line at which the program was when the control-C was entered is displayed on the screen:

```
BREAK IN 20
OK
```

At this point, the programmer can examine the program to find and alter the problem and then continue the execution of the program by typing:

```
CONT
```

In general, the control-C sequence may be used at any time that the programmer wants to interrupt a program. If a program does a lot of PRINTing, and the programmer wishes to stop the program before all of the printing has been completed, the control-C sequence may be used to abort the printing in progress and return control to BASIC.

ON...GOTO, Indexed Branching

A special form of the GOTO statement allows the programmer to specify several possible destinations of the branch, and make the selection of the one to be taken based upon the value of a particular variable. The form of this type of GOTO statement is illustrated at the top of the next page.

10 ON I GOTO 100, 200, 300, 400, 500, etc.

Here, the variable I is used as the index for the ON...GOTO statement. If the value of I is 1, then the GOTO will cause a branch to line 100. If I is equal to 2, then the branch will be to line 200, and so on.

ON GOTO

Notice that the value of the index to the ON...GOTO statement must be an integer, a whole number. It must also be greater than zero, and not greater than the total number of lines listed after the GOTO. If the index is zero, or greater than the total number of lines in the list, the next statement after the ON...GOTO statement will be executed. If the value of the index is negative, an error will result.

The ON...GOTO statement lends itself very well to making organized program branches such as are encountered when a function or operation is selected by the programmer by entering a number through the keyboard to the program. The program can then use the number as the index for the ON...GOTO statement, as in the following example:

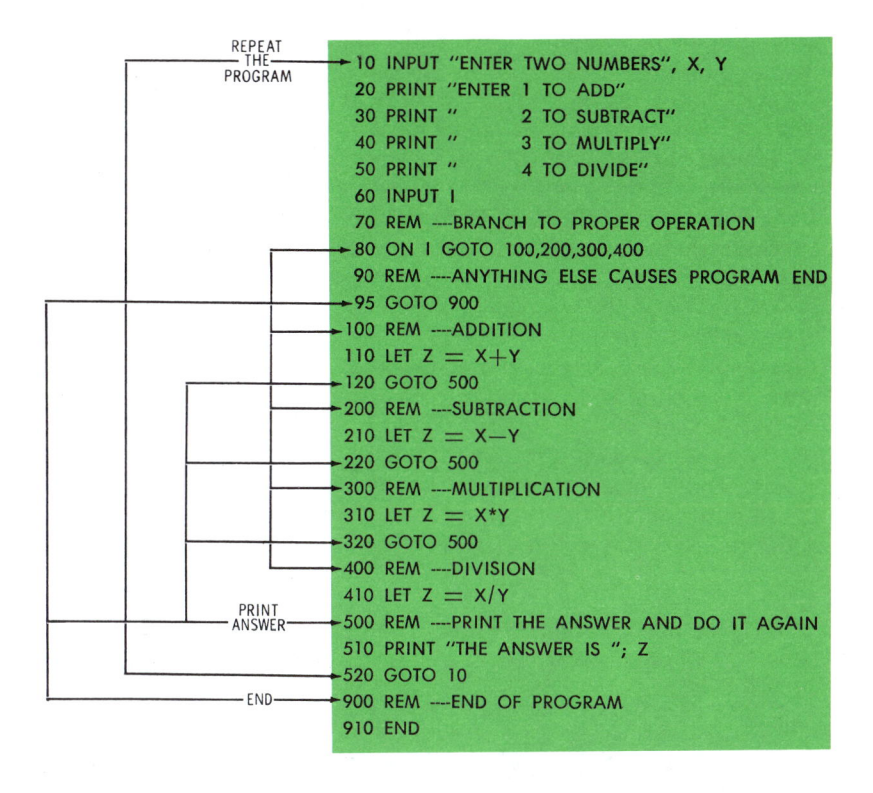

```
                REPEAT
                 THE         10  INPUT "ENTER TWO NUMBERS", X, Y
                PROGRAM      20  PRINT "ENTER 1 TO ADD"
                             30  PRINT "      2 TO SUBTRACT"
                             40  PRINT "      3 TO MULTIPLY"
                             50  PRINT "      4 TO DIVIDE"
                             60  INPUT I
                             70  REM ----BRANCH TO PROPER OPERATION
                             80  ON I GOTO 100,200,300,400
                             90  REM ----ANYTHING ELSE CAUSES PROGRAM END
                             95  GOTO 900
                             100 REM ----ADDITION
                             110 LET Z = X+Y
                             120 GOTO 500
                             200 REM ----SUBTRACTION
                             210 LET Z = X—Y
                             220 GOTO 500
                             300 REM ----MULTIPLICATION
                             310 LET Z = X*Y
                             320 GOTO 500
                             400 REM ----DIVISION
                             410 LET Z = X/Y
                 PRINT
                 ANSWER      500 REM ----PRINT THE ANSWER AND DO IT AGAIN
                             510 PRINT "THE ANSWER IS "; Z
                             520 GOTO 10
                 END         900 REM ----END OF PROGRAM
                             910 END
```

The ON...GOTO statement located at line 80 of this program serves to direct the program to the proper sequence of statements based upon the selected operation entered at line 60.

ENHANCING THE LOAN PROGRAM

Remember the Loan program we used in Chapter 1 to illustrate the use of the three laws of computing? Well, now we are going to modify that program to provide some additional information. As we recall, the program required as INPUT the following:

The amount of the loan L
The annual interest rate R
The term of the loan in years Y

By using the formula programmed into the LET statement, we were able to compute the monthly payment A. Now, we will enhance the program so that *for each payment,* it will compute the amount that is paid as interest, and also the amount that is applied to the principal of the loan. In addition, we will program it to accumulate the total amount of interest paid, and to compute the principal balance of the loan. Finally, we will have all of this information printed in columns, one line for each monthly payment.

To accomplish all of these wonderful things with this program we will use the "program control" statements that we just learned about. We will use the FOR...NEXT statements to control a loop which prints out the monthly information. The IF...THEN statements will be used for a special purpose in the program. Depending upon the loan amount and the interest rate, the last payment will not always be equal to the other monthly payments. You probably have noticed this on your own personal loans. So therefore, when we get down to computing the last payment, we will want to make sure that the amount of the payment which is applied to the principal is exactly equal to the outstanding balance.

So then, let us get into this program. We will break it up into logical segments for the purpose of illustration. First, the beginning of the program is very similar to the original version.

```
1000 REM ---LOAN AMORTIZATION PROGRAM
1010 REM ---INPUT SECTION
1100 INPUT "ENTER THE AMOUNT OF THE LOAN"; L
1110 INPUT "ENTER THE ANNUAL INTEREST RATE"; R
1120 INPUT "ENTER THE TERM IN YEARS"; Y
1200 REM ---CHANGE ANNUAL RATE TO MONTHLY RATE
1210 LET I = R/12
1220 REM ---CHANGE YEARS TO MONTHS
1230 LET M = Y*12
1300 REM ---COMPUTE THE MONTHLY PAYMENT AND PRINT
1310 LET A = (I*L)/((1—(I+1)^—M))
1320 PRINT "THE MONTHLY PAYMENT IS $"; A
```

The next thing that the program must do is prepare to print the amortization schedule. We will need to establish a variable for the current loan balance after a payment has been made B. We will also need a variable to accumulate the total interest paid T. To dress up the output, we will also print some column headings.

```
1400 REM ---INITIALIZE FOR AMORTIZATION SCHEDULE
1410 LET B = L
1420 LET T = 0
1430 PRINT "NUM", "INTEREST", "PRINCIPAL", "PRIN BAL", "TOT INT"
```

Now comes the payment loop. We will use the variable J as the "index" to the loop, and the number of monthly payments M as the "terminator" of the loop. For each payment, we will compute the amount which is paid as interest I1, and the amount which is applied to the principal P. Also, we will subtract the amount applied to the principal from the loan balance B, and accumulate the total interest paid T.

```
1500 REM ---DO THE LOOP FOR THE NUMBER OF PAYMENTS
1510 FOR J = 1 TO M
1520 REM ---COMPUTE THE INTEREST
1530 LET I1 = B*I
1540 REM ---COMPUTE THE PRINCIPAL
1550 LET P = A—I1
1560 REM ---FORCE OUT THE LAST PAYMENT
1570 IF J = M THEN LET P = B
1600 REM ---UPDATE THE LOAN BALANCE
1610 LET B = B—P
1620 REM ---UPDATE THE TOTAL INTEREST
1630 LET T = T+I1
```

Now, using the automatic column function of the PRINT statement we will print all of the information for the monthly payment and then end the loop.

```
1700 REM ---PRINT THE MONTHLY PAYMENT DETAIL
1710 PRINT J,I1,P,B,T
1720 NEXT J
```

At this point, we will add some statements that will provide the option either to go back to the beginning of the program to process another loan, or to end the program. See if you can figure out how this works.

```
1800 REM ---SEE IF DONE
1810 INPUT "PROCESS ANOTHER LOAN (YES/NO)"; A$
1820 IF A$ = "YES" THEN GOTO 1100
9999 END
```

Notice that we are using a "string variable" here. Remember that this is denoted by the "$" following the variable name. So, what is happening here is that we are inputting a string of characters at statement 1810, and if that string happens to be the word "YES" then the program will go back to statement 1100 where the entire process starts. If the input string is not the word "YES," then the program will proceed to the next statement which is the END statement at 9999. This causes the program to terminate.

Now you have a very useful little program. You can use this to find out what your monthly payment would be on a particular loan, and also to see just how much monthly interest you will pay.

Table 2-1 represents an example printout for a sample loan amortization. At the top of the table, the numbers that are underscored would have to be entered by the user as the program requested the input information. In this example, we are amortizing a loan of $5000.00, at an annual interest rate of 9% (entered as a decimal fraction .09), over a term of 4 years. The program computed the monthly payment to be $124.427 and printed that out first. Then

Table 2-1. Example of Printout for a Loan Amortization

```
ENTER THE AMOUNT OF THE LOAN? 5000.00
ENTER THE ANNUAL INTEREST RATE? .09
ENTER THE TERM IN YEARS? 4
THE MONTHLY PAYMENT IS $124.427
```

Num.	Interest	Prin. Pay	Prin. Bal.	Int. to Date
1	37.5	86.9273	4913.07	37.5
2	36.8481	87.5792	4825.49	74.3481
3	36.1913	88.236	4737.26	110.539
4	35.5296	88.8977	4648.36	146.069
5	34.8629	89.5644	4558.8	180.932
6	34.1912	90.2361	4468.56	215.123
7	33.5145	90.9128	4377.65	248.638
8	32.8327	91.5946	4286.05	281.47
9	32.1458	92.2815	4193.77	313.616
10	31.4537	92.9736	4100.8	345.07
11	30.7565	93.6708	4007.13	375.826
12	30.054	94.3733	3912.75	405.88
13	29.3463	95.081	3817.67	435.227
14	28.6333	95.7941	3721.88	463.86
15	27.9149	96.5125	3625.37	491.775
16	27.1911	97.2362	3528.13	518.966
17	26.4619	97.9654	3430.16	545.428
18	25.7272	98.7001	3331.46	571.155
19	24.987	99.4403	3232.02	596.142
20	24.2413	100.186	3131.84	620.383

Num.	Interest	Prin. Pay	Prin. Bal.	Int. to Date
21	23.49	100.937	3030.9	643.873
22	22.7331	101.694	2929.21	666.606
23	21.9704	102.457	2826.75	688.577
24	21.2021	103.225	2723.52	709.779
25	20.428	103.999	2619.52	730.207
26	19.6481	104.779	2514.74	749.855
27	18.8623	105.565	2409.18	768.717
28	18.0707	106.357	2302.82	786.788
29	17.2732	107.154	2195.67	804.061
30	16.4696	107.958	2087.71	820.531
31	15.6602	108.767	1978.94	836.191
32	14.8445	109.583	1869.36	851.035
33	14.0228	110.404	1758.96	865.058
34	13.1949	111.232	1647.72	878.253
35	12.3608	112.066	1535.66	890.614
36	11.5205	112.907	1422.75	902.134
37	10.6739	113.753	1309	912.808
38	9.8209	114.606	1194.39	922.629
39	8.96162	115.466	1078.93	931.591
40	8.09581	116.331	962.594	939.687
41	7.22375	117.204	845.391	946.91
42	6.34518	118.082	727.309	953.256
43	5.45965	118.968	608.341	958.715
44	4.56831	119.859	488.482	963.283
45	3.66998	120.757	367.725	966.953
46	2.76479	121.663	246.062	969.718
47	1.85405	122.573	123.489	971.572
48	.9375	123.49	−1.09863E-03	972.51

the program proceeds to print out the amortization schedule according to the format that we decided upon earlier. Notice that the column headings are printed first, followed by one line for each monthly payment. We can see that at first the amount paid as interest is relatively large, and decreases as the loan balance decreases. Likewise, the amount applied to the principal is relatively small at first, and then gets larger as the amount paid as interest decreases.

There are a few other things that we should notice at this time. One is that if we sum the amount paid as interest with the amount applied to the principal for each month, we do not always get the monthly payment, 124.427, as the answer. This is because the numbers printed here have not been rounded off after the computer performed the mathematics. For example, when the program converts the annual interest rate of 9% to a monthly interest rate, it comes out to a decimal fraction of .0075. (.09/12). Now, when the program computes the amount paid as interest on the second payment, the math actually comes out like this:

MONTHLY RATE × LOAN BALANCE = INTEREST AMOUNT
   .0075   ×   4913.07   =   36.848025

According to the table, the interest amount on payment two is 36.8481 (to six significant digits). This apparent discrepancy is due to the accumulated error inherent in the least significant digit of the arithmetic processes of the computer.

METRIC CONVERSION PROGRAM AND THE MENU CONCEPT

Here is an example of a very useful program written in BASIC (Fig. 2-1). We have all heard of the intended adoption of the metric system of measurement by the world at large. Many manufacturers of prepared foods are printing both the anglo and metric quantities on their products. Although this transition may seem to be difficult, there are many advantages to the metric system, which is always based upon the number 10. The anglo systems are all different. Length can be based upon a scale of 12 inches, or 3 feet, or 5,280 feet in a mile. The task of converting a length from yards to miles requires that two conversion factors be used. First, we must convert the length to feet, and then finally convert it to miles. The metric system, based upon ten, allows very simple conversion of lengths either measured in meters, or kilometers. All we need to do is to multiply or divide by a power of ten (10, 100, 1000, etc.) to perform the conversion. This then requires only that the decimal point be moved either to the right for multiplication, or to the left for division. For example, let us convert 500 meters to kilometers. First of all, we need to know the fact that 1 kilometer is equal to 1,000 meters. This is conveniently indicated by the prefix "kilo" meaning thousand. Therefore, to convert meters to kilometers, we simply divide by 1,000, or move the decimal point three places to the left. So, 500 meters is equal to .500 kilometers, or exactly half a kilometer.

During the world struggle to convert from the anglo system to the metric system, the major problem is that the new units do not have the inherent "sense" that the old ones did. How long is half a kilometer? Being conditioned to the old concepts of feet, yards, and miles, we find it hard to conceive of half a kilometer. But this is only due to our being unfamiliar with the metric terms. With a little practice, we can easily adapt to the metric system. In the

```
2000 REM ---METRIC CONVERSION PROGRAM
2010 REM ---DISPLAY THE MENU
2020 PRINT
2030 PRINT "METRIC CONVERSION PROGRAM"
2040 PRINT
2041 PRINT "1 - INCHES TO CENTIMETERS"
2042 PRINT "2 - POUNDS TO KILOGRAMS"
2043 PRINT "3 - QUARTS TO LITERS"
2049 PRINT "9 - TO END THE PROGRAM"
2050 PRINT
2060 REM ---GET THE SELECTION
2070 INPUT "ENTER YOUR SELECTION"; S
2080 REM ---DECIDE WHERE TO BRANCH
2081 IF S = 1 THEN GOTO 2100
2082 IF S = 2 THEN GOTO 2200
2083 IF S = 3 THEN GOTO 2300
2089 IF S>3 OR S<1 THEN GOTO 9999
2100 REM ---CONVERT INCHES TO CENTIMETERS
2110 PRINT
2120 INPUT "ENTER LENGTH IN INCHES "; I
2130 LET C = 2.54*I
2140 PRINT I;" INCHES IS EQUAL TO ";C;" CENTIMETERS"
2150 GOTO 2000
2200 REM ---CONVERT POUNDS TO KILOGRAMS
2210 PRINT
2220 INPUT "ENTER WEIGHT IN POUNDS "; P
2230 LET K = .4536*P
2240 PRINT P;" POUNDS IS EQUAL TO ";K;" KILOGRAMS"
2250 GOTO 2000
2300 REM ---CONVERT QUARTS TO LITERS
2310 PRINT
2320 INPUT "ENTER VOLUME IN QUARTS "; Q
2330 LET L = .9463*Q
2340 PRINT Q;" QUARTS IS EQUAL TO ";L;" LITERS"
2350 GOTO 2000
9999 END
```

Fig. 2-1. Listing of Metric Conversion program.

meantime, we can use BASIC to write a simple program that converts anglo measurements which we are now using to metric measurements.

The program has three major sections which we will discuss separately. First, the program will provide us with a "menu" from which we can select the conversion we want. Then, the program will have to interpret our request and branch to the proper statements to affect the conversion. Lastly, the desired conversion will be accomplished, and the answer printed out. Here is the first part of the program:

```
2000 REM ---METRIC CONVERSION PROGRAM
2010 REM ---DISPLAY THE MENU
2020 PRINT
2030 PRINT "METRIC CONVERSION PROGRAM"
2040 PRINT
2041 PRINT "1 - INCHES TO CENTIMETERS"
2042 PRINT "2 - POUNDS TO KILOGRAMS"
2043 PRINT "3 - QUARTS TO LITERS"
2049 PRINT "9 - TO END THE PROGRAM"
2050 PRINT
2060 REM ---GET THE SELECTION
2070 INPUT "ENTER YOUR SELECTION"; S
```

Note how we left room for you to add other conversion routines (4-8).

This is relatively straightforward. Using PRINT statements, the program displays the "menu" of the available conversion routines. In this example, we only included three conversion routines, but as we will see, it would be very easy to add others. Notice that we have made provision for ending the program from the menu by entering a selection of "9." Also, notice the PRINT statements on lines 2020, 2040, and 2050. These cause a blank line to be displayed which is like double-spacing on the typewriter.

The next section of the program uses the INPUT variable S to determine which conversion formula is to be used. This is accomplished using several IF...THEN statements.

```
2080 REM ---DECIDE WHERE TO BRANCH
2081 IF S = 1 THEN GOTO 2100
2082 IF S = 2 THEN GOTO 2200
2083 IF S = 3 THEN GOTO 2300
2089 IF S>3 OR S<1 THEN GOTO 9999
```

Could you replace the three IF...THENs with a single ON...GOTO?

Remember that if the premise is true in the IF statement then the result will be that the program performs the right side of the IF ...THEN statement. If the premise is not true, the program proceeds on to the next statement. So, the program checks the value of S to see if it is equal to 1, 2, or 3 and performs a GOTO branch to the proper statement for the selected conversion. Notice that if S is not equal to 1, 2, or 3, the program will end up at line 2089. Here, using a compound IF...THEN statement, the program will branch to line 9999 if S is greater than 3, *or* if S is less than 0. So, if anything other than 1, 2, or 3 is entered, the program will branch to line 9999, the end of the program. In this section again, we can see that it would be very easy to add additional IF...THEN statements to select more than three conversion routines.

The next section of the program is where the conversions actually are done. There are actually three "subsections," each consisting of the BASIC statements necessary to perform one of the three conversions. Let us look at the whole section at once, and notice how the three subsections are very similar.

```
2100 REM ---CONVERT INCHES TO CENTIMETERS
2110 PRINT
2120 INPUT "ENTER LENGTH IN INCHES "; I
2130 LET C = 2.54*I
2140 PRINT I;" INCHES IS EQUAL TO ";C;" CENTIMETERS"
2150 GOTO 2000

2200 REM ---CONVERT POUNDS TO KILOGRAMS
2210 PRINT
2220 INPUT "ENTER WEIGHT IN POUNDS "; P
2230 LET K = .4536*P
2240 PRINT P;" POUNDS IS EQUAL TO ";K;" KILOGRAMS"
2250 GOTO 2000

2300 REM ---CONVERT QUARTS TO LITERS
2310 PRINT
2320 INPUT "ENTER VOLUME IN QUARTS "; Q
2300 LET L = .9463*Q
```

79

```
2340 PRINT Q;" QUARTS IS EQUAL TO ";L;" LITERS"
2350 GOTO 2000

9999 END
```

Notice that each subsection begins with a blank PRINT statement to effect the double-spacing. Then an INPUT statement is used to get the particular anglo quantity to be converted. Next, a LET statement is used to perform the arithmetic conversion of the anglo quantity to a metric quantity. Notice that the conversion factors are "numeric constants" built into the statements. These can be found in any metric conversion table. Then, a PRINT statement is used to print out the answer in a sentence form. Notice how the variables representing both the anglo and metric values are imbedded right into the output line. Finally, after each subsection, a GOTO statement causes the program to branch back to the beginning where the menu is displayed again. This procedure is repeated as many times as desired until a value other than 1, 2, or 3 is entered as the desired selection, at which time the program is ended.

The following is an example of how the program runs:

```
METRIC CONVERSION PROGRAM
1 - INCHES TO CENTIMETERS
2 - POUNDS TO KILOGRAMS
3 - QUARTS TO LITERS
9 - TO END THE PROGRAM

ENTER YOUR SELECTION? 1

ENTER LENGTH IN INCHES? 6
6 INCHES EQUAL TO 15.24 CENTIMETERS

METRIC CONVERSION PROGRAM

1 - INCHES TO CENTIMETERS
2 - POUNDS TO KILOGRAMS
3 - QUARTS TO LITERS
9 - TO END THE PROGRAM

ENTER YOUR SELECTION? 2

ENTER WEIGHT IN POUNDS? 155
155 POUNDS IS EQUAL TO 70.308 KILOGRAMS
```

```
METRIC CONVERSION PROGRAM

1 - INCHES TO CENTIMETERS
2 - POUNDS TO KILOGRAMS
3 - QUARTS TO LITERS
9 - TO END THE PROGRAM

ENTER YOUR SELECTION? 3

ENTER VOLUME IN QUARTS? 4
4 QUARTS IS EQUAL TO 3.7852 LITERS

METRIC CONVERSION PROGRAM

1 - INCHES TO CENTIMETERS
2 - POUNDS TO KILOGRAMS
3 - QUARTS TO LITERS
9 - TO END THE PROGRAM

ENTER YOUR SELECTION? 9
```

Notice that each time a conversion is completed, the program returns to display the entire menu again. Since once would probably be sufficient, we might want to modify the program so that only the message "ENTER YOUR SELECTION?" would be displayed after the first time through the program. This can easily be done by replacing all of the GOTO 2000 statements following the conversions with GOTO 2070.

In a later chapter, we will use this same application for another example of a more powerful metric converson program that will provide a method for having many more conversion routines. The important things to learn from this example are the "menu" concept, and the use of the IF...THEN statement to selectively branch to different parts of the same program.

SIMPLE FUNCTION STATEMENTS

Many programming applications require that some operations be performed frequently. There are several of these functions that can be used by many different types of programs. For this reason, there are special "key words" used in BASIC to invoke these functions. There are quite a few different functions, some for use with numeric data, and others for use with string data. At this point, we will take a look at three of the most simple numeric functions. These are easy to understand, and can be used right away.

ABS, Absolute Value Function

The ABS function is used to get the "absolute value" of a number. This is defined as the actual numeric value of the number, ignoring the sign. The most common form of this statement looks like this:

    LET A = ABS(X)

Here, the variable (A) is replaced with the "absolute value" of the variable (X). For example:

    ABS(5) = 5
    ABS(13.25) = 13.25
    ABS(—25) = 25
    ABS(0) = 0
    ABS(5—12) = 7

Notice that the absolute value of a number can never be negative. It is always a positive number equal to the actual numeric value of the contents within the parentheses. This can be a numeric constant, a numeric variable, or an expression of numeric terms such as:

    LET A = ABS(12*X—6)

or,

    LET B = ABS(I+J+(K/3))

This function is useful for finding the actual difference between two numbers without being concerned as to whether they are positive or negative.

INT, Integerize Function

This INT function is especially useful for deriving the closest whole number to a numeric value. Really, all it does is to "truncate"

I'm integerizing this number with my trusty truncating saw

INT(345.897)

all of the digits of a number that are to the right of the decimal point. For example:

```
INT(25.035) = 25
INT(.95) = 0
INT(100.9999) = 100
INT(—12.2) = —12
```

So, this provides a way of getting rid of unwanted decimal positions. The common form used for the INT statement is:

```
LET A = INT(X)
```

where (X) is either a numeric constant, a numeric variable, or a numeric expression such as:

```
LET A = INT(12*B—2)
LET B = INT(.5*N)
```

One common usage of the INT statement is to allow for the rounding off of numeric variables to the nearest whole number. This is done very easily in BASIC as follows:

```
LET X = INT(X + .5)
```

For example, if;

$$X = 3.49999, \text{ then}$$
$$X + .5 = 3.99999, \text{ so}$$
$$INT(X + .5) = 3$$

However, if:

$$X = 3.50001, \text{ then}$$
$$X + .5 = 4.00001, \text{ so}$$
$$INT(X + .5) = 4$$

Using this technique, we can always guarantee that an answer that we are going to print out will be printed as a whole number.

RND, Randomize Function

This function allows the programmer to generate a random number. This is sort of like cutting a deck of cards, or spinning the wheel of fortune, or even throwing the dice. There is no way of knowing just what the result of the RND function will be. It will however always be returned as a number between 0 and 1. It might be .573 or .00941, or .0003 or any other number between 0 and 1. This random number can then be used to generate other numbers in other ranges simply by using multiplication. For example, if we wanted to program a deck of cards being cut, we would want the result of the RND function to be a number from 1 to 52. This can be done by multiplying the number returned by the RND function by the numeric constant 52 and then adding a numeric 1 to that. The general form of the RND function is as follows:

```
100 LET A = RND(X)
```

The variable (X) has a special purpose which is to control the way in which the random numbers are generated. If (X) is less than zero, a new sequence of random numbers is started. If (X) is greater than zero, the next random number in the sequence is returned. If (X) is equal to zero, the last used random number will

RND(1)

be returned again. The variable (A) is then set equal to the random value between 0 and 1.

This is not always the way that all forms of BASIC implement the RND function. Some of them begin generating new random numbers when the variable within the parentheses is equal to 0, while others will operate with only the keyword "RND" or "RANDOMIZE."

Combining Functions

In order to write even more sophisticated programs, it is possible to combine these functions within one statement. For example, we can write a statement like the following:

```
LET A = INT(2*ABS(X—1))
```

or,

```
LET B = ABS(INT(X)—INT(Y))
```

85

Let us say that what we really want is to get a random number between 1 and 52 to simulate a deck of cards being cut. We can use a combination of the RND and INT functions like this:

    LET C = INT(52*RND(—1))+1

The RND function would be done first because of the way that the parentheses are arranged, so that a random number between 0 and 1 would be generated. Then, the multiplication would follow, yielding a decimal number between 0 and 52. Next, the digits to the right of the decimal point would be stripped off using the INT function. This would result in an integer with a value ranging from 0 through 51. Finally, we will add one to the result so that we will end up with a number from 1 to 52.

We can use the same technique to simulate a throw of the dice as follows:

    LET T = INT(6*RND(—1))+1

or, we could "flip a coin" like this:

    LET F = INT(2*RND(—1))+1

Notice that we are always using the value of —1 to control the RND function so that we will get a new random sequence. Once a sequence has been started, it "seeds" itself, and we could change the argument of the RND function to 1 which would then continue to give us the next random number in the particular seeding sequence.

Another entertaining application of the RND function is in a little program that plays a number guessing game with you. The RND function is used to generate a number from 1 to 1,000. Then you have to guess what the number is and enter your guess through the keyboard. The program will then let you know if your guess was high or low, and give you another chance if you didn't guess it right. It also keeps track of how many chances it took for you to guess the number, and prints the total out at the end.

```
10 REM ----NUMBER GUESSING GAME USING RND
20 LET N = INT(1000*RND(—1))+1
30 LET T = 0
40 PRINT "OK, START GUESSING"
50 REM ----INPUT A GUESS AND COUNT IT
60 INPUT G
70 LET T = T+1
80 REM ----CHECK FOR A HIT
90 IF G = N THEN GOTO 160
100 REM ----CHECK FOR HIGH GUESS
110 IF G > N THEN PRINT "YOUR GUESS IS HIGH"
120 REM ----CHECK FOR LOW GUESS
130 IF G < N THEN PRINT "YOUR GUESS IS LOW"
140 GOTO 60
150 REM ----YOU GUESSED THE NUMBER
160 PRINT "YOU GUESSED THE NUMBER IN "; T; " TRYS"
170 PRINT "DO YOU WANT TO PLAY AGAIN? (Y/N)"
180 INPUT A$
190 IF A$ = "Y" THEN GOTO 20
200 END

RUN
OK, START GUESSING
?500
YOUR GUESS IS HIGH
?250
YOUR GUESS IS LOW
?375
YOUR GUESS IS HIGH
?300
YOU GUESSED THE NUMBER IN 4 TRYS
DO YOU WANT TO PLAY AGAIN? (Y/N)
?N
OK
```

THE SUBROUTINE CONCEPT

There are many occasions during the writing of a program on which it would be desirable to "chop up" a program into smaller parts. Sometimes, it is just too difficult to write one big program that takes care of everything. Other times, there is one series of operations that must be performed several times throughout the entire program. It would be tedious to write this series into the program every place that it is needed, and the resulting program would be unnecessarily large. These are two very good reasons for

GOSUB French Horn Solo

the development of the "subroutine." As its name implies, a subroutine is a "subpart" of a program. It is a routine which is performed at some specified time, and does the same thing each time. The subroutine need only be "written" once, somewhere within the program, and then "called" by the program when it's execution is necessary. When the subroutine has completed its operation, it "returns" to the main program at the point right after the line where the main program called the subroutine. This is especially useful in situations where a simple GOTO statement just doesn't quite handle it.

Subroutines are composed of BASIC statements just like any other program. The statements all have line numbers and must follow all of the rules that apply to any program statement. The subroutine is invoked through the use of a special BASIC statement called GOSUB. The form of the GOSUB statement is as follows:

```
100 GOSUB 2000
```

Directly following the word GOSUB must be a valid line number that represents the first line of the part of the program that is to be considered the subroutine. When the GOSUB statement is executed, the program branches to the line number specified in the statement. All of the subroutine statements are then executed until another special BASIC statement known as RETURN is encountered. At that time, the program branches back to the line directly following the GOSUB statement that caused the original branch. The following is a general example of the subroutine concept.

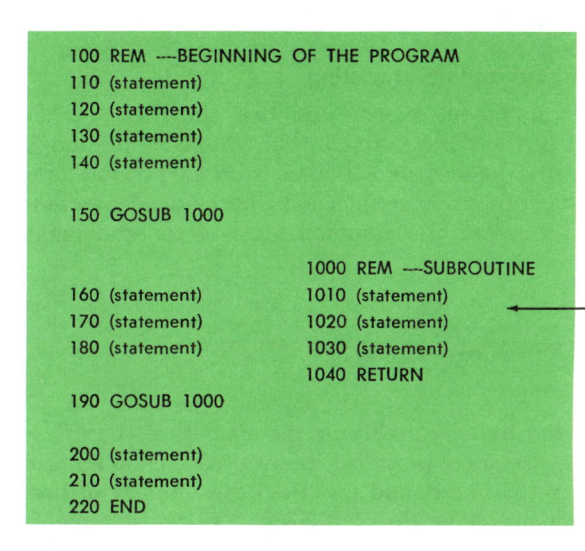

```
100 REM ---BEGINNING OF THE PROGRAM
110 (statement)
120 (statement)
130 (statement)
140 (statement)

150 GOSUB 1000

                        1000 REM ---SUBROUTINE
160 (statement)         1010 (statement)
170 (statement)         1020 (statement)
180 (statement)         1030 (statement)
                        1040 RETURN
190 GOSUB 1000

200 (statement)
210 (statement)
220 END
```

This is the subroutine. Note it would appear at the end of the program because it starts at line 1000.

Statements 100 through 140 are normal BASIC statements. At line 150 we see the first GOSUB statement which references line 1000. This is where the subroutine begins and at line 150 it is desired to branch to that subroutine and perform whatever statements are there. The subroutine is located at lines 1000 through 1400. On line 1400 we see the RETURN statement which causes the program to branch back to the line directly following the point at which the branch to the subroutine occurred. That will cause the program to go back to line 160 in the main program and continue executing statements there. Again at line 200, we see that there is another GOSUB statement which will cause a branch to line 1000 to occur. Again, the subroutine is executed until the RETURN statement at line 1400 is once again executed. The program then goes back to the next line after the GOSUB, which is line 210 this time. From here, the program keeps running until the END statement at line 240 is encountered.

In this particular example, we can see that if the statements that comprise the subroutine are found only once within the program, and that we can access these statements from several places in the main program, then the overall program has been made smaller through the use of the subroutine concept. Without the subroutine ability, we would have had to incorporate the same statements at two places in the main program, once after line 140, and again after line 190. In a sense, the GOSUB statement is like an unconditional branch with a return address telling it where to come back to when the RETURN statement is executed.

ON...GOSUB, Indexed Subroutine Branching

The ON...GOSUB statement works just like the ON...GOTO statement does. That is, there is a variable that is used as the index for the ON...GOSUB statement, and there is a list of possible line numbers to which the subroutine branch is to be made depending upon the value of the index. The common form of the statement looks like this:

```
100 ON K GOSUB 1000,2000,3000,4000,....
```

Again, the value of the index variable at the time that the ON... GOSUB statement is executed must be interpreted as an integer whole number greater than zero, and less than the number of line numbers in the list which follows the GOSUB part of the statement. In the example above, if the value of K is equal to one, the statement will cause a subroutine branch to line 1000. If the value is two, the branch will be made to line 2000, and so on. Again, if the value of K is zero or greater than the number of line numbers in the list, the program will ignore the ON...GOSUB statement completely, and resume execution on the next line in the program. If the value of K is negative, an error will result. After the subroutine has finished execution, the RETURN statement at its end will cause the program to come back to the next statement after the ON...GOSUB which caused the branch in the first place.

Here again, as with the ON...GOTO statement, the major advantage is that several different subroutines may be called depending upon the value of a variable in the program. This variable can be entered via an INPUT statement, or it may be computed in the program itself from some other data. In any case, its value at the time that the ON...GOSUB statement is executed will cause a controlled branch to a subroutine.

In the following pages, we will examine the use of the subroutine concept in two very common instances. The first involves the problem of getting the results of arithmetic operations to come out in whole pennies so that we can print an organized listing. The second example of subroutine usage provides a means of validating input data to make sure that it is within certain limits.

NUMERIC "ROUND-OFF" SUBROUTINE

If we remember the Loan program, there was a small problem encountered whenever we did certain types of airthmetic operations and then tried to print out the results. Because of the way that BASIC controls the PRINT operation, if we try to print a variable which has a current value of 7.50015, *that is exactly what will be printed*, even if we are dealing with dollars and cents and the amount should really be printed as 7.50. One way to overcome this small problem is to "round off" the results of any arithmetic operation which is to be printed. The procedure for doing this is quite simple. It uses one of the simple functions which we learned in the last section. The INT function, which allows us to integerize a variable, is used to get rid of any trailing decimal places. But, since we are using numbers representing dollars and cents, there must be two places to the right of the decimal point in all of the numbers. Also, we want to make sure that the number that is left after the trailing decimal places are removed is rounded to the nearest cent. To accomplish all of these things, we can use the following procedure:

ADD .005 to the number
MULTIPLY the number by 100
INTegerize the new number
DIVIDE the integerized number by 100

Let us go through a few examples of this procedure to see how it works. We will start with the number we used a few lines back.

Original number	7.50015
ADD .005 to the number	7.50515
MULTIPLY by 100	750.515
INTegerize the number	750
DIVIDE by 100	7.5

Well, it still doesn't read 7.50 does it? This is because BASIC doesn't print trailing zeros after numbers. But, let us accept this for now. At least it doesn't print out 7.50015. Let us take another example that will work—a number like 3.466666.

Original number	3.466666
ADD .005 to the number	3.471666
MULTIPLY by 100	347.1666
INTegerize the number	347
DIVIDE by 100	3.47

There, now that is better. Next, let us take a look at how we go about writing a subroutine to do this operation. We could use a LET statement for each of the numeric operations that must be done, where the variable X represents the original number. It would look like this:

```
5000 REM ---ROUND OFF SUBROUTINE
5100 LET X = X+.005
5200 LET X = 100*X
5300 LET X = INT(X)
5400 LET X = X/100
5500 RETURN
```

Well, that seems to work just fine. However, the whole thing could be done with just one statement like this:

```
5000 REM ---ROUND OFF SUBROUTINE
5100 LET X = (INT(100*(X+.005)))/100
5200 RETURN
```

This approach uses "nested parentheses" to accomplish the same thing as the previous example. Because of the way that the parentheses are arranged, first the addition of .005 will be done then the multiplication by 100, then the INTegerization function and finally, the division by 100 to get back to the right decimal place, and then the variable X is replaced with the new value.

So then, how would we go about using this subroutine? Let us take a look at some examples. First of all, we would have to set up the variable X to contain whatever number we wanted to round off. This could be done with just a LET statement. Then we would have to GOSUB to the subroutine to perform the rounding operation. When the subroutine is finished, the RETURN statement will bring the program right back to the next line after the GOSUB. This would probably be a PRINT statement since we now have the number rounded off for printing. One ideal place to use this new subroutine would be in the Loan program. Let us see how we might modify the program to incorporate this subroutine. Fig. 2-2 is a reproduction of the entire Loan program with some additional notes.

```
1000 REM ---LOAN AMORTIZATION PROGRAM
1010 REM ---INPUT SECTION
1100 INPUT "ENTER THE AMOUNT OF THE LOAN"; L
1110 INPUT "ENTER THE ANNUAL INTEREST RATE"; R
1120 INPUT "ENTER THE TERM IN YEARS"; Y
1200 REM ---CHANGE ANNUAL RATE TO MONTHLY RATE
1210 LET I = R/12
1220 REM ---CHANGE YEARS TO MONTHS
1230 LET M = Y*12
1300 REM ---COMPUTE THE MONTHLY PAYMENT AND PRINT
1310 LET A = L*1*(1+I)^M/((1+I)^(M—1))
1320 PRINT "THE MONTHLY PAYMENT IS $"; A
1400 REM ---INITIALIZE FOR AMORTIZATION SCHEDULE
1410 LET B = L
1420 LET T = 0
1430 PRINT "NUM", "INTEREST", "PRINCIPAL", "PRIN BAL", "TOT INT"
1500 REM ---DO THE LOOP FOR THE NUMBER OF PAYMENTS
1510 FOR J = 1 TO M
1520 REM ---COMPUTE THE INTEREST
1530 LET I1 = B*I
1540 REM ---COMPUTE THE PRINCIPAL
1,550 LET P = A—I1
1560 REM ---FORCE OUT THE LAST PAYMENT
1570 IF J = M THEN LET P = B
1600 REM ---UPDATE THE LOAN BALANCE
1610 LET B = B—P
1620 REM ---UPDATE THE TOTAL INTEREST
1630 LET T = T+I1
1700 REM ---PRINT THE MONTHLY PAYMENT DETAIL
1710 PRINT J,I1,P,B,T
1720 NEXT J
1800 REM ---SEE IF DONE
1810 INPUT "PROCESS ANOTHER LOAN (YES/NO)"; A$
1820 IF A$ = "YES" THEN GOTO 1100
9999 END
```

Fig. 2-2. Listing of Loan program.

```
1000 REM ---LOAN AMORTIZATION PROGRAM
1010 REM ---INPUT SECTION
1100 INPUT "ENTER THE AMOUNT OF THE LOAN"; L
1110 INPUT "ENTER THE ANNUAL INTEREST RATE"; R
1120 INPUT "ENTER THE TERM IN YEARS"; Y
1200 REM ---CHANGE ANNUAL RATE TO MONTHLY RATE
1210 LET I = R/12
1220 REM ---CHANGE YEARS TO MONTHS
1230 LET M = Y*12
1300 REM ---COMPUTE THE MONTHLY PAYMENT AND PRINT
1310 LET A = (I*L)/((1—(I+1)^—M))
```

Here is one place where the round-off subroutine will come in very useful. At this point, the monthly payment A could be equal to a variety of different decimal places, depending upon the number of decimals in the interest rate R, and what happens to all of these numbers when the arithmetic operations at line 1310 are performed. The monthly payment amount might be as simple as 332.60, or it might come out as weird as 124.12507. So this is the first place in the LOAN program where we are about to PRINT out the monthly payment, and we don't want it to come out with five places to the right of the decimal. Let us add a few lines of program right here then, to GOSUB to a subroutine to round off the monthly payment amount. It looks like this:

```
1312 LET X = A
1314 GOSUB 5000
1316 LET A = X
```
— *Line 5000 is where the round-off subroutine starts.*

Notice that we can add lines into the program by using line numbers that are available because we planned ahead when we assigned the original line numbers. Here again, we are trying to leave a little slack in the line numbering scheme in the event that we might need to further modify this section of program in the future. We need to add three lines of program here in order to do the rounding operation. First, since the round-off subroutine always rounds off the variable called X, we must make X equal to the number that we want to be rounded. Therefore, we use the LET statement at line 1312 to get X equal to the monthly payment amount A. Next comes the GOSUB statement that will cause the program to branch to line 5000 where the round-off subroutine is located. After the subroutine has finished, the program will branch back to the next line after the GOSUB statement. That would be line 1316, where we must now replace the value calculated for A with the rounded off version which the subroutine has left stored in the variable X. Now, we can let the program go ahead and PRINT the new rounded off value of A.

Now, you may be wondering just how effective it is to use three lines of additional program just to be able to use the subroutine. Why not just insert the round-off formula as *one* line of program at the same place in the program. In this case, it is probably a trade-off. The amount of memory needed to accommodate the round-off formula is probably about the same as is required to store the three additional statements needed to use the subroutine. But, in other cases this is not always true. We have chosen a rather simple example to illustrate how subroutines work. The same principles would apply to much more complex subroutines.

```
1320 PRINT "THE MONTHLY PAYMENT IS $"; A
1400 REM --INITIALIZE FOR AMORTIZATION SCHEDULE
1410 LET B = L
1420 LET T = 0
1430 PRINT "NUM", "INTEREST", "PRINCIPAL", "PRIN BAL", "TOT INT"
1500 REM --DO THE LOOP FOR THE NUMBER OF PAYMENTS
1510 FOR J = 1 TO M
1520 REM --COMPUTE THE INTEREST
1530 LET I1 = B*I
```

Recall here we use a FOR...NEXT statement (FOR J = 1 TO M) to make a loop for each month of the schedule. The index J will vary from 1 to M (M = the term of the loan in months). The NEXT J statement for this loop is coming up later, so don't worry. Now let us continue with the loan program.

This is also another place in the Loan program where the result of the arithmetic operation at line 1530 is undependable. The amount of interest for the particular monthly payment may come out to be some funny looking number with lots of digits to the right of the decimal point. So, to eliminate this problem, we will insert three more lines of program here to allow the round off subroutine to take care of the extra digits.

```
1532 LET X = I1
1534 GOSUB 5000
1536 LET I1 = X
```

Line 5000 is the round-off subroutine. I1 is the interest for a particular month J.

Here again, we follow the same procedure. First we set the variable X equal to the value of I1 which was just computed. Then, using the GOSUB statement we branch to the subroutine. Upon return from the subroutine, we must replace I1 with the new "rounded off" version.

From here on, there is no further need for rounding things off. The results of addition or subtraction operations will always yield a number with the same decimal places as the number with the most decimals which was involved in the arithmetic. For example, if we subtract:

$$\begin{array}{r} 1{,}500.00 \\ -125.35 \\ \hline 1{,}474.65 \end{array}$$

the answer has two digits to the right of the decimal, just like both of the numbers involved in the subtraction. Likewise,

$$\begin{array}{r} 800.0 \\ -57.25 \\ \hline 742.75 \end{array}$$

Again, the answer has the same number of digits to the right of the decimal point as that of the number with the largest that was involved in the arithmetic. So, since all the rest of the arithmetic operations in the LOAN program are either addition or subtraction, there will be no further need for the round-off subroutine.

Here is the rest of the program. Recall line 1550 calculates the principal part of the monthly payment ($P = A - I1$), line 1570 forces the last payment (when $J = M$) to be equal to the actual remaining amount on the loan ($P = B$), line 1610 calculates the new principal balance B, line 1630 accumulates the total interest paid, and line 1710 prints out the five items in the loan schedule (NUM, INTEREST, PRINCIPAL, PRIN BAL, TOT INT) in neat columns across the page. The NEXT J statement at line 1720 causes the process to repeat for the next month J. The statements 1800-1820 check if you wish to process another loan.

```
1540 REM ---COMPUTE THE PRINCIPAL
1550 LET P = A—I1
1560 REM ---FORCE OUT THE LAST PAYMENT
1570 IF J = M THEN LET P = B
1600 REM ---UPDATE THE LOAN BALANCE
1610 LET B = B—P
1620 REM ---UPDATE THE TOTAL INTEREST
1630 LET T = T+I1
1700 REM ---PRINT THE MONTHLY PAYMENT DETAIL
1710 PRINT J,I1,P,B,T
1720 NEXT J
1800 REM --SEE IF DONE
1810 INPUT "PROCESS ANOTHER LOAN (YES/NO)"; A$
1820 IF A$ = "YES"THEN GOTO 1100
```

The last thing we do is insert the round-off subroutine. There is one other thing that we need to insert just before the subroutine. At line 1820, if the result of the IF statement is false, the branch to line 1100 will not be taken, and the *next line* will be executed. Since we don't want to execute the subroutine when we get here, the first thing that we must add is an unconditional branch to the END statement at line 9999. Here is the rest of the program.

```
1830 GOTO 9999
5000 REM ----ROUND OFF SUBROUTINE
5010 LET X = (INT(100*(X+.005)))/100
5020 RETURN
9999 END
```

Fig. 2-3 shows the complete listing of the enhanced loan program with the numeric round-off subroutine.

ERROR-CHECKING SUBROUTINE

Another simple use of the subroutine concept can be illustrated by the example of checking for errors in INPUT data. There is an old programmer's proverb that says, "Garbage in, garbage out." This simply means that if you enter invalid information into a computer program, you cannot depend on the results. In some situations, the program might be "faked out" by the invalid information, and go right ahead and process it anyway. This usually yields an invalid answer, or output. In other cases, the INPUTing of invalid information may cause a program error to occur which might result in the total malfunction of the program. This is especially true if the INPUT information is to be used in a program-control statement such as a FOR...NEXT loop where the use of an invalid loop parameter could cause the loop to go on forever.

This subroutine provides the most basic error-checking capability and can be used in both the Loan program and the Metric Conversion program. What it will do is:

1. Check for a positive, nonzero number.
2. Check that the number does not exceed some predetermined maximum value.
3. Display an error message if either of these conditions is not correct, and re-INPUT the data.

The subroutine looks like this:

```
6000 REM ----NUMERIC ERROR CHECKING SUBROUTINE
6100 IF X > 0 AND X <=Z THEN RETURN
6200 INPUT "INVALID ENTRY, TRY AGAIN"; X
6300 GOTO 6100
```

```
1000 REM ---LOAN AMORTIZATION PROGRAM
1010 REM ---INPUT SECTION
1100 INPUT "ENTER THE AMOUNT OF THE LOAN"; L
1110 INPUT "ENTER THE ANNUAL INTEREST RATE"; R
1120 INPUT "ENTER THE TERM IN YEARS"; Y
1200 REM ---CHANGE ANNUAL RATE TO MONTHLY RATE
1210 LET I = R/12
1220 REM ---CHANGE YEARS TO MONTHS
1230 LET M = Y*12
1300 REM ---COMPUTE THE MONTHLY PAYMENT AND PRINT
1310 LET A = (I*L)/((1—(I+1)^—M))
1312 LET X = A
1314 GOSUB 5000
1316 LET A = X
1320 PRINT "THE MONTHLY PAYMENT IS $"; A
1400 REM ---INITIALIZE FOR AMORTIZATION SCHEDULE
1410 LET B = L
1420 LET T = 0
1430 PRINT "NUM", "INTEREST", "PRINCIPAL", "PRIN BAL", "TOT INT"
1500 REM ---DO THE LOOP FOR THE NUMBER OF PAYMENTS
1510 FOR J = 1 TO M
1520 REM ---COMPUTE THE INTEREST
1530 LET I1 = B*I
1532 LET X = I1
1534 GOSUB 5000
1536 LET I1 = X
1540 REM ---COMPUTE THE PRINCIPAL
1550 LET P = A—I1
1560 REM ---FORCE OUT THE LAST PAYMENT
1570 IF J = M THEN LET P = B
1600 REM ---UPDATE THE LOAN BALANCE
1610 LET B = B—P
1620 REM ---UPDATE THE TOTAL INTEREST
1630O LET T = T+I1
1700 REM ---PRINT THE MONTHLY PAYMENT DETAIL
1710 PRINT J,I1,P,B,T
1720 NEXT J
1800 REM ---SEE IF DONE
1810 INPUT "PROCESS ANOTHER LOAN (YES/NO)"; A$
1820 IF A$ = "YES" THEN GOTO 1100
1830 GOTO 9999
5000 REM ---ROUND OFF SUBROUTINE
5010 LET X = (INT(100*(X+.005)))/100
5020 RETURN
9999 END
```

Fig. 2-3. Listing of the enhanced Loan program with numeric round-off subroutine included. Old parts of program are shaded with green.

The real work here is done by the IF...THEN statement on line 6100. The first thing that happens here is that it checks to see that the value of the variable X is greater than zero. It also checks to see that X is less than or equal to another variable called Z. Remember how the IF...THEN statement works? If *both* of the premises are true, then the result is also true; meaning that the RETURN statement is executed, taking the program back to where the subroutine branch was made because X passed the test. Here again, we are using a variable called X which must be set up in the main program to be equal to the current value of the INPUT data to be checked. Also, the variable Z must be set up by the main program prior to the branch to the subroutine, to be equal to the maximum value that the INPUT data can have. If either of the two premises in the IF...THEN statement is *not* true, the next line following the IF...THEN statement is executed. This is the INPUT statement which causes an error message to be output, and then the data to be INPUT again. The GOTO on line 6300 takes the subroutine back to check the new value.

We will use this subroutine to modify the Metric Conversion program so that we can check the INPUT data as desired. Here is the program listing up to line 2120.

```
2000 REM ---METRIC CONVERSION PROGRAM
2010 REM ---DISPLAY THE MENU
2020 PRINT
2030 PRINT "METRIC CONVERSION PROGRAM"
2040 PRINT
2041 PRINT "1 - INCHES TO CENTIMETERS"
2042 PRINT "2 - POUNDS TO KILOGRAMS"
2043 PRINT "3 - QUARTS TO LITERS"
2049 PRINT "9 - TO END THE PROGRAM"
2050 PRINT
2060 REM ---GET THE SELECTION
2070 INPUT "ENTER YOUR SELECTION"; S
2080 REM ---DECIDE WHERE TO BRANCH
2081 IF S = 1 THEN GOTO 2100
2082 IF S = 2 THEN GOTO 2200
2083 IF S = 3 THEN GOTO 2300
2089 IF S>3 OR S<1 THEN GOTO 9999
2100 REM ---CONVERT INCHES TO CENTIMETERS
2110 PRINT
2120 INPUT "ENTER LENGTH IN INCHES "; I
```

Here is a likely place to use the error-check subroutine. At line 2120 the program has just INPUT a value for the variable I which represents the number of inches that is to be converted to centimeters. If we are going to use the error-check subroutine to test this value, we must first establish the allowable maximum value for I. For the purpose of demonstration, let us suppose that we don't want to convert anything greater than 36 inches. Since we will have to get the variable X equal to the value that was INPUT for (I), why not INPUT X directly by changing line 2120 also. The new statements look like this:

```
2120 INPUT "ENTER LENGTH IN INCHES "; X
2122 LET Z = 36
2124 GOSUB 6000
2126 LET I = X
```

Notice that when the subroutine returns to the main program we must finally set I equal to the INPUT value X (line 2126). In a similar manner, we can insert statements in the other conversion sections of the program in order to check the INPUT data and choose other values for the allowable maximum. Here is how the program continues to line 2220.

```
2130 LET C = 2.54*I
2140 PRINT I;" INCHES IS EQUAL TO ";C;" CENTIMETERS"
2150 GOTO 2000
2200 REM ---CONVERT POUNDS TO KILOGRAMS
2210 PRINT
2220 INPUT "ENTER WEIGHT IN POUNDS "; P
```

We will set a maximum weight of 2000 pounds to convert to kilograms and add a GOSUB to our error-checking subroutine.

```
2220 INPUT "ENTER WEIGHT IN POUNDS "; X
2222 LET Z = 2000
2224 GOSUB 6000
2226 LET P = X
```

Notice again, that we have replaced the INPUT statement with one which INPUTs the value of X directly. Then once the value is determined to be correct, we set P equal to X. Continuing with the program we have:

```
2230 LET K = .4536*P
2240 PRINT P;" POUNDS IS EQUAL TO ";K;" KILOGRAMS"
2250 GOTO 2000
2300 REM ---CONVERT QUARTS TO LITERS
2310 PRINT
2320 INPUT "ENTER VOLUME IN QUARTS "; Q
```

Here is the last part to be inserted into the program. The allowable maximum liquid volume to be entered will be 100 quarts.

```
2320 INPUT "ENTER VOLUME IN QUARTS "; X
2322 LET Z = 100
2324 GOSUB 6000
2326 LET Q = X
2330 LET L = .9463*Q
2340 PRINT Q;" QUARTS IS EQUAL TO ";L;" LITERS"
2350 GOTO 2000
```

Here is where we will insert the subroutine itself.

```
6000 REM ---ERROR CHECKING SUBROUTINE
6100 IF X>0 and X<=Z THEN RETURN
6200 INPUT "INVALID ENTRY, TRY AGAIN "; X
6300 GOTO 6100

9999 END
```

Fig. 2-4 shows the complete listing of the metric conversion program with the error-checking subroutine and code added.

We've learned a large number of powerful new BASIC statements and a couple of useful program methods. The next thing we will learn about will allow your programming to jump to a higher level of sophistication through the use of the "array" concept—so lets get moving.

```
2000 REM ---METRIC CONVERSION PROGRAM
2010 REM ---DISPLAY THE MENU
2020 PRINT
2030 PRINT "METRIC CONVERSION PROGRAM"
2040 PRINT
2041 PRINT "1 - INCHES TO CENTIMETERS"
2042 PRINT "2 - POUNDS TO KILOGRAMS"
2043 PRINT "3 - QUARTS TO LITERS"
2049 PRINT "9 - TO END THE PROGRAM"
2050 PRINT
2060 REM ---GET THE SELECTION
2070 INPUT "ENTER YOUR SELECTION"; S
2080 REM ---DECIDE WHERE TO BRANCH
2081 IF S = 1 THEN GOTO 2100
2082 IF S = 2 THEN GOTO 2200
2083 IF S = 3 THEN GOTO 2300
2089 IF S>3 OR S<1 THEN GOTO 9999
2100 REM ---CONVERT INCHES TO CENTIMETERS
2110 PRINT
2120 INPUT "ENTER LENGTH IN INCHES "; I
2122 LET Z = 36
2124 GOSUB 6000
2126 LET I = X
2130 LET C = 2.54*I
2140 PRINT I;" INCHES IS EQUAL TO ";C;" CENTIMETERS"
2150 GOTO 2000
2200 REM ---CONVERT POUNDS TO KILOGRAMS
2210 PRINT
2220 INPUT "ENTER WEIGHT IN POUNDS "; X
2222 LET Z = 2000
2224 GOSUB 6000
2226 LET P = X
2230 LET K = .4536*P
2240 PRINT P;" POUNDS IS EQUAL TO ";K;" KILOGRAMS"
2250 GOTO 2000
2300 REM ---CONVERT QUARTS TO LITERS
2310 PRINT
2320 INPUT "ENTER VOLUME IN QUARTS "; X
2322 LET Z = 100
2324 GOSUB 6000
2326 LET Q = X
2330 LET L = .9463*Q
2340 PRINT Q;" QUARTS IS EQUAL TO ";L;" LITERS"
2350 GOTO 2000
6000 REM ---ERROR CHECKING SUBROUTINE
6100 IF X>0 and X<=Z THEN RETURN
6200 INPUT "INVALID ENTRY, TRY AGAIN "; X
6300 GOTO 6100
9999 END
```

Fig. 2-4. Metric Conversion program with error-checking subroutine and code added. Old parts of program are shaded with green.

CHAPTER
3

Getting Organized

So far in our study of BASIC we have learned how to deal with information which is made up of a single part. We can manipulate numbers by giving each a variable name, or groups of letters by giving each string a string-variable name. In order to make BASIC programming more powerful, the originators decided to allow you to take a single variable name and use it to represent information that is made up of several parts. In this section we will explore the concept of "arrays and subscripted variables," a method whereby information may be divided into several subelements or parts, and each part can be organized and referenced by your program with ease. Such a method means we can represent information inside the computer in a more organized manner than is possible with single-value variables. As a way of illustrating the array idea we will show how to make a program that plays TIC-TAC-TOE against you by using the array concept throughout its operation. As a by-product of the program we will see how a computer game is made, the steps involved in converting a popular game into a series of program steps called "flowcharting," and how a game "algorithm" is formed which gives it the machine intelligence to figure out how to win.

ARRAYS AND SUBSCRIPTED VARIABLES

Arrays are items of data arranged and stored under a single variable name. An array has a simple name like regular variables but instead of that variable only representing a single value, an array represents several values. The parts that make up an array are called its "elements." Each element can be a number or a string. An array element is identified by an array name followed by an integer number which can be as low as 0 or as large as 255. The number is enclosed in parentheses and follows the array name. The number serves to identify a unique element in the array. We call a variable with a referencing number following it a "subscripted variable." The general form of a subscripted variable looks like this:

> ARRAYNAME (integer constant)

The ARRAYNAME part of a subscripted variable is any legal BASIC variable name as described in Chapter 1. The "subscript" is the integer constant following the ARRAYNAME and surrounded by parentheses. The subscript tells us which item of the variable we are referencing.

In order to make this concept of arrays more lucid consider this "loaf of bread" analogy. Imagine that a loaf of bread is a variable in a program. The loaf has a name, say L, and we can talk about the variable loaf just like it is a BASIC variable. Now without arrays we can only talk about a single loaf of bread when we use the letter L. We cannot indicate a particular piece of the bread, like the center of the loaf, or the heels, or any other part of the loaf. Further, we cannot tell if the bread is wheat, white, or rye unless we make up some new variable to stand for these different items of information. To talk about a loaf of wheat bread we must create a new variable, say L2, or W for Wheat. If the bread was sliced and sold in a varying number of slices in a loaf, we could not easily represent these in BASIC because we would soon run out of variable names for each slice.

But, if we represent the loaf as an array, things become much more efficient and organized. What we can do is divide the loaf into several slices and use the array element to reference a certain slice in the loaf. The first slice would be L(1), the second L(2), the third L(3), and so on. The last slice would be determined by the largest numbered element which for now we will say is L(10). With subscripted variables unique for each slice, we can add more information about the bread. For example, if the loaf was raisin bread, we could specify how many raisins were in each slice, rather than just the total number of raisins in the loaf. If slice number one has 7 raisins in it we could represent this in BASIC as:

```
L(1) = 7
```

This is read as "L sub 1 equals 7" and means the value of element 1 of the array L is 7.

Suppose we wanted to set up the bread array (L) so that each slice contained exactly five raisins. We could do this two ways: (1) with explicit LET statements for each element, or (2) with a FOR...NEXT loop. The LET approach is rather straightforward, but requires quite a bit of code. Assuming we have five slices in the loaf, the LET approach looks like this:

```
100 LET L(1)=5
110 LET L(2)=5
120 LET L(3)=5
130 LET L(4)=5
140 LET L(5)=5
```

Now each element of the array L contains the constant 5.

The other approach is to use a FOR...NEXT loop and is possible because we can make the subscript (the value between parentheses) an integer variable. The integer variable subscript can be the index of the loop and each time it is incremented we are locating or referencing the specified element, like this:

```
100 FOR I=1 TO 5
110 LET L(I)=5
120 NEXT I
```

In this example, the array subscript is a variable called I. As I is incremented by the FOR...NEXT statement, the array changes to the next element, which is then set to the constant 5 by statement 110. As you can see, this approach requires less statements to accomplish the same thing as did the five LET statements.

In a similar manner we can make the elements of the array be displayed on the screen or terminal device by using another FOR ...NEXT loop with an imbedded PRINT statement in it like this:

```
200 FOR I=1 TO 5
210 PRINT L(I),
220 NEXT I
```

These statements make the elements of the array L appear on the screen in columns because of the comma following the LET statement.

We can also make the subscript of the array an expression, as long as the results of the expression evaluate to an integer. (An array subscript must be an integer because there is no such thing as a fractional element—L(1.5) just doesn't exist.) An example of an expression for a subscript would be when we want to reference the elements in some special order, such as just the last 5 elements of a 10 element array, like this

```
300 FOR I=1 TO 5
310 LET L(I+5)=5
320 NEXT I
```

Obviously array and subscripted variables make our programming job much easier and more flexible. But arrays are not limited to just a series of linear parts. We can further divide an array with the aid of a concept called "dimension."

DIMENSION WITH DIM

Arrays and subscripts are not limited to a single element. We can, for example, consider organizing our bread analogy into even more detail. Suppose you wanted to not just specify the particular slice in the loaf, but wanted to organize the loaf into sections, say a front, middle and an end. Now we have to specify two items: section and slice. How is this done? The answer is to consider that the loaf has two "dimensions." The first dimension is the slice. The second dimension is the section. BASIC accomplishes this concept by allowing you to specify a second independent subscript between the parentheses. These two subscripts must be separated by a comma, like this:

```
L(I,J)
```

Here the subscript I indicates the slice in the loaf L, and the subscript J indicates the section in the loaf L. For each section J there is a number of slices I which depends on the size of the array. We can call a dual subscripted array, a *two dimensional* array, because it has the equivalent of dimensions, just like height and width describe a room.

Now when we specify the loaf we talk about a particular section and a particular slice in that section. For example, to specify that we set the middle section (section 2) and the third slice in that section we would write:

```
LET L(3,2)=5
```

To help visualize the array we can imagine that the elements are arranged in the computer like this (assuming there are three sections and five slices per section):

```
L(1,1)  L(2,1)  L(3,1)  L(4,1)  L(5,1)
L(1,2)  L(2,2)  L(3,2)  L(4,2)  L(5,2)
L(1,3)  L(2,3)  L(3,3)  L(4,3)  L(5,3)
```

For each of the five slices there is one particular section it is associated with, (1-3). Thus we now have a total of 5 × 3 or 15 slices in the loaf. We say that array L is an I by J array in BASIC.

What is nice about BASIC arrays is that we can keep adding information, or dimensions, to the array by increasing the number of subscripts. For example, if we wanted to specify a particular section, slice, and *bakery* that the bread is found in we could add a third subscript, like this:

> L(I,J,K)

Here the subscript K stands for the bakery that the bread is found in and the subscripts I and J are as previously described. We now have a three dimensional array, or an I by J by K array.

Visualizing three dimensions is certainly not as easy as two, but for convenience you can imagine that the third dimension is like the length of a space, and the other two stand for height and width.

In order for BASIC to set aside the proper amount of memory space for holding the element values of the array we need to specify this before the array is used. BASIC provides a special keyword called DIM for this purpose. DIM appears at the beginning of a program that uses an array, and describes to the computer how many dimensions are in the array and how many elements are in each dimension. The general form of DIM is:

> DIM arrayname(I,J,K, . . .), arrayname(I,J,K, . . .), . . .

where arrayname is the symbolic name of the array which follows the convention for variable names and I, J, and K stand for the *maximum elements* of the array dimensions. For example, the two-dimensional array in the loaf analogy with three sections and five slices per section would be dimensioned as:

> DIM L(5,3)

The 5 indicates that the first dimension has a maximum of five elements in it and the second dimension has a maximum of three elements. Thus the computer sets aside 15 memory locations (or more if the values take up more than one byte each) for the array L.

For a three-dimensional array we would write:

```
DIM L(5,3,10)
```

where the 10 indicates that there are 10 bakeries each of which contains a loaf with 3 sections and 5 slices per section. Obviously the array needs $3 \times 5 \times 10$ elements or 150 total elements to fully describe all combinations.

As the general form of the DIM statement shows, we can have several arrays dimensioned on the same DIM statement by simply separating each with a comma. This saves us having to write separate DIM statements for each array we wish to dimension.

Is there any limit to the number of dimensions an array can have? The answer is yes, but the actual maximum number of dimensions is a function of which BASIC you are using. The simple BASICs such as the 4K and integer BASICs, only allow a single dimensional array. The 8K and extended BASICs allow a maximum number of dimensions usually determined by the longest line you can use. Thus the maximum dimensions may range up to 127, depending on how many elements are specified for each dimension. The maximum number of elements for a particular dimension is usually limited to about 255 in most BASICs.

Is the element 0 a legal element? In most cases the zero element means the same thing as the simple variable without dimension, i.e., $L(0)$ is the same as L. In general you should consult your BASIC manual to make sure this is the way your version actually works.

GAME BASIC: TIC-TAC-TOE

Arrays, as we have learned, are most useful for accessing information that is ordered in a special way. Games, particularly those employing a board and men or marks that move on the board, lend themselves well to simulation in BASIC using an array. In fact, games in BASIC have quickly become the most popular use for computers today, offering the proverbial battleground between man and machine.

In this section we will learn how the game of TIC-TAC-TOE can be represented in BASIC. The program will enable you to play against the computer. The computer will take care of everything—displaying the game board, moving the men, checking for ties or a winner, and allowing you to input your move. A special "move" algorithm" which allows the computer to decide what move to make will be developed. But before we get into the program let us review the rules of the game. Then, we will see how to translate these rules into program steps and how to expand them for an improved game.

Remember The Rules?

For review, there are two players in the game of TIC-TAC-TOE. One player uses an "X" marker and the second player (in this case the computer) uses a "O" marker. The playing board consists of a square divided into nine smaller squares, and the object of the player is to get three of his own markers in a straight line by filling a row, line, or diagonal. Plays are made on the board in alternate moves. If no player gets a line and all squares are filled the game is a tie, or "cat."

The moves of a typical game may go like this:

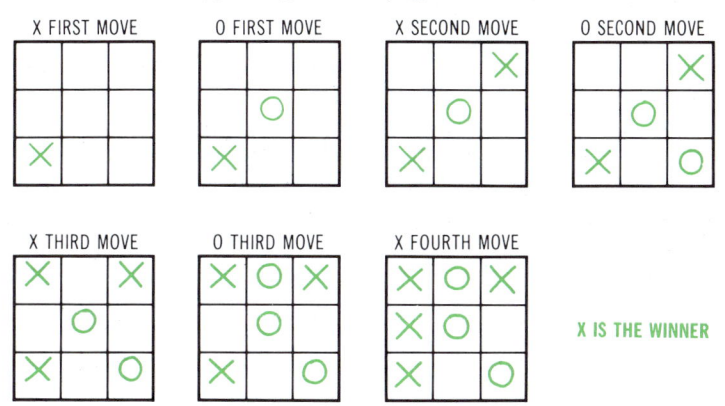

X FIRST MOVE   O FIRST MOVE   X SECOND MOVE   O SECOND MOVE

X THIRD MOVE   O THIRD MOVE   X FOURTH MOVE

X IS THE WINNER

There are a few simple strategies you can employ to make your chances of winning more likely. If you move first, take the center square. If you move second take the center square if it is unoccupied. If the center is already occupied, take a corner square. Then play to either block your opponent, or to win a line.

Representing the Board

Our first problem is to represent the board. A simple way to do this is to use a 9-element two-dimensional array called A(3,3). Since there are nine elements in the array, and there are three columns and three rows, the array will be dimensioned as:

```
DIM A(3,3)
```

The squares of the game board are referenced in the array like this:

A(1, 1)	A(1, 2)	A(1, 3)
A(2, 1)	A(2, 2)	A(2, 3)
A(3, 1)	A(3, 2)	A(3, 3)

Representing the Men

We also need some way to represent the two different players' marks, i.e., the X and the O. One way to do this allows the program to make decisions rapidly. We will use the number −1 to stand for the computer's man, and the number +1 (or just 1) to stand for the player's (opponent against the computer) man. The value of any element thus tells us who is in that particular square. An empty square will be represented by a 0 (zero) value. Thus, if $A(2,2) = -1$ then the computer has a man on the center square. If $A(3,3) = 1$ then the player has a man on the lower right corner of the board.

Overall Flow of the Game

In order to make the methods of converting a game like TIC-TAC-TOE to play on the computer we need to acomplish several steps. One way to visualize these steps is to use what is called a "flowchart." A flowchart is simply a diagram of the logic of the game, showing us what happens as the game proceeds and what decisions must be made. There are several special flowchart symbols for doing this and we will learn these as we develop the flowchart. A flowchart can have several levels of meaning, each of which gives more information about the action of the game itself. The most general flowchart explains the overall flow of the program and is shown in Fig. 3-1.

In this flowchart the boxes indicate the processes the game follows. The triangle symbol indicates a decision-making step. The flowchart shows that the game starts by displaying the rules of the game to the user, and then requests that the user select who goes first. After this the computer makes a move (or the player if he goes first) and then the board is displayed, the game checked for a tie or a winner, and the next player proceeds with a move. This generalized flowchart helps us visualize the overall logic of the game, but to use the flowchart we must expand it.

Fig. 3-2 shows the flowchart for the game in more detail. Processes that involve input and output are illustrated with a parallelo-

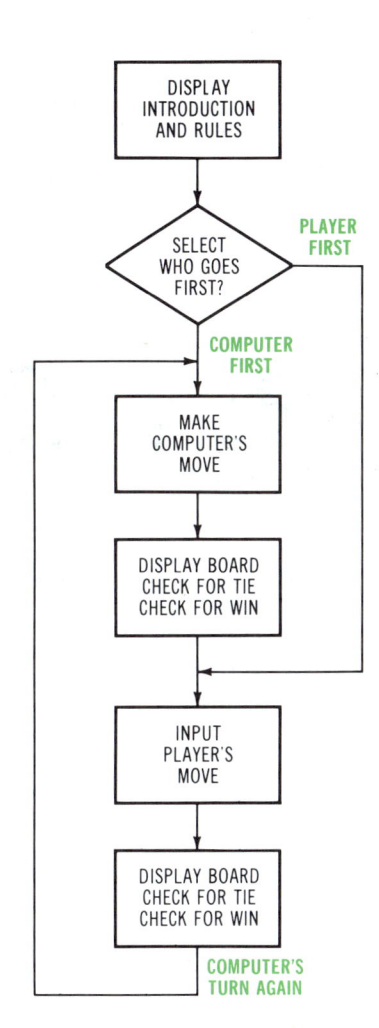

Fig. 3-1. Overall flowchart for TIC-TAC-TOE.

gram symbol. Decisions are made in triangle symbols and subroutines are set up as rectangles with pointed sides.

As you can see in the flowchart we have represented three important functions—display the board, check for a tie, and check for a winner as subroutines. Let us take a look at how they work.

Displaying the Board

One of the most important things the computer program must do is display the board after each player has made a move. This is accomplished in a simple subroutine that simply increments through each array element and prints it out on the screen.

113

To increment through the array we use the subscript I to stand for the row element and the subscript J to stand for a column element. Then I and J are used as the indexes of two FOR...NEXT loops. I is incremented after J has been incremented three times, and a PRINT statement makes the array elements appear on the screen just like the real board would. The code for the subroutine for displaying the game board looks like this:

```
6997 REM
6998 REM            DISPLAY THE BOARD
6999 REM
7000 PRINT: PRINT
7005 FOR I=1 TO 3: PRINT TAB(20): FOR J=1 TO 3: PRINT A(I,J);" ";
7010 NEXT J: PRINT: NEXT I: PRINT:PRINT: RETURN
```

The first thing to notice about this program is that we have more than one statement on some lines. Most BASICS allow multiple statement lines by using a "continuation" or "separator" character between the statements. In our BASIC we use the colon symbol (:) to separate statements with the same line number. For example, line 7000 (PRINT:PRINT) simply means two PRINT statements are executed before line 7005 gets executed. Line 7005 starts a FOR... NEXT loop, does a PRINT and a TAB, starts a second loop, then PRINTs the referenced element of array A, and finally executes line

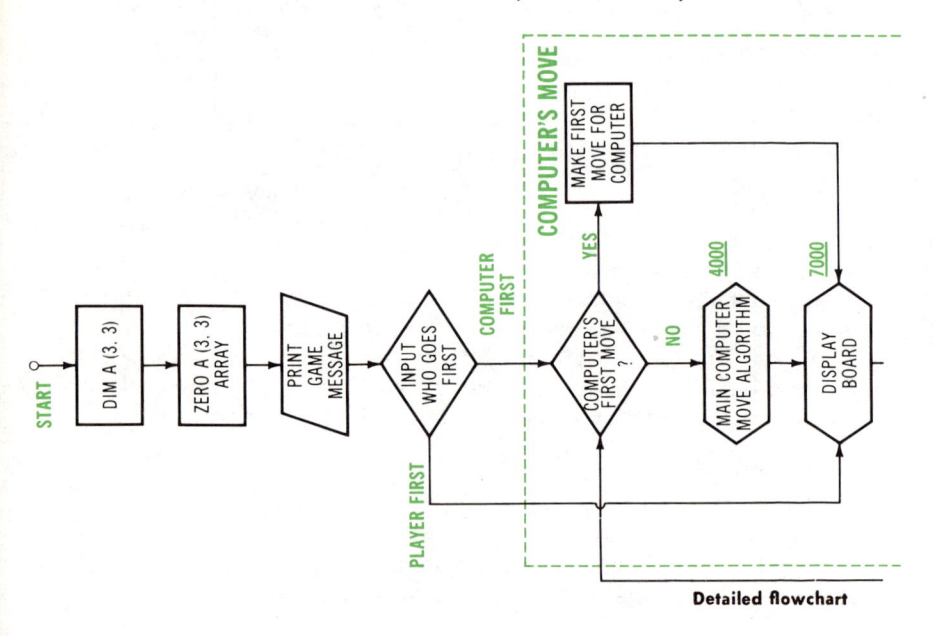

Detailed flowchart

7010. Some BASICs use a reverse backslash symbol (/) to indicate continuation of a line.

Notice the way the PRINT statement is set up. The quote marks contain three blank spaces which cause the elements of the board to be separated so you can easily see what values they are. The TAB statement spaces the board over 20 spaces on the screen so it is in the approximate middle of the display area. The flowchart for the display board subroutine looks like Fig. 3-3.

Notice also that we are placing the REM statements before the actual subroutine with line numbers that are less than the line numbers of the subroutine itself. By keeping the line numbers for the REM statements out of the main body of the subroutine we can easily remove them later to save precious memory space.

Assuming that the elements of the board array are all zero when we start the game (you may have to zero them yourself if your BASIC does not guarantee this), we can display the board by running the subroutine:

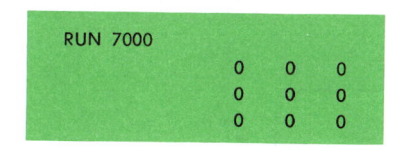

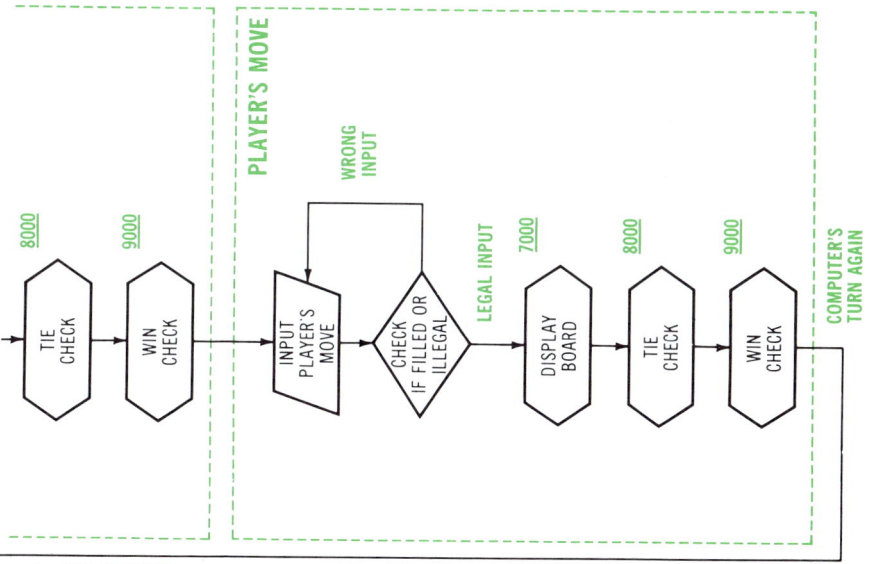

```
RUN 7000
            0    0    0
            0    0    0
            0    0    0
```

for TIC-TAC-TOE.

Notice how the display moved over 20 spaces before printing out. Later we will see how to add lines so the squares are easier to see, but now you can just imagine they exist.

Check for a Tie

In order to tell if the game is over or not we use a second subroutine to check for a tie game. The code for this function is quite simple. All we need to do is to loop through the elements of the board array looking for a zero (0) element. If we find a zero it

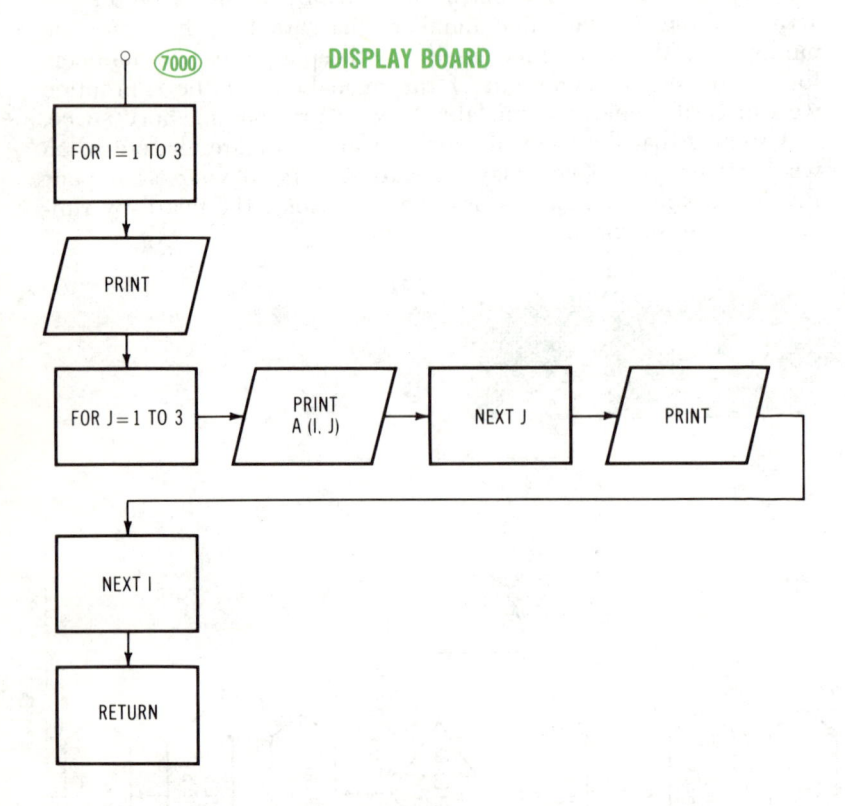

Fig. 3-3. Subroutine to display board.

means there is still an unfilled square on the board. In this case we must return to the main program because the game is not over until all squares are filled. If *no* zero squares are found by the subroutine then the board must be filled and we cause the message "TIE GAME" to be printed, and a new game begins. Here is the code for the tie-checking subroutine:

```
7997 REM
7998 REM            TIE CHECK
7999 REM
8000 FOR I=1 TO 3: FOR J=1 TO 3: IF A(I,J)=0 THEN 8020
8010 NEXT J: NEXT I: PRINT TAB(20) "TIE GAME": GOTO 20
8020 RETURN
```

The flowchart for the tie-checking subroutine looks like Fig. 3-4.

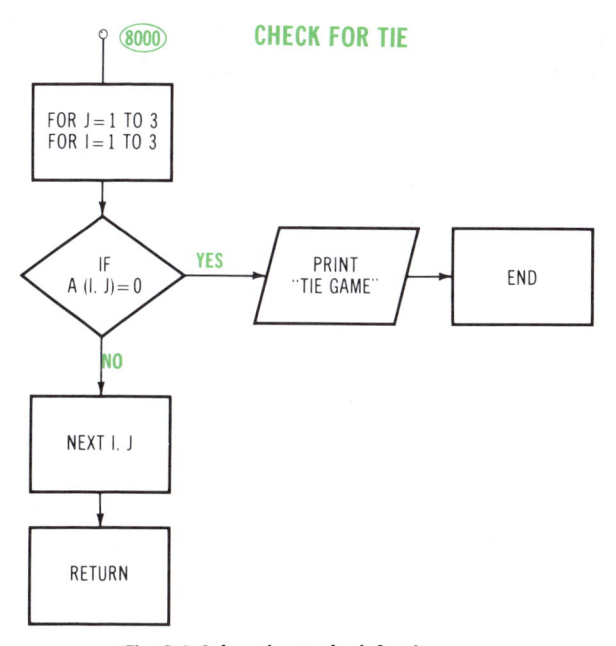

Fig. 3-4. Subroutine to check for tie game.

Check for a Winner

Finally our TIC-TAC-TOE program must be able to tell if a player has won, and end the game. To accomplish this we must be able to tell if the computer has won or the opponent has won. We can tell if a player has won by adding up all the columns, rows, and diagonals and seeing if the sum of any of these is +3. We do the same thing for the computer, but a sum of −3 indicates that it has won. The code for doing this is shown below. R is used to hold the sum of a row, C holds the sum of a column, and D1 and D2 hold the sums for the two diagonals of the board. Here is the program:

```
8997  REM
8998  REM            WIN CHECK
8999  REM
9000  LET D1=0: LET D2=0
9010  FOR I=1 TO 3: LET D1=A(I,I)+D1: LET D2=A(I,4—I)+D2
9020  LET R=0: LET C=0
9030  FOR J=1 TO 3: LET R=A(I,J)+R: LET C=A(J,I)+C: NEXT J
9040  IF D1=—3 OR D2=—3 OR R=—3 OR C=—3 THEN 9070
9050  IF D1=3 OR D2=3 OR R=3 OR C=3 THEN 9080
9060  NEXT I:RETURN
9070  PRINT TAB(20) "COMPUTER WINS": GOTO 20
9080  PRINT TAB(20) "YOU'RE THE WINNER": GOTO 20
```

Notice in line 9010 that we add up the value of the diagonal D1 with D1=A(I,I)+D1. If I varies from 1 to 3 then we will make D1 the sum of the squares A(1,1)+A(2,2)+A(3,3). Likewise D2 is set up so D2=A(I,4—I)+D2. If you follow the values for I in this expression you will see that we are adding up the squares like this A(1,3)+A(2,2)+A(3,1) which represents the second diagonal on the board. This nicely illustrates the way we can use arrays by simply making expressions inside the parentheses. The rows and columns are summed in a similar manner. The IF...THEN statements in lines 9040 and 9050 are used to tell if we have a winner and if so the respective PRINT statement in lines 9070 or 9080 is executed and the message "THE COMPUTER WINS" or "YOU'RE THE WINNER" is displayed and the game begins over.

The flowchart for the win check subroutine is shown in Fig. 3-5.

Input Players Move

What we have now are the three simple subroutines for "housekeeping" the game. Looking at our flowchart again we now need some code that allows the user to enter his or her move. The computer must check the entry for legality and make sure the numbers are in the proper range and that the square isn't already filled. Then the square must be filled (or the player is requested to make the entry over because it is an illegal move) and the three subroutines we developed must be called.

Here is the code for inputting the player's move. (Note that because the input part of the program is not a subroutine we will place it in the beginning part of the program, with line numbers in the hundreds.)

```
298 REM              INPUT PLAYERS MOVE
299 REM
300 PRINT: INPUT "ENTER THE ROW, COLUMN FOR YOUR MOVE"; I,J
310 PRINT
320 IF I<1 OR I>3 OR J<1 OR J>3 THEN 360
325 IF A(I,J)<>0 THEN 365
330 LET A(I,J)=1
335 GOSUB 7000       'DISPLAY BOARD
340 GOSUB 8000       'CHECK FOR TIE
345 GOSUB 9000       'CHECK FOR WINNER
350 GOTO 60          'COMPUTERS TURN
360 PRINT TAB(20) "YOUR NUMBERS ARE ILLEGAL": GOTO 300
365 PRINT TAB(20) "SORRY THAT SQUARE IS FILLED": GOTO 300
```

In this section of the program the desired square must be entered as two numbers between 1 and 3. The numbers must be separated by commas. The first number is the row and the second is the column of the square you wish to fill. After checking with statements 320 and 325 if an out of range number or filled square is found in the element the player specified, the computer prints out the respective message and the INPUT statement is repeated. If the numbers are legal, then statement 330 sets the desired element in the board array to a 1, and executes the three subroutines so the board is displayed and the game is checked for a tie or a winner.

Note that we also used a special form of remark statement. The single quote character on a line after a statement indicates the following message after the quote is a comment or remark. This sometimes can make our programs easier to read and can save us from writing a separate line for each remark.

Now even though the program is hardly finished, it is good practice to run it and see if the code you have written checks out and works correctly. In our case we have the three subroutines and the input from the player sections done, so we can at least check that the computer puts the players' marks (1s) in the correct squares. To check the subroutines that look for a tie or a winner we can add some statements so the program branches back to the input section and allows us to fill the board array. When we get three marks in a row the subroutine that checks for wins should operate and print out the message "YOU'RE THE WINNER"?

To do this program checkout we temporarily add a line:

```
60 GOTO 300
```

CHECK FOR WINNER

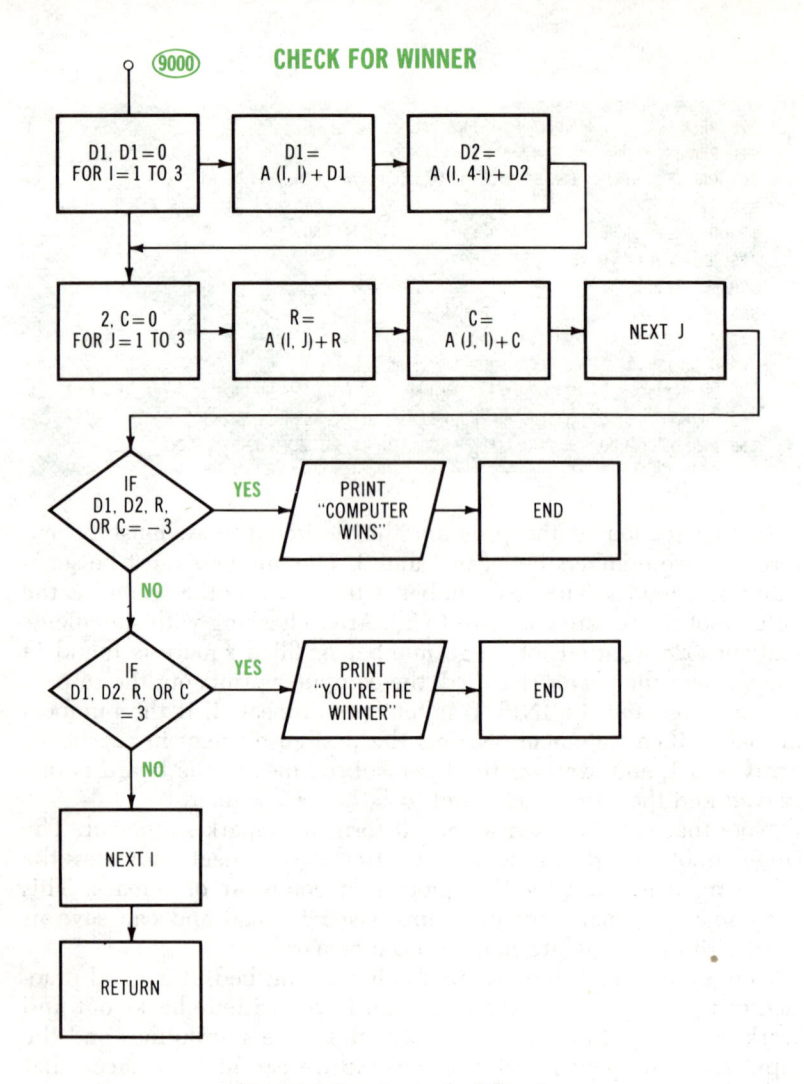

Fig. 3-5. Subroutine to check for winner.

which causes the computer to go back to the input routine after it has implemented all the subroutines.

Here is a run of the program so far:

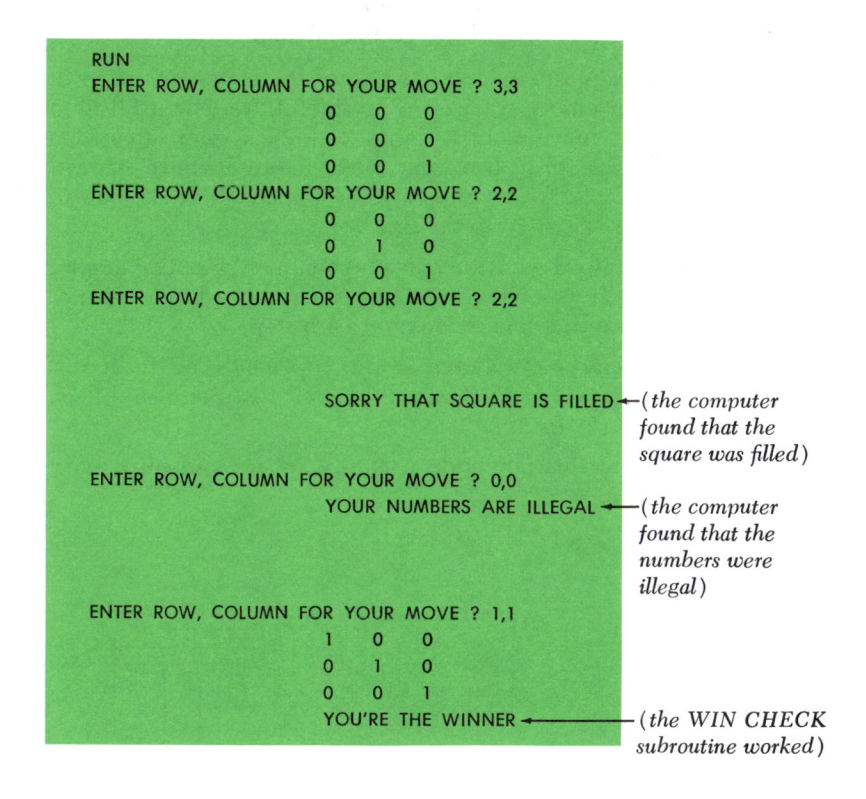

```
RUN
ENTER ROW, COLUMN FOR YOUR MOVE ? 3,3
              0    0    0
              0    0    0
              0    0    1
ENTER ROW, COLUMN FOR YOUR MOVE ? 2,2
              0    0    0
              0    1    0
              0    0    1
ENTER ROW, COLUMN FOR YOUR MOVE ? 2,2


                    SORRY THAT SQUARE IS FILLED
```
← (*the computer found that the square was filled*)

```
ENTER ROW, COLUMN FOR YOUR MOVE ? 0,0
                    YOUR NUMBERS ARE ILLEGAL
```
← (*the computer found that the numbers were illegal*)

```
ENTER ROW, COLUMN FOR YOUR MOVE ? 1,1
              1    0    0
              0    1    0
              0    0    1
                    YOU'RE THE WINNER
```
← (*the WIN CHECK subroutine worked*)

As we can see in the program output, everything seems to check out properly. The next logical step in the development of the program is the computer's move algorithm.

Computer Move Algorithm

In order for the computer to make an intelligent move it must be able to analyze the current board array and decide the best move to make in light of the squares that are occupied. In essence the computer program must mimic the way we would go about making a decision to move. If you examine the thought process carefully around playing TIC-TAC-TOE you can discover that a certain series of steps, almost like a formula, can be determined. One way to express the series of steps so we can devise a program around it is in "algorithmic" form. First we must identify the specific steps involved in making a good TIC-TAC-TOE move.

1st step Is there any line (row, column, or diagonal) that has two of your men in it and the third square in the line empty? If yes, fill it to win; if no, go to 2nd step.

2nd step Is there any line which has two of the opponent's men in it and an empty square in the line? If yes, then fill it to block the move from winning. If there is more than one line in this form, take any move because you can't win unless a mistake is made by the opponent. If no line in this form exists, go to the 3rd step.

3rd step Is there any line with one of your men and two empty squares? If yes, fill one of the squares to develop a potential winning line. If no, go to 4th step.

4th step Is there any line with one of the opponent's men in it and two empty squares? If yes, fill one of the squares to block. If no, go to 5th step.

5th step If you are this far, find an empty square and fill it with your man.

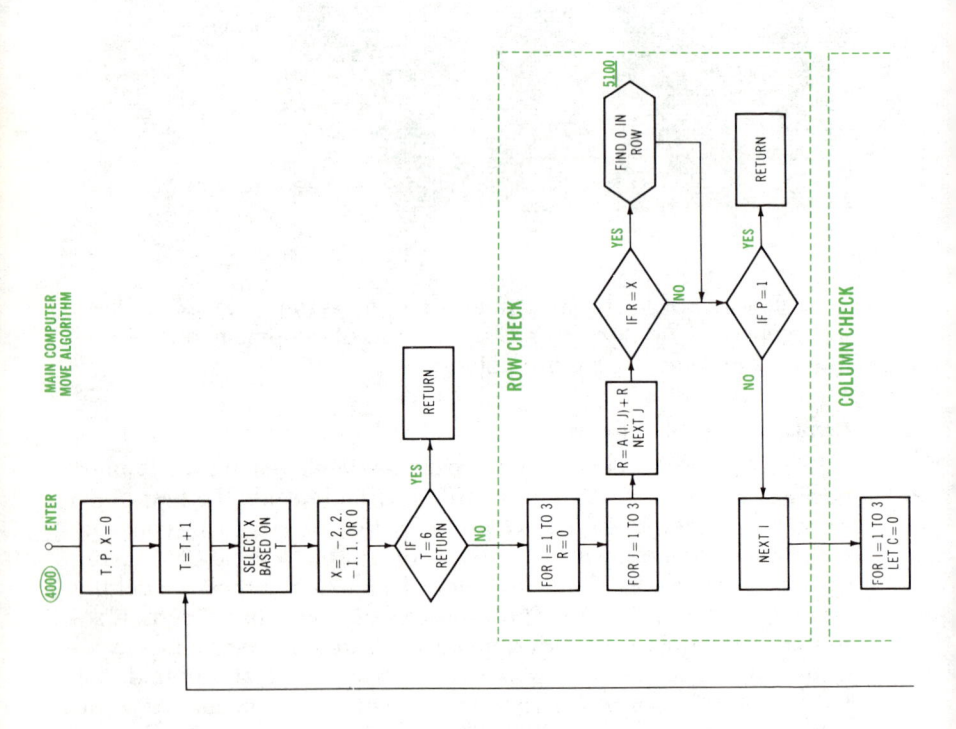

Fig. 3-6. Main computer

122

Now to implement this series of steps as an algorithm in BASIC we must figure out a way to determine the various conditions for the lines in the program and, based on what we find, fill the respective empty square. One way to do this is to look at the board array mathematically. That is, for each line condition in the five steps there is a unique mathematical sum to the elements in the lines. For example, in step 1 a line meeting this condition would have a sum, if you added up all the elements in that line, of +2. The only way we could get the sum of the elements in a line to add up to +2 (assuming the men are either +1 or −1) is for two squares to contain +1s and one square to contain a zero (0), meaning it is empty. Thus we can loop through all the lines on the board (that is three rows, three columns, and two diagonals) and if we find any line equal to 2, then we only need to find and fill the empty square in that line.

Look at step two. It is just like step 1 except we are looking for a sum of −2 to block a potential loss. The only way we could get a line to add up to −2 is if two squares are −1 and one square is empty.

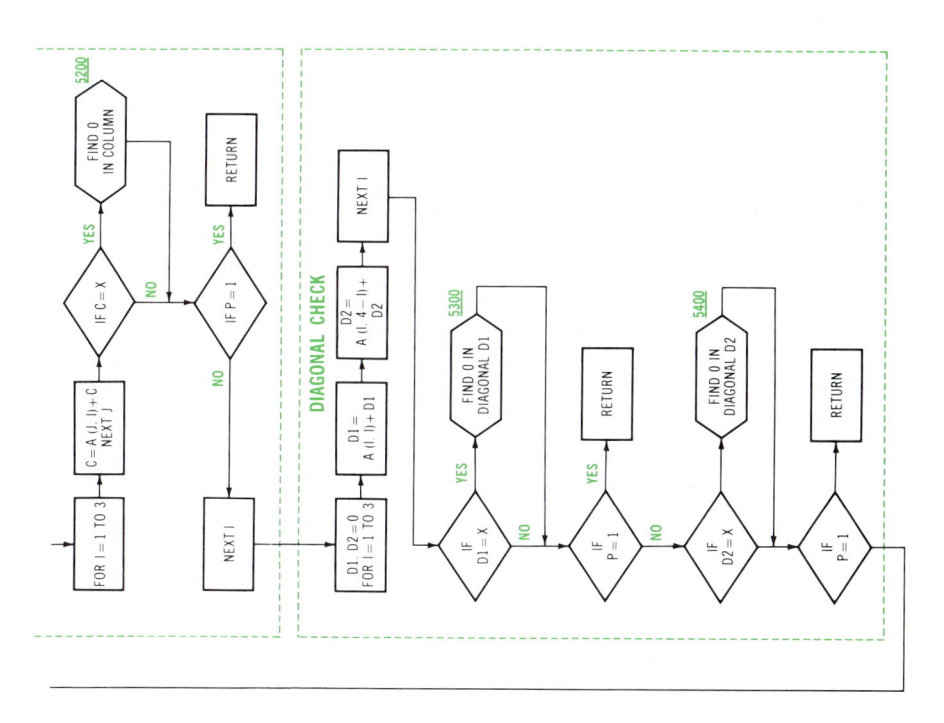

move algorithm.

123

The third step involves searching for a sum of +1. This condition could occur if two squares were empty and one square was a +1, or it could happen if two squares were +1 and one was a −1. We could still use the same kind of mathematical process, except we must arrange to continue after finding the condition of no empty square to fill.

The fourth and fifth steps are easily seen to be just the same logic process.

In summary what we want is a routine that allows us to check sequentially through each step of the algorithm, looking for each of the conditions (a sum in a line of +2, −2, +1, −1, or 0) and making a move based on the first one satisfied. What we can do is write three separate routines that check the rows, check the columns, and then check both of the diagonals. We put these in a loop and make the number the routines are looking for start at −2, then change to +2, then to −1 and so on. Each of the routines will contain the ability to search through a row, column, or diagonals looking for a line that adds up to some value X. The value of X will be set by IF...THEN statements which change it after we have executed all the routines with one value of X and found no conditions to fill a square. Also to consider is what happens when we find a line which adds up to −2, +2, etc? How do we decide which square in that line is empty so we can fill it? The solution is that once we have determined that a line adds up to a certain number, we branch to another subroutine which scans the line looking for the empty square. If none is found we have one of those conditions where a sum was met but the squares were all full. If this happens we jump back to where the subroutine sent us to check for an empty square and continue with the move checking. If we do find an empty square we do two things. First we fill the square with a −1 mark for the computer's move. Second we set a software switch (a flag) which is a variable called P, to the value 1. P is normally 0. When we return from the routine now, the routine that is looking through the lines for a sum will check to see if switch P is a 1. If it is, then we don't need to look any further for a move because the computer has already made one. So we RETURN to the main program and implement the steps after the computer move subroutine. If P is still 0 we continue checking for a valid move.

The flowchart for the computer move algorithm is shown in Fig. 3-6. Note that there are boxes around the row check portion, column check, and diagonal check portions. This helps us see how things operate. The subroutines used by it for finding an empty square are in Fig. 3-7 in flowchart form.

The complete program listing for the TIC-TAC-TOE game is

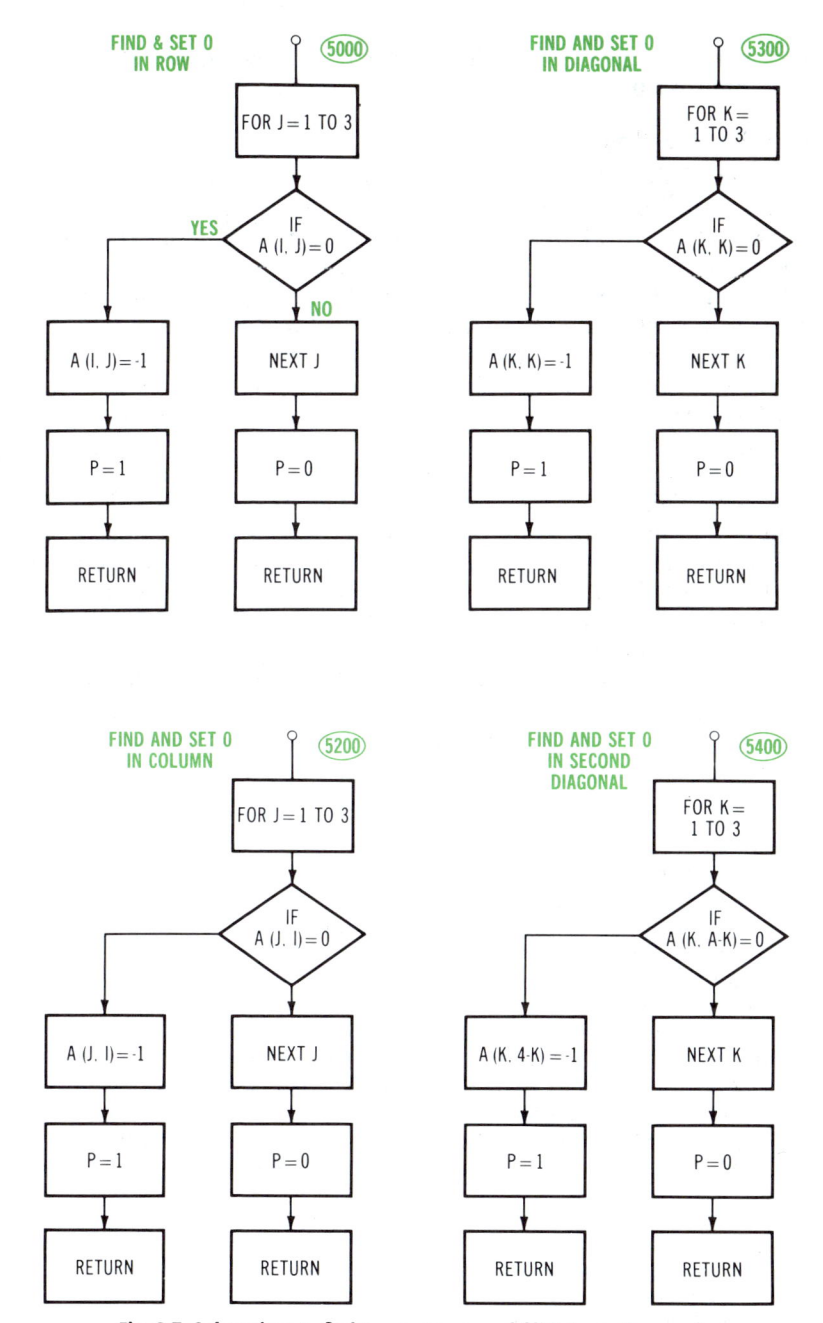

Fig. 3-7. Subroutines to find empty square and fill it (part of computer move algorithm).

shown in Fig. 3-8. The code for the computer's move algorithm is in lines 4000 to 5900.

Finishing the Program

To finish the TIC-TAC-TOE program we must add a few more things to it. First we must have a way to deal with the situation of an opening move; in other words, what do we do if the computer goes first. The solution is to use a series of IF...THEN statements which (assuming this is the computer's first turn) cause the favored strategies of grabbing the center square first to be implemented. We also must consider the condition of the computer's second move if the player has occupied the center square first. In this case the IF...THENs must occupy a corner square. Lines 100 to 150 in the listing in Fig. 3-8 take care of this.

We also need to allow the user of the program to choose who goes first. This is taken care of by the statements in lines 31 to 50. And in order for our game player to play again, we must clear the old board before a new game begins. This is accomplished by the FOR...NEXT loop in line 30 of the program. Variables used in the program are also cleared at this statement.

Finally we add a beginning message to the game user in a series of PRINT statements (lines 15 to 24). These tell the rules of the game and how to enter moves. Also REMs are added to the beginning of the program to define to the programmer who wrote the code and who owns the program.

```
0  REM    TIC-TAC-TOE GAME
1  REM    WRITTEN: JULY 1978
2  REM    BY MITCHELL WAITE
3  REM    USED AS AN EXAMPLE IN BASIC PRIMER
4  REM    ALL RIGHTS RESERVED WORLDWIDE
5  REM
10 DIM A(3,3)
15 PRINT TAB(20) "***** TIC-TAC-TOE *****":PRINT
20 PRINT "TIC TAC TOE REPRESENTS AN INTERESTING GAME OF LOGIC.":
21 PRINT "YOU TRY TO BEAT THE COMPUTER. +1 = YOUR MEN."
22 PRINT "—1 = COMPUTER'S MEN.  0 = EMPTY SQUARE"
23 PRINT "ENTER YOUR MOVES BY SPECIFYING A ROW AND COLUMN FOR"
24 PRINT "YOUR MAN, I.E. CENTER SQUARE IS 2,2.":PRINT
25 PRINT
26 REM            CLEAR ARRAY AND ZERO VARIABLES
27 REM
30 FOR I=1 TO 3: FOR J=1 TO 3 A(I,J)=0:NEXT J,I
31 LET C9=0: LET F=0
32 PRINT "SELECT WHO GOES FIRST"
```

Fig. 3-8. Complete program listing for TIC-TAC-TOE game.

```
35  INPUT "TYPE 1 FOR COMPUTER, 2 FOR YOU ";F
40  IF F=2 THEN 215
45  IF F<1 OR F>2 THEN 30
50  PRINT:PRINT TAB(20) "COMPUTER GOES FIRST":PRINT
58  REM
59  REM             COMPUTER'S MOVE STARTS
60  LET M=0
97  REM
98  REM             CHECK FOR OPENING MOVE
99  REM
100 IF A(2,2)<>0 THEN 115
110 LET A(2,2)=-1: GOTO 200
115 IF C9>=1 THEN 155
120 IF A(1,1)<>0 THEN 130
125 LET A(1,1)=-1: GOTO 200
130 IF A(1,3)<>0 THEN 140
135 LET A(1,3)=-1: GOTO 200
140 IF A(3,3)<>0 THEN 150
145 LET A(3,3)=-1: GOTO 200
150 LET A(3,1)=-1: GOTO 200
152 REM
153 REM             CALL COMPUTER MOVE ALGORITHM
154 REM
155 GOSUB 4000
200 PRINT "COMPUTERS MOVE": LET C9=C9+1
213 REM
214 REM             GO DISPLAY THE BOARD
215 GOSUB 7000
229 REM             CHECK FOR A TIE
230 GOSUB 8000
239 REM             CHECK FOR A WINNER
240 GOSUB 9000
298 REM             INPUT PLAYERS MOVE
299 REM
300 PRINT :INPUT "ENTER ROW,COLUMN FOR YOUR MOVE ";I,J
310 PRINT
320 IF I<1 OR I>3 OR J<1 OR J>3 THEN 360
325 IF A(I,J)<>0 THEN 365
330 LET A(I,J)=1
335 GOSUB 7000      'DISPLAY BOARD
340 GOSUB 8000      'CHECK FOR TIE
345 GOSUB 9000      'CHECK FOR WINNER
350 GOTO 60         'COMPUTERS TURN
360 PRINT TAB(20) "YOUR NUMBERS ARE ILLEGAL": GOTO 300
365 PRINT TAB(20) "SORRY THAT SQUARE IS FILLED": GOTO 300
3997 REM
3998 REM            COMPUTER MOVES ALGORITHM
3999 REM
```

Fig. 3-8 cont. Complete program listing for TIC-TAC-TOE game.

```
4000 LET T=0: LET P=0: LET X=0
4010 LET T=T+1: IF T=1 THEN  LET X=-2
4015 IF T=2 THEN  LET X=2
4020 IF T=3 THEN  LET X=-1
4025 IF T=4 THEN  LET X=1
4030 IF T=5 THEN  LET X=0
4035 IF T=6 THEN  RETURN
4097 REM
4098 REM            ROW CHECK FOR -2,+2,-1,+1,0
4099 REM
4100 FOR I=1 TO 3: LET R=0
4110 FOR J=1 TO 3: LET R=A(I,J)+R: NEXT J: IF R=X THEN  GOSUB 5100
4120 IF P=1 THEN 5900
4130 NEXT I
4197 REM
4198 REM            COLUMN CHECK FOR -2,+2,-1,+1,0
4199 REM
4200 FOR I=1 TO 3: LET C=0
4210 FOR J=1 TO 3: LET C=A(J,I)+C: NEXT J: IF C=X THEN  GOSUB 5200
4220 IF P=1 THEN 5900
4230 NEXT I
4297 REM
4298 REM            DIAGONAL CHECK FOR -2,+2,-1,+1,0
4299 REM
4300 LET D1=0: LET D2=0
4310 FOR I=1 TO 3: LET D1=A(I,I)+D1: LET D2=A(I,4-I)+D2: NEXT I
4320 IF D1=X THEN  GOSUB 5300
4430 IF P=1 THEN  RETURN
4450 IF D2=X THEN  GOSUB 5400
4460 IF P=1 THEN  RETURN
4470 GOTO 4010
4999 REM
5000 REM            FIND IF A 0 EXISTS IN THE "I-TH" ROW AND MAKE -1
5001 REM
5100 FOR J=1 TO 3: IF A(I,J)=0 THEN 5120
5110 NEXT J: LET P=0: RETURN
5120 LET A(I,J)=-1: LET P=1: RETURN
5197 REM
5198 REM            FIND IF A 0 EXISTS IN THE I-TH COLUMN, ETC.
5199 REM
5200 FOR J=1 TO 3: IF A(J,I)=0 THEN 5220
5210 NEXT J: LET P=0: RETURN
5220 LET A(J,I)=-1: LET P=1: RETURN
5297 REM
5298 REM            FIND IF A 0 EXISTS IN THE DIAGONAL D1, ETC.
5299 REM
5300 FOR K=1 TO 3: IF A(K,K)=0 THEN 5320
5310 NEXT K: LET P=0: RETURN
```

Fig. 3-8 cont. Complete program listing for TIC-TAC-TOE game.

```
5320 LET A(K,K)=—1: LET P=1: RETURN
5397 REM
5398 REM            FIND IF A 0 EXISTS IN THE DIAGONAL D2, ETC.
5399 REM
5400 FOR K=1 TO 3: IF A(K,4—K)=0 THEN 5420
5410 NEXT K: LET P=0: RETURN
5420 LET A(K,4—K)=—1: LET P=1: RETURN
5430 PRINT "STOPPED AT 5430": END
5900 RETURN
6997 REM
6998 REM            DISPLAY BOARD
6999 REM
7000 PRINT:PRINT
7005 FOR I=1 TO 3:PRINT TAB(20): FOR J=1 TO 3:PRINT A(I,J);" ";
7010 NEXT J: PRINT: NEXT I: PRINT: PRINT: RETURN
7020 RETURN
7997 REM
7998 REM            TIE CHECK
7999 REM
8000 FOR I=1 TO 3: FOR J=1 TO 3: IF A(I,J)=0 THEN 8020
8010 NEXT J: NEXT I: PRINT TAB(20) "TIE GAME":GOTO 20
8020 RETURN
8997 REM
8998 REM            WIN CHECK
8999 REM
9000 LET D1=0: LET D2=0
9010 FOR I=1 TO 3: LET D1=A(I,I)+D1: LET D2=A(I,4—I)+D2
9020 LET R=0: LET C=0
9030 FOR J=1 TO 3: LET R=A(I,J)+R: LET C=A(J,I)+C: NEXT J
9040 IF D1=—3 OR D2=—3 OR R=—3 OR C=—3 THEN 9070
9050 IF D1=3 OR D2=3 OR R=3 OR C=3 THEN 9080
9060 NEXT I: RETURN
9070 PRINT TAB(20) "COMPUTER WINS": PRINT: GOTO 20
9080 PRINT TAB(20) "YOU'RE THE WINNER": PRINT: GOTO 20
```

Fig. 3-8 cont. Complete program listing for TIC-TAC-TOE game.

We now have a complete TIC-TAC-TOE game written in BASIC. If you play it you'll see that the computer seems to almost be thinking longer on some moves than on others. Did we say "thinking?" Oh well, perhaps it only seems like thinking. In the next chapter we'll see that BASIC can be even more sophisticated and if you'll permit . . . smarter.

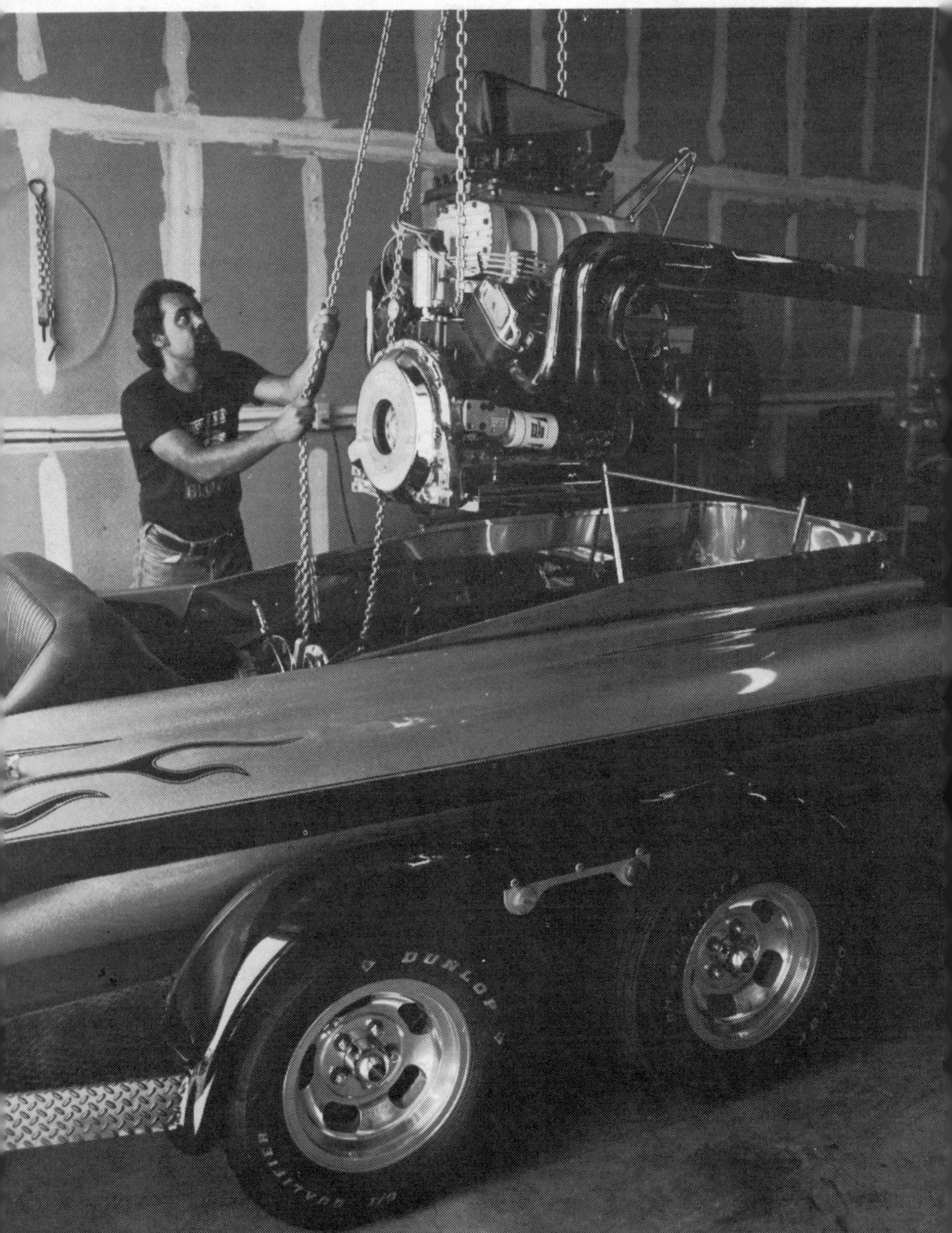
DUNLOP

CHAPTER
4

Adding More Power

Because BASIC is used by so many beginners in the computing field, it is often thought of as a "simple language" that is not capable of doing very sophisticated tasks. This is far from the truth. Although BASIC lends itself very well to simple programs, it can also be used for quite complex programs as we shall learn in this chapter. In fact, today there are many computers being used in all kinds of application areas which have been programmed in BASIC. Generally, what happens is that a particular computer manufacturer will modify the BASIC language for his computer so that it is even better at doing the specific kind of job required. There are several forms of "business BASIC" languages available today. These are versions of BASIC which lend themselves especially well to processing large amounts of information, and producing long report printouts for business accounting purposes.

Ordinary garden variety BASIC has quite a bit of computing power in itself. In this chapter we will discuss some of the more commonly used capabilities of the language. They are:

DATA and READ statements which allow information to be defined by the program.

Numeric functions which can provide extensive mathematical capability.

String functions for manipulating characters and words.

DATA AND READ STATEMENTS

Many times it is necessary or advantageous to include some type of fixed information right within the body of the program. This information may be too lengthy to be INPUT into the program through the normal manner, and may always be the same anyway. This would mean that each time the program was used, the same information would have to be INPUT at the beginning so that the program could operate properly. Examples of fixed information include such things as tax tables, prices of merchandise, dates, names, instructions, and the like. In order for information to be used by any program, it must be stored with a variable name of some sort. Remember that numeric information is stored using one format, while string information is stored using another. If there are only a few items of fixed information which must be included in a program, then these might be easily set up using LET statements. However, when the volume of information starts to increase, there has to be a better way.

The purpose of the DATA and READ statements is to allow large volumes of fixed information to be set up within a program with relative ease. The information is included as part of the DATA statement, and it is transferred into a variable by the READ statement when the program is run. Once this has been done, the variable can be used throughout the program. The format for the DATA statement is as follows:

```
DATA (information separated by commas)
```

The format of the READ statement is like this:

```
READ (list of variables separated by commas)
```

Below are some examples of various types of DATA and READ statements.

```
DATA 1,2,3,4,5
READ A,B,C,D,E
```

This pair of statements would cause the variables A, B, C, D, and E to be initialized to the values of 1, 2, 3, 4, and 5 respectively. The same thing could have been done using the following DATA and READ statements.

```
DATA 1,2,3,4,5
READ A,B,C
READ D,E
```

This is because BASIC uses an internal pointer to keep track of where in the DATA statement to get the next element of data. This pointer is set to 1 at the beginning of the program, and then is incremented each time that a variable is READ from a DATA statement. After the first READ statement above has set up the variables A, B, and C, the pointer is pointing at the next data element in the DATA statement. When the next READ statement is encountered by the program, the variables D and E are READ from the same DATA statement beginning at the fourth data element. This procedure can go on and on as long as there is enough data in the DATA statements to fill up the variables that are to be read. If all of the data gets used up and another READ is attempted, an error will result.

There is one other BASIC statement associated with the DATA and READ statements. It is the RESTORE statement. What it does is to reset the internal pointer which BASIC uses to sequentially get the information from the DATA statement. After a RESTORE statement is executed, the next READ statement will access the first DATA statement in the program regardless of where the internal pointer happened to be pointing prior to the RESTORE.

Let us look at some other DATA and READ combinations.

```
DATA 12,14.5,18,75.66,100,500,1000
READ A1,A2,A3,A4,A5,A6,A7
```

In this example, the variable A1 is initialized to a value of 12, A2 is set to a value of 14.5, A3 is set to 18, and so on.

```
DATA "JAN", "FEB", "MAR", "APR", "MAY", "JUN"
READ A$,B$,C$,D$,E$,F$
```

In this example, the string variables A$ through F$ are initialized by the READ statement to the names of the months which are described in the DATA statement.

Probably the most useful form of the DATA and READ statements is that of initializing arrays. As we learned in the previous chapter, an array is a group of variables which usually have something in common, and are all referenced by the same variable name. A specific element of an array may then be referenced through the use of a subscript, such as A(5), M$(2) and so on.

It should be noted here that there are some differences in the way that different versions of BASIC handle string arrays. Some require that the length of each string within the array be defined in the DIM statement. For example,

```
DIM A$(12)
```

would define a string containing 12 characters. The same DIM statement in other BASICS would define a string array that contained 12 strings, each with a dynamic length determined by the actual number of characters stored in it at any given time, up to a maximum of 255. For the sake of the examples in this book, we will adhere to the latter of these conventions. That is:

```
DIM M$(2)
```

defines an array of two strings of dynamic length. In order to use DATA and READ to initialize an array, we must first make sure that the array has been defined with a DIM statement. Then, there are two ways of getting the information from the DATA statement into the array variables. We will discuss both of them below.

```
10 DIM M$(12)
20 DATA "JAN","FEB","MAR","APR","MAY","JUN"
30 DATA "JUL","AUG","SEP","OCT","NOV","DEC"
40 READ M$(1),M$(2),M$(3),M$(4),M$(5),M$(6)
50 READ M$(7),M$(8),M$(9),M$(10),M$(11),M$(12)
```

First of all, notice here that we have split up the names of the twelve months into two DATA statements, and we have also split up the twelve elements of the array M$ into two READ statements. This is possible due to the fact that when the first READ statement in a program is encountered, the information is gotten from the first DATA statement found in the program. The variables in the READ statement are initialized until they have all been taken care of. When the next READ statement is encountered, the variables in its list are initialized beginning with the next DATA statement in the program. Notice that the first six elements of the array M$ are initialized, and then the last six are initialized on line 50.

This method will work just fine. However, it does not take full advantage of the convenience of arrays. In the next example, we will achieve the same thing, but in a different way.

```
10 DIM M$(12)
20 DATA "JAN","FEB","MAR","APR","MAY","JUN"
30 DATA "JUL","AUG","SEP","OCT","NOV","DEC"
40 FOR I = 1 TO 12
50 READ M$(I)
60 NEXT I
```

Notice the difference here? Instead of spelling out each and every array element, we have used a FOR...NEXT loop to cause the index I to go from 1 to 12. Then the READ statement at line 50 reads only one element of the array M$ from the DATA statements. Notice also here that there are two DATA statements, and only one READ statement with only one variable name in its list. However, the READ statement is in a loop so that it is actually executed 12 times. Each time that it is executed, it gets the next element of information from the DATA statements.

Both of the above methods will work just fine. The first method will probably work better when there are only a few variables which must be initialized. But, when the number of variables starts to increase, the second method using the FOR...NEXT loop will definitely be easier to program. Imagine having to initialize a hundred or more variables using the first method.

METRIC CONVERSION PROGRAM ENHANCED

Earlier in the book, we used as an example a program that converts anglo units to metric units. In order to explain some of the beginning concepts of BASIC, the approach that we used to write this program was quite simple. Now, we will use the same application as an example of the use of the DATA and READ statements. You will notice that this will make the program much more flexible and general-purpose usable. We will use the same conversion formulas that we used in the previous example, but in a completely new way. What we are going to do is to store all of the "literal" or string information in string arrays. Also, we will store the conversion factors themselves in a numeric array. Then, we can access the string and numeric information which we will need through the use of a subscript to the arrays. So, let us set up the beginning of the program.

```
1000 REM ----METRIC CONVERSION PROGRAM
1010 REM ----USING DATA AND READ
1020 REM ----INITIALIZE THE ARRAYS
1030 LET N = 3
1040 DIM M$(N),Q$(N),A$(N),B$(N),F(N)
```

The variable N is used to determine how many different conversions the program is capable of doing. This is set to 3 for our example, since we will use the same three conversions that the old program used, namely, "INCHES TO CENTIMETERS," "POUNDS TO KILOGRAMS," and "QUARTS TO LITERS." Others can easily be added as we shall see. At line 1040 we see the DIM statement which sets up the size of the various arrays which are going to be used in this program. They are all set up to the length defined by the variable N, and are:

N—number of functions.

M$—a string array containing the menu.

Q$—a string array containing the "input question."

A$—a string array containing the first part of the answer.

B$—a string array containing the last part of the answer.

F—a numeric array containing the conversion factors.

The next part of the program consists of the DATA statements which will be used to READ the arrays dimensioned above.

```
1090 REM ----DATA FOR ARRAYS
1100 DATA "1 - INCHES TO CENTIMETERS", "ENTER LENGTH IN INCHES",
     " INCHES "," CENTIMETERS",2.54
1200 DATA "2 - POUNDS TO KILOGRAMS", "ENTER WEIGHT IN POUNDS",
     " POUNDS "," KILOGRAMS" .4536
1300 DATA "3 - QUARTS TO LITERS","ENTER VOLUME IN QUARTS",
     " QUARTS "," LITERS ",.9463
```

Here we have three DATA statements. Each one contains all of the information necessary for one of the conversion routines. The different pieces of information are separated by commas in the DATA statement. First, there is the string information which will be used to display the menu. Then, there is the question which is asked just before the quantity to be converted is entered. Next comes the two string parts of the answer which is printed, and finally there is the actual numeric conversion factor itself. Now, let us write the statements to READ this information into the proper arrays.

```
1980 REM ----READ THE ARRAYS
1990 FOR I = 1 TO N: READ M$(I),Q$(I),A$(I),B$(I),F(I): NEXT I
```

This is how the information in the DATA statements is finally READ into the arrays. We use a FOR...NEXT loop to cycle the program through the DATA statements in such a way as to make sure that all of the information pertinent to each of the conversion routines is READ into its proper place in the arrays. Now, we can go ahead with the rest of the program.

```
2000 REM ----DISPLAY THE MENU
2100 PRINT: PRINT "METRIC CONVERSION PROGRAM": PRINT
2200 FOR I = 1 TO N: PRINT M$(I): NEXT I
2300 PRINT "9 - TO END THE PROGRAM": PRINT
```

First, at line 2100 we PRINT the heading. Line 2200 consists of the FOR...NEXT loop which PRINTs the menu itself. Lastly, on line 2300 we must PRINT the option to end the program. At this point, we are ready to INPUT our selection.

```
3000 REM ----ENTER SELECTION
3100 INPUT "ENTER YOUR SELECTION "; S
3200 IF S<1 OR S>N THEN GOTO 9999
```

This part of the program is similar to the original version except that we are not going to need all the IF...THEN statements to decide where in the program to branch to do the actual work. Here, all we need to do is to see if the value of S is outside of the range of defined selections, and if it is, we branch to the end of the program. The next part of the program is where the actual conversion takes place.

```
4000 REM ----DO THE CONVERSION
4100 PRINT: PRINT Q$(S): INPUT X
4200 PRINT X; A$(S); "IS EQUAL TO "; X*F(S); B$(S)
4300 GOTO 2000
```

and of course,

```
9999 END
```

See how it works? First, on line 4100 we PRINT the appropriate question according to the selected conversion routine. Then, we enter the value to be converted, X. On line 4200, we accomplish the same thing that the previous program did. First, we PRINT back the value to be converted, followed by the string A$ which contains the name of the units that we are converting. Then we PRINT the literal data "IS EQUAL TO", followed by the value of the converted quantity which is arrived at by simply multiplying X by the appropriate numeric factor contained in the array F. Lastly, we PRINT the string data which contains the description of the new units.

This program works exactly the same as the one in the previous chapter. Notice however, that it can be expanded very easily to to include many other conversion routines just by changing the LET statement in the beginning which defines the value of N, and by adding more DATA statements in the form that we have designed here. This has been a very good example of how arrays, together with the DATA and READ statements can make a simple program into a powerful program (Fig. 4-1).

NUMERIC FUNCTIONS

Earlier in this book, we introduced three simple numeric functions: ABS, INT, and RND. In this section we will introduce some additional numeric functions which will be useful in many different programs. Most of these functions are common to all the varieties of the BASIC language. Some particular languages may have more of them depending upon the general nature of the language. Some of the functions are strictly for use in situations of a mathematical nature, like the trigonometric functions and the square root functions. Others may be useful in a variety of different applications, including business programs and even games. We will discuss these

```
1000 REM ----METRIC CONVERSION PROGRAM
1010 REM ----USING DATA AND READ
1020 REM ----INITIALIZE THE ARRAYS
1030 LET N = 3
1040 DIM M$(N),QS(N),A$(N),B$(N),F(N)

1090 REM ----DATA FOR ARRAYS
1100 DATA "1" - INCHES TO CENTIMETERS", "ENTER LENGTH IN INCHES",
     " INCHES "," CENTIMETERS",2.54
1200 DATA "2" - POUNDS TO KILOGRAMS","ENTER WEIGHT IN POUNDS",
     " POUNDS "," KILOGRAMS",.4536
1300 DATA "3 - QUARTS TO LITERS","ENTER VOLUME IN QUARTS",
     " QUARTS "," LITERS",.9463

1980 REM ----READ THE ARRAYS
1990 FOR I = 1 TO N: READ M$(I),Q$(I),A$(I),B$(I),F(I): NEXT I

2000 REM ----DISPLAY THE MENU
2100 PRINT: PRINT"METRIC CONVERSION PROGRAM": PRINT
2200 FOR I = 1 TO N: PRINT M$(I): NEXT I
2300 PRINT "9 - TO END THE PROGRAM": PRINT

3000 REM ----ENTER SELECTION
3100 INPUT "ENTER YOUR SELECTION "; S
3200 IF S<1 OR S>N THEN GOTO 9999

4000 REM ----DO THE CONVERSION
4100 PRINT: PRINT Q$(S): INPUT X
4200 PRINT X; A$(S); "IS EQUAL TO "; X*F(S); B$(S)
4300 GOTO 2000

9999 END
```

Fig. 4-1. Listing of enhanced Metric Conversion program.

functions rather briefly here, and show only simple examples. In actual application, you should consult the BASIC manual of your computer for a more detailed explanation of how it operates.

AND, OR, and NOT

These three functions are sometimes called the Boolean logic functions because they perform the truth-table operations on each bit of the bytes as arguments. (See Appendix A for more information about binary and other numbering systems.) The general form of their usage follows:

```
100 LET X = A AND B
200 LET X = C OR D
300 LET X = NOT Z
```

Notice that for the AND and OR functions that there are two variables involved in the operation, while for the NOT function there is only one. Let us take a look at the truth table for each of these functions. Remember that the operation is carried out at the

bit level. Corresponding bits of the two arguments are used in the following way to produce the answer.

A	B	A AND B	C	D	C OR D	Z	NOT Z
1	1	1	1	1	1	1	0
1	0	0	1	0	1	0	1
0	1	0	0	1	1		
0	0	0	0	0	0		

In the first truth table, notice that for the AND function, both bits must be "1" in order for their ANDed value to be "1." If either of them is "0" then the result will be "0." The OR function on the other hand will yield a "1" for a result if either of the argument bits is a "1." Only when they are both "0" will the result become "0." The NOT function, as you can see produces the complement of the argument bit. Now, let us take a look at some examples using complete 8-bit bytes as arguments.

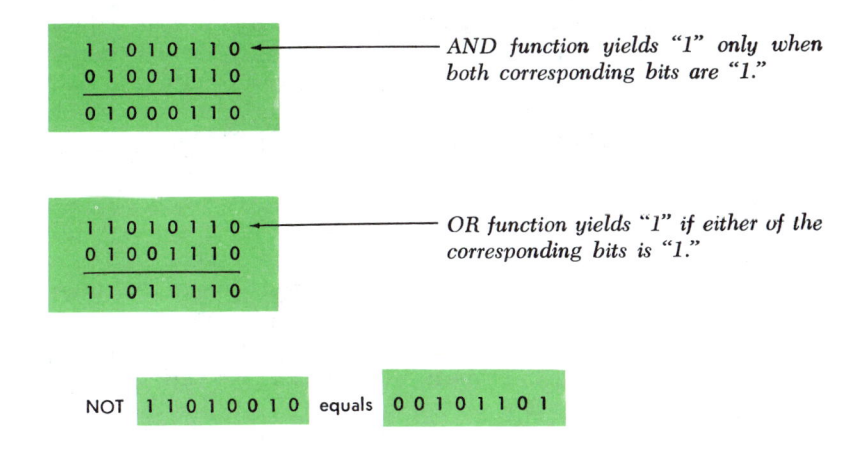

```
1 1 0 1 0 1 1 0  ◄──────────  AND function yields "1" only when
0 1 0 0 1 1 1 0               both corresponding bits are "1."
─────────────────
0 1 0 0 0 1 1 0
```

```
1 1 0 1 0 1 1 0  ◄──────────  OR function yields "1" if either of the
0 1 0 0 1 1 1 0               corresponding bits is "1."
─────────────────
1 1 0 1 1 1 1 0
```

NOT `1 1 0 1 0 0 1 0` equals `0 0 1 0 1 1 0 1`

The NOT function simply reverses all of the bits in the argument byte.

These functions AND and OR are the same ones that we used to produce compound IF...THEN statements. Their operation in that usage is not readily apparent, and in most cases need not be a concern. Used as we have described here, however, these functions can be very useful in dealing with data at the "bit level." For example, if we are only interested in the last four bits of a given byte of data, we can use the AND function to strip off the first four bits as follows:

`100 LET X = X AND 15`

Suppose that X is the variable that we wish to strip down. Looking at this function at the bit level, we see that

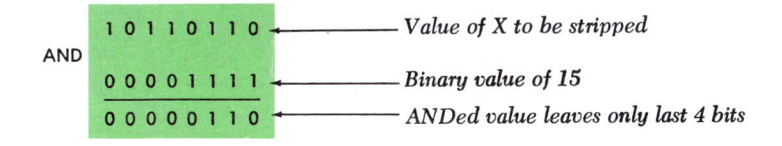

```
        1 0 1 1 0 1 1 0  ◄──────── Value of X to be stripped
AND
        0 0 0 0 1 1 1 1  ◄──────── Binary value of 15
        ─────────────────
        0 0 0 0 0 1 1 0  ◄──────── ANDed value leaves only last 4 bits
```

Another convenient example of the use of the AND function is regarding the use of a technique known as "bit-coding." This provides a means of economically storing the status of various conditions, which can have a value of either "true" or "false." Such conditions might include the status of various programs in a business data processing system. Other examples may be whether or not a file has been updated, or a particular program run in the right sequence. One way of doing these things would be to use a whole variable for each status indicator that is needed. If there are only a few indicators required, then this will be no problem. If, however, there are to be many indicators, then the use of a whole byte to store a "1" or a "0" is going to cost memory space. To save this space, we can use individual bits in a byte to store the condition of many different things. We can then use the AND function to interrogate the bit in question, and the OR function to change the bit. Let us suppose that the third bit of a byte of data indicates the update status of a file. A "1" means that the file has been updated, and "0" means that it has not been updated. We will call the byte S and interrogate it as follows:

```
100 IF S AND 32 = 32 THEN PRINT "FILE IS UPDATED"
200 END
```

Here is how this works. Let us assume that the file has been updated. Then the bits look like this.

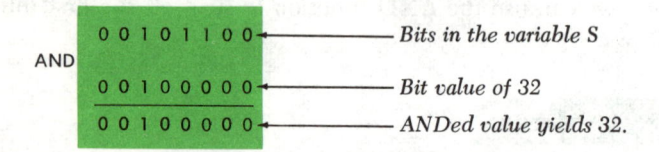

```
        0 0 1 0 1 1 0 0 ←————— Bits in the variable S
AND
        0 0 1 0 0 0 0 0 ←————— Bit value of 32
        ─────────────────
        0 0 1 0 0 0 0 0 ←————— ANDed value yields 32.
```

The result of the AND function yields the value of 32 which will then cause the message "FILE IS UPDATED" to be printed. If the third bit was a "0" then the result of the AND function would have yielded all "0s" and the message would not have been printed.

Now suppose that the indicator is a "0," indicating that the file has not been updated, and we wish to change it to a "1" without disturbing any of the other bits in the variable. For this we can use the OR function as follows

```
100 LET S = S OR 32
```

The bits then look like this:

OR
```
0 0 0 1 1 1 0 0    ── Bit value of the variable S
0 0 1 0 0 0 0 0    ── Bit value of 32
0 0 1 1 1 1 0 0    ── ORed value results in bit 3, a "1"
```

SIN, COS, and ATN

If you ever took trigonometry in high school or college then you probably remember vaguely that there were some special relationships between the sides of a right triangle and the angles themselves. These "laws of trigonometry" are very useful in many problems involving distances and relative angles. We will briefly review the basic definitions of three of the trig functions here.

The SINE of an angle is defined as the ratio of the side of the triangle which is opposite the angle in question, divided by the hypotenuse of the right triangle. Remember that the hypotenuse is the side that is opposite the right angle. Graphically, the SINE looks like this:

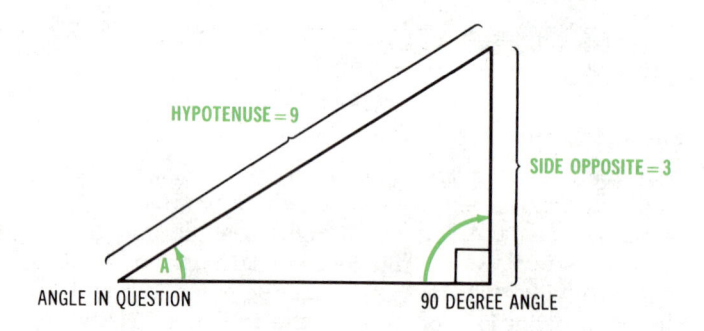

$$\text{SINE}(A) = \frac{\text{side opposite}}{\text{hypotenuse}} = \frac{3}{9} = \frac{1}{3} = .3333$$

Similarly, the COSINE of an angle is defined as the ratio of the side of the triangle which is adjacent to the angle in question, divided by the hypotenuse. Graphically, this can be represented as follows:

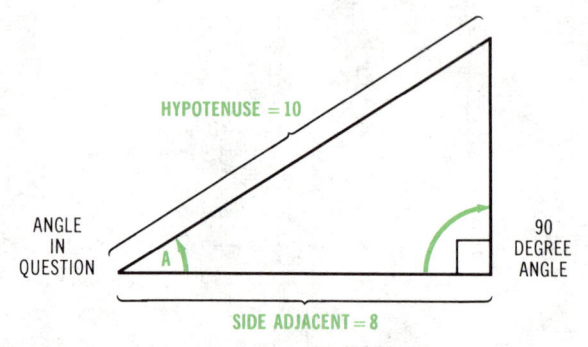

$$\text{COS}(A) = \frac{\text{side adjacent}}{\text{hypotenuse}} = \frac{8}{10} = .8$$

The ARCTANGENT is a little different from the SINE and COSINE functions. Both of them used an angle as the argument to the function in order to derive the particular ratio of the sides of the triangle in question. The ATN function works in reverse. Given the TANGENT of an angle, the ATN function will produce the angle itself. First, we should take a quick look at what the TANGENT of an angle is. It is defined as the ratio of the side opposite the angle in question, divided by the side adjacent to the angle. This looks like the following:

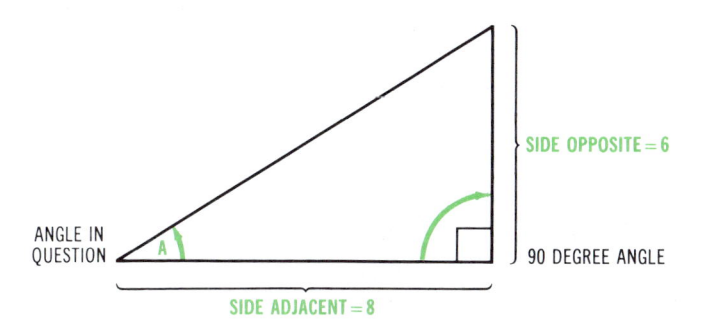

[Diagram of a right triangle with ANGLE IN QUESTION labeled A at left, SIDE ADJACENT = 8 along the bottom, SIDE OPPOSITE = 6 on the right, and 90 DEGREE ANGLE at the bottom right corner.]

$$\text{TAN}(A) = \frac{\text{side opposite}}{\text{side adjacent}} = \frac{6}{8} = \frac{3}{4} = .75$$

Now, the arctangent (ATN) is just the opposite of this definition. Given that we already know what the tangent is, we can then find out what the angle is by using the ATN function like this:

The angle A = ATN(.75)

This usually returns the angle measured in radians rather than degrees. Since there are 2 pi radians in a complete circle, one radian is equal to 360 degrees divided by 2 pi, or about 57.3 degrees per radian.

In actual usage, these trig functions would be very cumbersome if we had to draw little right triangles every time that we wanted to know the sine or cosine of an angle. That is why there are books which contain large tables of these values which can be used to get the required information. If we have a computer at our disposal, which happens to support these trig functions, then we don't even need the books full of tables. We can simply program the computer to give us the information that we want using the trig functions. Most all of the BASIC languages provide the three trig functions that we have described here. Some even offer more, but these are the most commonly used, and the other trig functions can be derived from them. Using BASIC, the form of the usage of these functions is as follows:

```
100 LET X = SIN(A)  ←――――― where A is the angle in radians
200 LET X = COS(A)  ←――――― again A is the angle in radians
300 LET A = ATN(X)  ←――――― where X is the known tangent,
                            and A will be returned as the angle
                            in radians.
```

EXP and LOG

These two functions are related in the sense that they both have to do with natural logarithms. If you remember your high school math, you will recall that the logarithm of a number is the power to which the "base" must be raised to obtain the number. Natural logarithms use a special number for the base known as "base e." The value of this base is approximately 2.718 which may seem like an unusual value to base a system of logarithms on, but proves very useful in higher mathematics. To further clarify the logarithm principle:

$$\text{If } Y = e^X, \text{ then } LOG(Y) = X$$

So, the log of a number is the power to which the base (e) must be raised in order to obtain the number. This is just how the LOG function is used in a program. The typical form is:

```
100 LET X = LOG(Y)
```

The LOG function may also be used in any of the usual combinations such as imbedded in a PRINT statement, or compounded with other functions.

The EXP function is sort of the reverse of the LOG function. It will produce the result of raising the base (e) to some power. In other words:

$$EXP(X) \text{ is the same as } e^X$$

The typical usage of the function is as follows:

```
100 LET Y = EXP(X)
```

One very useful application of the LOG function is regarding the conversion from one logarithm base to another. The general form of this relationship is as follows:

$$\text{LOG}_b(X) = \frac{\text{LOG}_e(X)}{\text{LOG}_e(b)}$$

That is, the logarithm of a number X in base b is equal to the natural log base (e) of the number, divided by the natural log of the base. To find the base 10 log of 100 we would write:

```
100 LET Y=LOG(100)/LOG 10
```

SQR function

The SQR function is used to produce the square root of a number. Of course the number must be positive, since the square root of a negative number is not real and cannot be dealt with by this function. Remember that the square root of a number is a number which when multiplied by itself yields the original number. The general form of the SQR function is:

```
100 LET Y = SQR(X)
```

One common example of the use of the square root function has to do with some more geometry known as the Pythagorean theorem. This describes the relationship of the sides of a right triangle. Simply stated, it says that the length of the hypotenuse of a right triangle is equal to the square root of the sum of the squares of the other two sides. Using the figure below, the formula is expressed as:

$$C = \sqrt{A^2 + B^2}$$

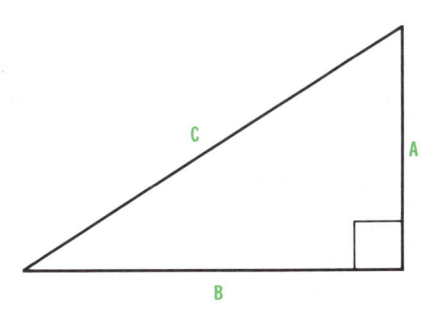

Translating this formula into BASIC, we would use the following:

```
100 LET C = SQR(A*A + B*B)
```

Notice that to square the values of the two sides A and B, we have simply multiplied them by themselves. Some BASICs also include a numeric function that allows a number to be raised to a power. In that case, we could use the appropriate arithmetic operator and write the expression as follows:

```
100 LET C = SQR(A^2 + B^2)
```

This would yield the same results as the statement above.

SGN function

The function SGN which stands for "sign" is very handy for encoding the arithmetic sign of a number (+ or −). The general usage form is:

```
100 YET Y = SGN(X)
```

The variable Y will be set equal to 1 if X is positive, 0 if X is zero, or −1 if X is a negative number.

One very common use of this function is in rounding off a number to the nearest whole number. If we are going to be dealing with only positive numbers, then they could be rounded off using the following statement:

```
100 LET X = INT(X+.5)
```

By adding 0.5 to any positive number and then integerizing it with the INT function, we will obtain the nearest whole number. This does not work however when the number is negative. Adding 0.5 to a negative number will actually reduce its value toward zero. Therefore, we can use the SGN function as follows:

```
100 LET X = INT(X+.5*SGN(X))
```

Since multiplication takes precedence over addition, the 0.5 will be multiplied by either 1 if X is a positive number, −1 if X is a negative number, or by 0 if X is zero. This will then be added to the value of X that is then INTegerized to produce the nearest whole number.

MOD function

Occasionally, it is useful to know what the value of the remainder of an arithmetic division is. This is the purpose of the MOD function, which is short for "modulus." The general form of the MOD function is as follows:

```
100 LET C = A MOD B
```

In the above example, A is divided by B, and the remainder is stored in the variable C. Some examples:

$$12 \text{ MOD } 6 = 0$$
$$47 \text{ MOD } 13 = 8$$
$$5 \text{ MOD } 2 = 1$$

One use of the MOD function involves the case where several code numbers have been consolidated into one number for the sake of memory savings. For example, a date such as April 21, 1945 can be abbreviated 04/21/45. This can then be represented as a number 42145. Now suppose that we want to extract the year portion of this number. We can use the MOD function as follows:

```
100 LET Y = X MOD 100
```

In this case, the variable X will contain the composite date 42145. When the MOD operation is performed, dividing by 100, the remainder 45 is stored in the variable Y. This is then the year part of the date. The rest of the date can be extracted in a similar manner. Here is the whole program:

```
100 LET X = 42145
110 YET Y = X MOD 100
120 REM ----SHIFT THE DIGITS RIGHT
130 LET X = INT(X/100)
140 LET D = X MOD 100
150 REM ----ONE MORE TIME
160 LET M = INT(X/100)
```

STRING FUNCTIONS

Most BASIC languages provide several functions for manipulating string variables, and converting string variables to numeric variables and vice-versa. This section deals with some of the more common string functions.

ASC and CHR$

These two functions are somewhat related in that they are both used to convert between string and numeric variables. The ASC function produces the ASCII decimal value of the first character of a string variable which is given as the argument to the function.

My inherent string functions made doing this mailing list for the Marin Peacock Feather Society a breeze.

Remember that ASCII (pronounced "ass-key") is the name of a special type of coding used to represent the characters of the alphabet and the numerals, as well as several special characters. The name stands for "American Standard Code for Information Interchange." There is a table of all of the ASCII values listed in Appendix B.

The common form of the ASC function is as follows:

```
100 LET X = ASC(A$)
```

It should be noted that the ASC function only produces the ASCII decimal value of the first character in the string. The other characters are ignored. Let us look at an example.

```
100 LET A$ = "SAN FRANCISCO"
200 LET X = ASC(A$)
300 PRINT X
```

Can you figure out what will be printed for the value of X? From the table in Appendix B, we can see that the ASCII decimal value for an upper case "S" is 83. Since only the first character of the string A$ is used by the ASC function, the value which is printed is the ASCII decimal value for the "S" which is 83.

The ASC function is useful in situations when the program must deal with characters which are not part of the normal alphabet. For example, most computer keyboards include a key called "ESCAPE." This key usually has some special use, and does not create a regular character when it is pressed. It does however create an ASCII value of 27. If we had a program that was expecting to be INPUTing a string variable, and we wanted to see if the ESCAPE key was pressed, we could use the following statements:

```
100 INPUT A$
200 IF ASC(A$) = 27 THEN GOTO 9000
```

The above statements would first INPUT a string variable called A$ and then test the first character of that string to see if it was equal to the ESCAPE character. If it is, then the program will unconditionally branch to line 9000.

The CHR$ function operates just the reverse of the ASC function. It takes an ASCII decimal value as the argument and converts it into a one character string. The common form of the CHR$ function is as follows:

```
100 LET A$ = CHR$(X)
```

The CHR$ function is also useful for dealing with characters which are not part of the normal character set consisting of the alphabet, the numerals, and a few special characters. Most terminals have some form of audible alarm such as a bell, horn, buzzer, beeper, etc. This can be used to attract the operator's attention when displaying error messages and the like. This alarm can be activated by sending a special ASCII character to the terminal. This character cannot be enclosed in quotes like a normal string variable, so it must be generated using the CHR$ function like this:

```
100 PRINT CHR$(7)
```

When the CHR$ function converts the decimal value of 7 into an ASCII character and sends it to the terminal, the result will be that the terminal recognizes it as a command to beep the horn. You should notice that the string which is created by the CHR$ function is only one character in length.

LEFT$, MID$ and RIGHT$

These three string functions are all used to break up string variables into substrings. The LEFT$ function allows the program to move a certain number of characters from the left end of a string variable into another string. Likewise, the RIGHT$ function allows the program to move characters from the right end of a string into another string. The MID$ function, as we might guess from its name, allows characters to be moved out of the middle of one string, and into another string. Let us take a closer look at each of these functions.

The general form of the LEFT$ function is:

```
100 LET B$ = LEFT$(A$,N)
```

Notice that there are two arguments inside the parentheses of the LEFT$ function. The first, A$ is the string variable upon which the function is to be performed. The variable N is used to define just how many characters on the left end of A$ will be moved into the string B$. For example:

```
100 LET A$ = "MILL VALLEY"
200 LET N = 4
300 LET B$ = LEFT$(A$,N)
400 PRINT B$
```

Can you figure out what will be printed by the PRINT statement at line 400? Since the LEFT$ function will only move the leftmost N characters of the string A$ into the new string B$ only the word 'MILL' will be printed. By the way, the characters in the string A$ are not disturbed. They are just the same after the LEFT$ function as they were before.

There are some restrictions on the variable N with this function. The value of N must never be negative, or greater than 255. If N is greater than the current length of the string argument, then the entire string will be moved. If N is equal to zero, the result will be a string with no length.

The RIGHT$ function works just the opposite of the LEFT$ function. That is, it moves N characters from the right end of the argument string. The general form is:

```
100 LET B$ = RIGHT$(A$,N)
```

Here again, the same rules apply as for the LEFT$ function. For example:

```
100 LET A$ = "GRAND TOTAL"
200 LET N = 6
300 LET B$ = RIGHT$(A$,N)
400 PRINT B$
```

Since this function will move the rightmost N characters from the argument string, we would expect that after the function was performed, the string B$ would contain 'TOTAL.' Notice that since the rightmost 6 characters are moved, the blank preceding the word TOTAL is also moved.

The MID$ function operates just a bit differently from the LEFT$ and RIGHT$ functions. Basically, it is still used to move characters from one string into another string, but the difference is that it takes them from the middle of a string. In order to do this, the MID$ function requires one additional argument. The general form of the MID$ function is as follows:

```
100 LET B$ = MID$(A$,N,M)
```

Here, the variable N is used to define the starting position within the string A$ from which characters will be moved. This is relative to the left end of the string. The variable M is used to define the number of characters to be moved. For example:

```
100 LET A$ = "GOLDEN GATE BRIDGE"
200 LET N = 8: LET M = 4
300 LET B$ = MID$(A$,N,M)
400 PRINT B$
```

Because of the values of the variables N and M, the MID$ function will begin with the eighth character in the string A$ and move four characters into the string B$. After this is done, the string B$ will contain just the word 'GATE.' The same restrictions apply to the variable N as for the other functions LEFT$ and RIGHT$. The variable M also has the same restrictions of value.

Here again, we must stop and recognize that due to the fact that some versions of BASIC require that the string variables have a declared length, the LEFT$, MID$, and RIGHT$ functions are not permitted. Therefore, there are other means of extracting part of a string. For example,

```
LET B$ = LEFT$(A$,N)
```

would be accomplished by;

```
LET B$ = A$(1,N)
```

Thus moving the characters from A$ into B$ beginning with the first character, and including the Nth character. Likewise,

```
LET B$ = RIGHT$(A$,N)
```

is done using;

```
LET B$ = A$(LEN(A$)—N,+1,LEN(A$))
```

The LEN function shown in the above example produces the current length of the string given as the argument. We will explore the LEN function later in this chapter. Finally,

```
LET B$ = MID$(A$,N,M)
```

is written in some BASICs as

```
LET B$ = A$(N,N+M−1)
```

In general, these alternate forms of the string manipulation statements all use the same type of arguments, namely:

```
LET B$ = A$ (first character position, last character position)
```

STR$ and VAL

These two functions are very useful to the BASIC programmer, especially when programming a business application. They are used to convert string variables into numeric variables, and numeric variables into strings. The form of the STR$ function is:

```
100 LET A$ = STR$(X)
```

What this function does is evaluates the numeric variable X and puts the characters into the string A$ which represents the value of X. For example:

```
100 LET X = 357
200 LET A$ = STR$(X)
300 PRINT A$
```

The string A$ is set up by the STR$ function to contain the characters '357' as a result of evaluating the numeric variable X. Now, the string can be printed out in any way that the programmer de-

155

sires instead of leaving the choice to the BASIC way of printing numeric variables.

The VAL function is used to accomplish the opposite of the STR$ function. It takes a string variable containing characters which represent a numeric value, and evaluates them so as to create a numeric variable. The general form of the VAL function is:

```
100 LET X = VAL(A$)
```

An example of the operation of the VAL function is:

```
100 LET A$ = "25.79"
200 LET X = VAL(A$)
300 PRINT X
```

After the VAL function is complete, the variable X will contain the numeric value 25.79. The original string A$ is not disturbed, and still contains the original characters. Negative values may be converted by placing a minus sign in the first position of the string as follows:

```
100 LET A$ = "−62"
```

An error will occur if there are any characters in the argument string which are not numerals, a decimal point, or a minus sign in the first position of the string.

LEN function

This is one of the most useful of the string functions. It is used to determine the "current length" of a string variable. Each time that a string variable is redefined with new characters, its current length changes. Especially when a string is INPUT, the length is quite variable depending upon how many characters are input. The form of the LEN function is:

```
100 LET N = LEN(A$)
```

If the string A$ happened to contain the characters 'TYPEWRITER' then the LEN function would return a value of 10 in the variable N. Remember that this will only be the current length of the string, and that if it is changed by the program, or by an INPUT statement, then the length will change also.

We have now explored the major bulk of the instructions that make the BASIC language capable of manipulating letters and numbers in powerful ways. The next chapter deals with the more specialized BASIC statements not found in all versions.

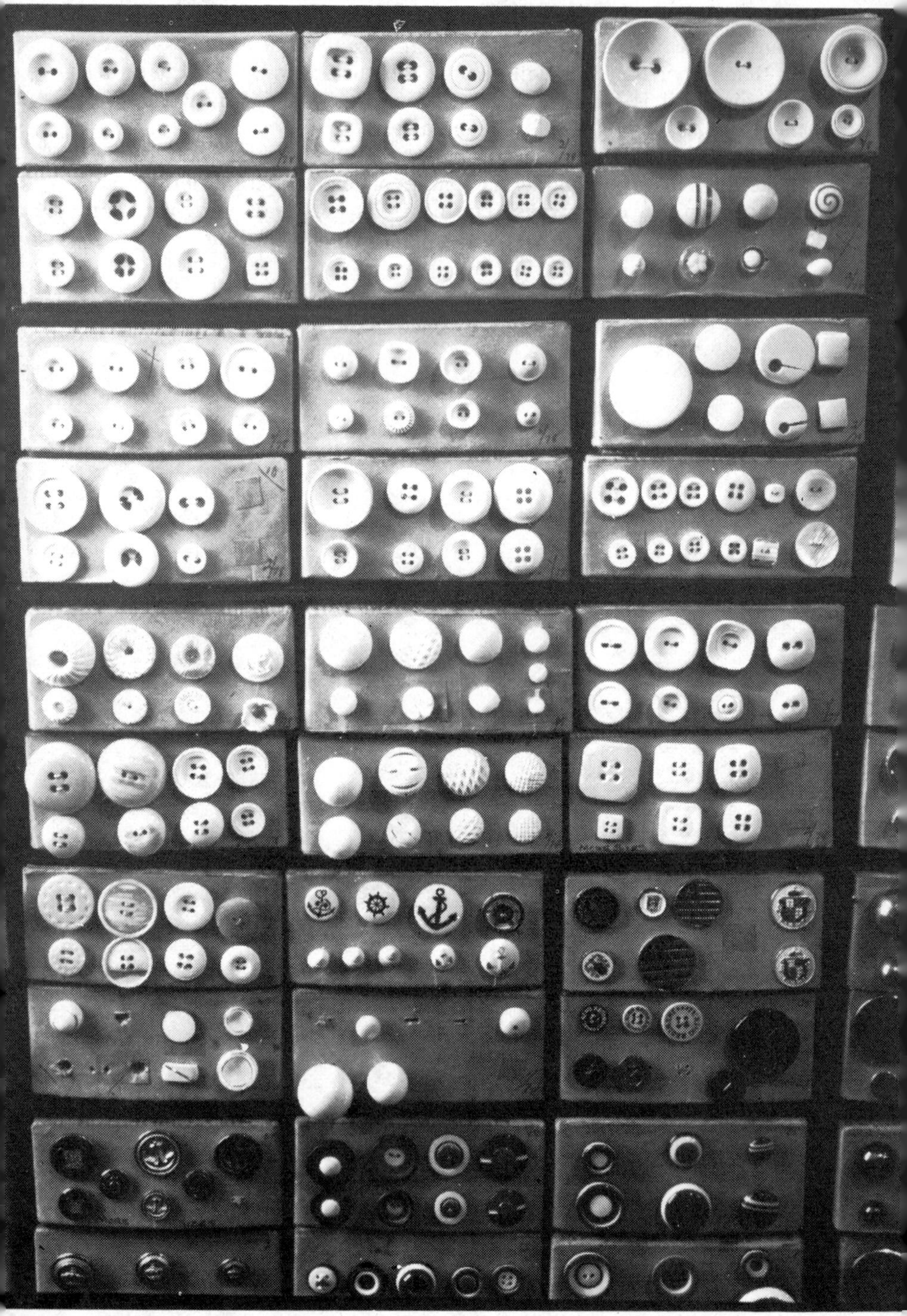

CHAPTER
5

Variations

Chapters 1 through 4 dealt with those features of the BASIC language most common to the variety of computers on the market today. In this chapter we will explore the more advanced BASIC language features. The keywords that control these features are not always available in all versions of BASIC, but are nonetheless extremely useful in your programs. Chances are that you will find at least 50% of these keywords in any particular version of BASIC. The disk and extended BASICs usually incorporated all these topics and more. The particular keywords and topics we will cover include:

PEEK/POKE	direct memory access from BASIC
IN/OUT	I/O port access
CALL/USR	machine language subroutine linkage
CSAVE/CLOAD	cassette tape program storage
AUTO, REN, NEW, etc.	BASIC utility commands
TRON, TROFF, DSP	BASIC debug trace commands

PEEK AND POKE

PEEK and POKE (EXAM and FILL in some BASICS) allow direct control over individual memory locations from BASIC. Recall that a memory location is made up of 8 bits, which is commonly referred to as a "byte." An 8-bit byte can represent a number between 0 and 255. Thus a single memory byte can hold a number between 0 and 255. Also recall that the computer memory can have up to approximately 64,000 of these memory locations.

In BASIC we can place a number (0-255) in any of these memory locations with POKE. POKE works like this:

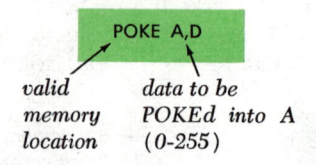

> POKE A,D
>
> *valid*   *data to be*
> *memory*   *POKEd into A*
> *location*   *(0-255)*

Here A is a positive integer expression, variable, or constant which is equal to the memory location we wish to put the data D into. It varies from 0 to the highest memory location in your computer. D is a number or expression between 0 and 255 that you want to go into location A.

For example:

> POKE 800,127

causes memory location 800 to be filled with the value 127. The previous contents of location 800 are lost. And consider this:

```
100 FOR I=800 TO 1000: POKE I,15: NEXT I
```

This example causes memory locations 800 to 1000 to be filled with the number 15. We can say that POKE *writes* data into memory. We can visualize the operation of POKE like this:

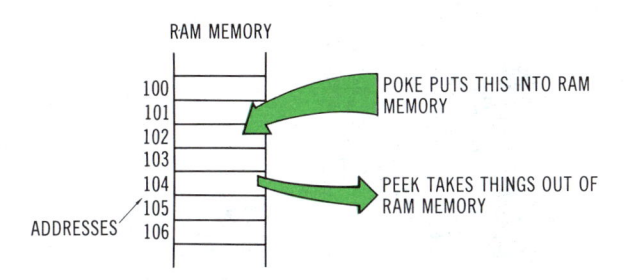

```
                    RAM MEMORY
                100  ┌────────┐
                101  │        │──── POKE PUTS THIS INTO RAM
                102  │        │     MEMORY
                103  │        │
                104  │        │
                105  │        │──── PEEK TAKES THINGS OUT OF
     ADDRESSES  106  │        │     RAM MEMORY
                     └────────┘
```

The memory is visualized as a huge ladder of memory cells or locations. We can see that each location has a fixed address and can be made to contain any number between 0 and 255.

The keyword PEEK does the complementary function of POKE. PEEK is used to *read* data from memory. PEEK is a *function* and therefore is used like this:

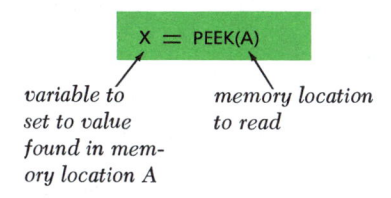

```
              X = PEEK(A)
```
variable to   *memory location*
set to value   *to read*
found in mem-
ory location A

Here the variable X is set to the value found in memory location A by PEEKing at A. Being a function, PEEK *returns* a value to a variable. The argument of PEEK is the memory address A, which may be an expression, variable, or an integer constant. It must not exceed the memory range of your computer.

For example:

```
X=PEEK(4096)
```

causes X to be set to the number found in memory location 4096. And:

```
100 FOR I=0 TO 1023
110 PRINT PEEK(I)
120 NEXT I
```

causes the contents of memory locations 0 to 1023 to be printed out on the screen. (We sometimes refer to this as a memory *dump*.) Note that PEEK(I) may appear alone in the PRINT statement just as if it were an expression.

By now you are probably wondering what is so special about direct memory access with PEEK and POKE. There are many uses, but we will cover three of the most common here. They include: controlling external devices, controlling screen information (graphics), and setting option switches in the BASIC operating system.

Controlling the External World with PEEK and POKE

One of the more important uses of PEEK and POKE is in the manipulation of external hardware devices connected to the computer. Devices that may be hooked up to the computer include speakers, joysticks, lights, oscillators, a/d and d/a converters, sensors, and so on. The way PEEK and POKE are used is based on what kind of hardware device is hooked up, and how the designer has implemented the "interface" between the device and the computer. In most cases the external device contains circuitry that decodes a unique fixed address of some memory location in RAM. We can think of the external device as just another memory location. PEEK will allow us to read any information produced by an external device. POKE will allow us to send information to an external device.

For example, consider a speaker connected to the computer memory through an interface that simply pulses the speaker whenever the memory address it is attached to is POKEd from BASIC.

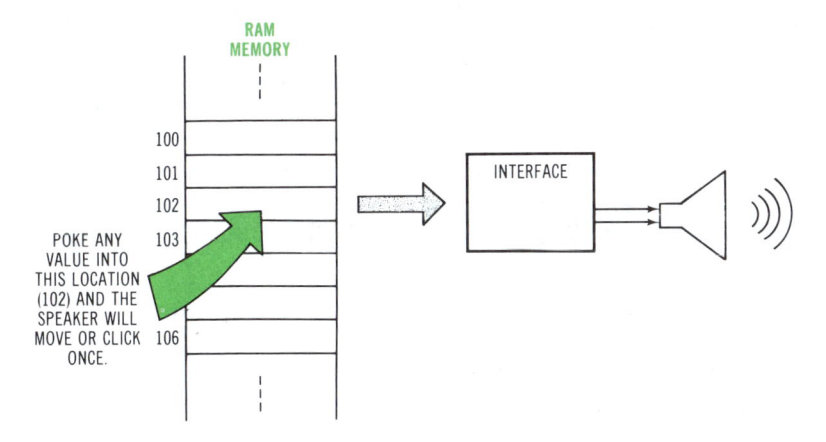

The interface is designed so that a "flip flop" hooked up inside the device, moves the speaker cone whenever the memory location is POKEd into with a value, or when it is PEEKed at. The action of PEEKing or POKEing to the location containing the speaker causes the cone to move regardless of the actual data PEEKed or POKEd. This is because the flip-flop is connected to the address bus of the computer.

Because PEEK is somewhat faster in execution than POKE we can write a simple program that causes the speaker to click several times, and simulate the sound of a ball hitting a wall:

```
100 X = PEEK(102)—PEEK(102)+PEEK(102)—PEEK(102)+PEEK(102)—
       PEEK(102)+PEEK(102)—PEEK(102)+PEEK(102)—PEEK(102)
```

Here we alternately PEEK at location 102 ten times. Address 102 is the location that the speaker flip-flop decodes. The reason we alternately add and subtract the PEEKs is that we end up with X equal to zero.

We can also make tones and melodies with the speaker by adding a little more programing. Suppose we wrote this program:

```
100 FOR I=1 TO 100: POKE 102,0: NEXT I
```

This program will pulse the speaker 100 times by POKEing into location 102. The result will be a medium pitched tone of about 1000 to 5000 hertz. We can see that the program can be expanded so the user could INPUT the length of the FOR...NEXT loop to control how long the tone lasted (duration). Furthermore, we can place another delay inside the main loop to slow down the time *between* pulses. This will have the effect of lowering the tone, like this:

```
100 FOR I=1 TO 100: POKE 102,0: FOR J=1 TO 10: NEXT J:NEXT I
```

Now the tone lasts longer and has a much lower pitch than before.

Manipulating Screen Data with PEEK and POKE

One particularly useful application of PEEK and POKE involves manipulating character and graphics on the terminal screen without using PRINT statements. This technique is made possible on some computers which represent character positions on the screen in a special chunk of RAM memory called the "screen memory." In this method the computer automatically scans these memory locations, converts the contents to a specific ASCII character, and then displays the characters on the screen in a unique position. Computers that represent screen information in memory are said to be "memory mapped." The memory containing the screen data can be visualized as shown on the following page.

In this example memory locations 0 to 1919 hold the screen information. This is about 2K bytes of memory, which represents the upper limit that can be displayed on a standard video terminal without smearing from loss of bandwidth. The screen is usually organized as 80 columns by 24 rows for a total of 80 × 24 or 1020 characters. Although the screen is organized as rows and columns, the actual memory is organized as one long series chain of bytes.

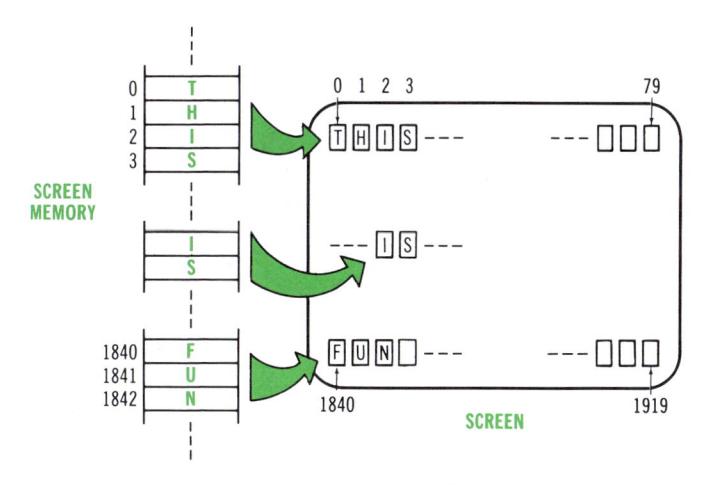

Thus every 80th memory location is the beginning of a new row on the screen. Keep in mind that the scanning of the screen memory is done automatically and is invisible to the user.

We can easily use POKE to put any character we want in any particular location on the screen from BASIC. For example suppose we want to draw a horizontal line of asterisks (*) on the screen, perhaps for a boundary. Assuming the screen memory begins at 0, the code is:

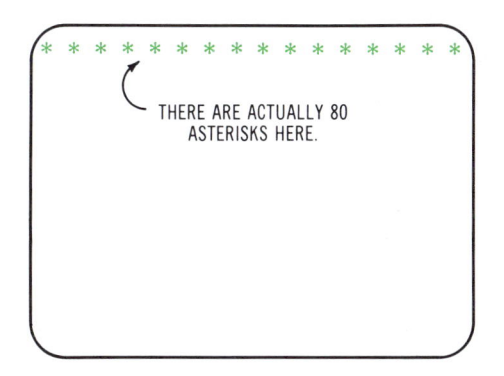

```
100 FOR I=0 TO 79
110 POKE I,ASC("*")
120 NEXT I
```

Here the index of the FOR...NEXT statement I is used as the address of the screen row. ASC("*") converts the asterisk character to its equivalent ASCII code so it can be stored in screen memory. The FOR...NEXT loop causes successive * characters to be stored in the first row of screen memory which automatically places the characters on the screen itself.

If we wish to place a specific character on the screen using X-Y rectangular coordinates we can use statements that convert X and Y to values that access the proper memory location corresponding to the X-Y coordinate. Note that the actual screen memory may not start at location 0 as we have shown so far. In this case a base value B must be added to our results to offset the locations so they fall into the screen memory area:

```
198 REM ---C IS THE ASCII CODE FOR A CHARACTER
199 REM ---B IS THE BASE ADDRESS OF THE SCREEN MEMORY
200 POKE B+(Y*80)+X,C
```

This code POKEs the character code C into memory location specified by X and Y. Y determines the row and X determines the column in the row.

Setting Controls and Options with PEEK and POKE

In many computers PEEK and POKE are used to set various operating modes for BASIC and to obtain the status of certain functions.

For example, in one particular computer, POKE 50,127 turns on the inverse video flag so subsequent characters sent to the screen appear in reverse video (black characters on a white background). POKE 50,255 sets the video back to the normal mode. POKE 33,W1 sets the width of the scrolling window according to the value of W1. POKE −16304,0 sets the computer to operate in the color graphics mode.

Notice that in this last example, the address that the POKE instruction will affect is given as a negative number. This happens because of the fact that internally most computers represent numbers, so that the most significant bit in the number is used to store the arithmetic sign of the number. If it is a positive number, then this bit is a 0. If the number is negative, then the bit is a 1. Since most computers also use 16 bits to store memory addresses, then the highest memory address that can be stored is 65,535 using all 16 bits. If however, the first bit is used to store the sign, then only 15 bits are left for the address itself. This means that the highest address that can be stored in 15 bits is 32,767. If we want to address memory locations that are above this using a signed integer, we must determine what negative number will result in the proper bits being on so as to represent the memory address. This is a somewhat difficult process, since most computers store negative numbers in a form called "twos complement." The point is that it can be done if you really need to PEEK or POKE into memory location above 32,767.

Thus, to access memory 42,000 with POKE you can write:

```
POKE 32767—42000,1
```

In using POKE to control software options, the internal software continually checks the various bytes in memory that have been set by POKE, and uses the value found there to control certain routines while the computer operates. The POKE, in essence, turns a software switch on or off, or provides a certain parameter that is used in the computer's internal processing.

PEEK has similar uses, but is mainly used for checking the status or value of some external or internal event. For example, in a certain computer PEEK(−16384) reads the keyboard and returns the ASCII equivalent of the key pressed. This way no carriage return is needed in a program that accepts keyboard entry (good for programs for children to keep input simple). PEEK(−16336) toggles the external speaker attached to the computer, and X=PEEK(−16286) reads an external push-button switch on the game paddle and if X is greater than 7.27, it means the switch was pressed.

These uses of PEEK and POKE suggest that our programs can communicate even more actively with the intended user, and provide a more exciting and "earthy" computer interaction.

INP AND OUT

Certain computers that are built around the Intel 8080 and Zilog Z-80 microprocessors have special input and output locations called I/O ports. The purpose of the I/O ports is to provide a method for communicating 8-bit data from the computer to and from the outside world. Other computers use memory mapped I/O which means any memory location can serve as an I/O port. The port approach is actually a special page of 256 addresses in memory. The chip is designed so that the hardware engineer can decode these special addresses and easily hook up various devices to them such as keyboards, external displays and lights, d/a and a/d converters, speakers, and so on.

In order to access these ports from a BASIC program two special keywords called INP and OUT are provided. INP is a function statement which accepts an integer byte argument (0-255) which specifies the port, and returns an 8-bit value from the port. The value of the 8-bits is determined by what kind of device is connected to the port, and how many bits are being used. As an example of INP, imagine an analog to digital converter (ADC) which is hooked up to port 255:

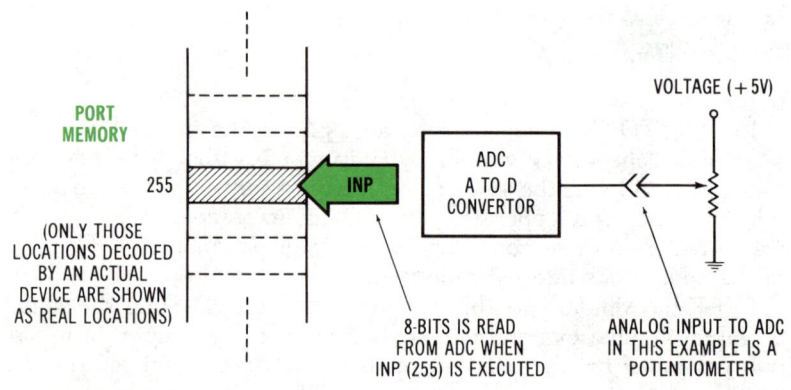

```
PORT
MEMORY
   255                    INP         ADC
                                      A TO D
(ONLY THOSE                           CONVERTOR
LOCATIONS DECODED
BY AN ACTUAL
DEVICE ARE SHOWN
AS REAL LOCATIONS)           8-BITS IS READ      ANALOG INPUT TO ADC
                             FROM ADC WHEN       IN THIS EXAMPLE IS A
                             INP (255) IS EXECUTED   POTENTIOMETER
```
VOLTAGE (+5V)

At the input of the ADC we have attached a potentiometer (pot) to a voltage reference and the wiper is connected to the ADC single input. Varying the pot shaft changes the input voltage to the ADC and the ADC produces a varying digital output in response to this.

If we write the statements:

```
100 PRINT INP(255)
110 GOTO 100
```

it will cause the computer to read the output of the ADC and PRINT this value on the terminal over and over. As we vary the pot shaft the number displayed on the screen should change in step. We now have a neat way to input position information from a user to the computer program. BASIC could use this result to move an object on the screen, change the rate of some process, etc.

In BASIC, OUT performs the complementary function of INP, that is, OUT is a statement that *sends* an 8-bit value in the range of 0 to 255 to a specified output port in the range 0 to 255. For example consider a DAC (digital to analog converter) connected to port zero of the computer, with a speaker attached to its output. The DAC takes an 8-bit digital value from the port zero and converts it into an equivalent voltage. Thus, depending on how the value sent to the DAC varies, we can make the speaker vary to make sounds.

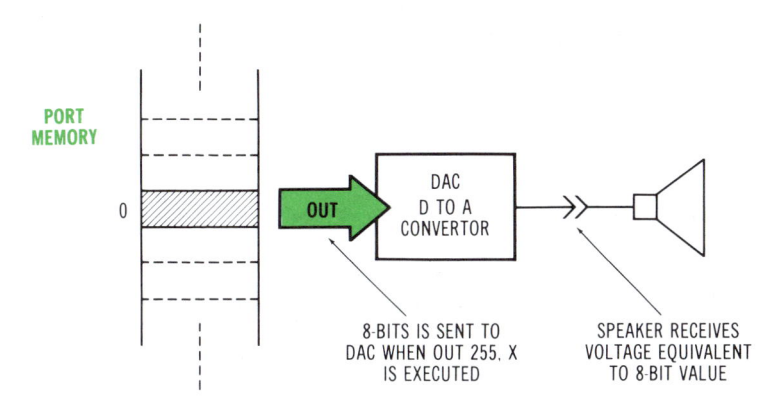

In this example we could make a tone by writing the code:

```
100 I=1
110 I=—I
120 OUT 255,I
130 GOTO 110
```

This will make the computer OUTput alternately a +1 and a −1 to the DAC and will result in a square wave coming from the speaker. Other uses for OUT can be devised in a similar manner. For example, a simple pure tone could use the SIN function like this:

```
100 FOR I=0 TO 2*3.14159
110 R=I/100
120 OUT 255, R
130 NEXT R
140 GOTO 100
```

CALL OR (USR)

To understand the CALL (or USR) statement we must first realize that there is a second kind of programming language available to the microcomputer, that is different than BASIC. This second language is the one that operates the microprocessor chip itself. This second language has its own special instruction set, rules of usage and formatting conventions. The language is referred to as the "machine language" of the computer. It uses special codes and instructions that look like this:

LDA F000

To the computer this means "load the accumulator register inside the microprocessor with data (8-bits) that is located at memory address F000 (where F000 is a hexadecimal address which equals 61440 in decimal). There are other machine language instructions for the microprocessor, and these allow 8-bit data to be moved back and forth between registers inside the microprocessor, data to be placed in memory or read from memory into the microprocessor, simple binary arithmetic to be performed, and so on. In essence, the machine language program controls the elementary logic of the microprocessor operations.

Machine language programs allow us to do things that would be very difficult, if not impossible, to do with BASIC alone. A machine language program resides in an area of memory that is not occupied by BASIC. It has a starting address somewhere in the free memory space not used by BASIC and is treated like a special form of subroutine.

The machine language subroutine has its own return statement which is usually designated by the instruction RET. What CALL does is provide a way for us to branch out of BASIC and execute a specific machine language subroutine. The machine language program does something special until it finds the RET instruction which is usually at the end of the program. RET tells the computer to transfer control back to BASIC and exit from the machine language program. BASIC begins executing again as if nothing happened. The format of the CALL statement is something like the GOSUB statement:

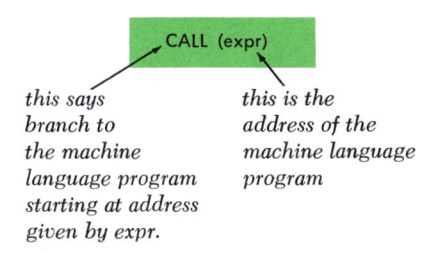

CALL (expr)

this says branch to the machine language program starting at address given by expr.

this is the address of the machine language program

The expression *expr* represents the memory address of the beginning of the user's machine language program. It may also be the address of a machine language program provided in the systems firmware or monitor. This means you can take advantage of the many machine language utility subroutines that are available in the operating system of the computer. As an example of how to visualize the CALL statement imagine you want to use a machine language subroutine that begins at memory location 10 and then later in your BASIC program you want to use one that begins at location 20. The sequence might look like that shown on the top of the following page.

What we have here are two machine language subroutines located in memory, one starting at location 10 and the other starting at location 20. The BASIC program executes one statement at a time until the first CALL is found. Then the CALL 10 statement sends the computer off to execute the machine language program that starts at location 10 in RAM (or ROM in some cases). None of the variables or arrays are changed in the BASIC program, and their values are automatically saved by BASIC when it leaves the main program. The machine language program then operates and performs its specific function (which we will describe soon). When the RET is encountered the control is sent back to the next state-

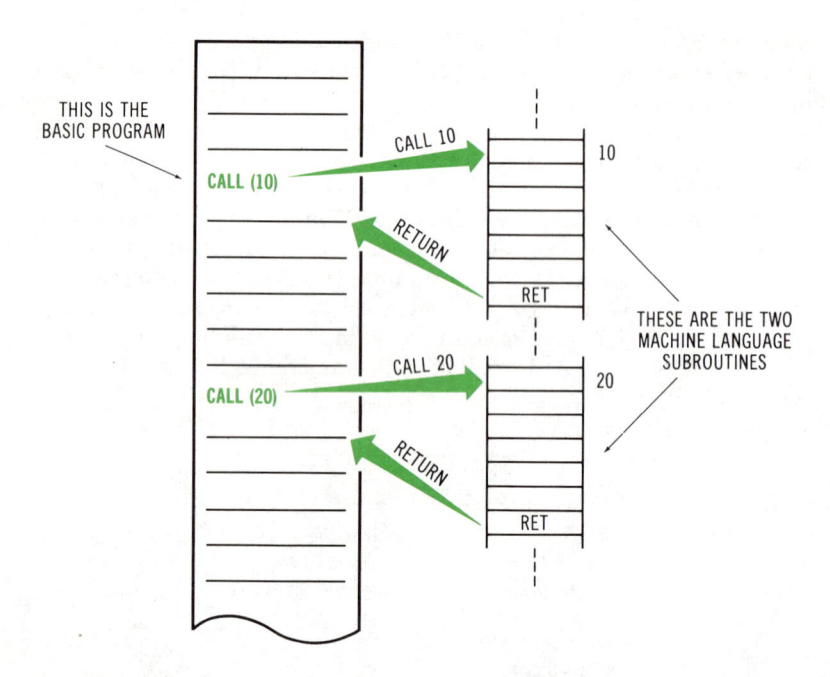

THIS IS THE BASIC PROGRAM

CALL (10) → CALL 10 → 10
← RETURN ← RET

CALL (20) → CALL 20 → 20
← RETURN ← RET

THESE ARE THE TWO MACHINE LANGUAGE SUBROUTINES

ment after the CALL in BASIC. The second CALL 20 works in the same manner.

What CALL Can Do

What can we do with the CALL statement and the subroutines it can access? There are literally hundreds of uses for machine language programs and we will outline just a few of the more popular uses here.

Because of its microprocessor controlling capabilities, machine language programs can do things extremely fast. One typical use is in producing fixed time delays from microseconds to seconds, minutes, and hours. You can, for example, write a machine language program that simply goes into a loop for a specified period of time when it is called from BASIC. The delay could be used for controlling some external event, like how long a process works, making musical tones which have a precise frequency depending on the delay time, and so on.

A simple delay program, written in the machine language of the 8080 might look like this program. Its function is to simply loop for exactly 256 times. Since the microprocessor instructions execute at a precisely defined rate that you can look up on a data sheet, we can precisely know how long the loop takes by multiplying the instruction time by the number of cycles it operates. The code would look like this:

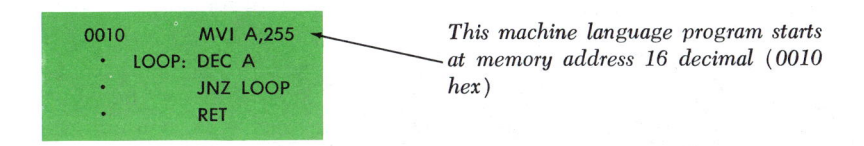

```
0010        MVI A,255
     LOOP:  DEC A
            JNZ LOOP
            RET
```

This machine language program starts at memory address 16 decimal (0010 hex)

This says load the accumulator register inside the microprocessor with the value 255, decrement the accumulator with DEC by 1, and then jump to the label LOOP if the accumulator is not zero yet. This causes the same series of instructions to execute until the value in the accumulator is decremented down from 255 to 0. When 0 is finally reached, we skip to the next instruction after the JNZ which, as it should be, is a RETurn.

We have looked up on our microprocessor data sheet that the instructions in the main loop (DEC and JNZ) take the total of 7.5 microseconds with a 2 MHz clock frequency. Thus the loop takes 7.5 microseconds × 256 loop cycles which equals 1930 microseconds, or 1.9 milliseconds. The MVI instruction takes 3.5 microseconds and the RET takes 5 microseconds so the total time to execute the loop is 1930 + 3.5 + 5 which equals 1938.5 microseconds. We have to add the time it takes to make the CALL itself which is about 25 to 50 microseconds. Thus the total delay time is fairly close to 2000 microseconds, or 2 milliseconds.

Now if we want to produce a 2 millisecond pause in our BASIC program we could write:

```
100 CALL (16)
```

and the program would stop for about 2 milliseconds. We could increase the delay time easily by putting the CALL (10) statement in a loop. For example consider you want a delay of one second. This would do it:

```
100 FOR I=1 TO 500: CALL (16): NEXT I
```

Now the CALL statement is executed 500 times which gives an overall delay of about 500 × 2 mS, or 1000 ms which is one second. Actually the time will be slightly larger than this because the

173

FOR...NEXT instruction takes up time independently of the machine language program.

To see how the delay program is useful, let us suppose that we have a speaker hooked up to a memory mapped I/O port so when we address the memory location it causes the speaker cone to move once. We can use POKE(−16336), where −16336 is the address of the speaker port, to make the cone move once. We can then put this statement inside the loop we wrote and the CALL will control how long the delay is between successive POKEs at the speaker, or the overall frequency:

```
100 FOR I=1 TO 500: POKE −16336,0: CALL (16): NEXT I
```

This should begin to give you an idea of what we can do with the CALL statement. However, you can use CALL and never write a bit of machine language program. What can be done is this. We can use CALL to access a machine language program that is provided within the system monitor. The manufacturer will usually document the address of various subroutines of the utility type so that you can CALL them from your BASIC program. These utility routines consist of programs that home the cursor and clear the screen, clear the cursor from end of page or end of line, produce a line feed, scroll up or down one line of text, and so on. What actually happens when the call is made is that the address in the CALL specifies a utility machine language subroutine that performs the desired function without you doing anything. Exit is like in the normal CALL. For example, to clear the screen normally we would have to issue a succession of PRINT statements that caused enough line feeds to move any text off the screen, like this for a 24 line screen:

```
100 FOR I=1 TO 24: PRINT:NEXT I
```

Look how much simpler this is with a CALL:

```
100 CALL (−936)
```

Not only does this clear the screen it also homes the cursor to the top left corner of the screen. The previous statements left the cursor at the bottom left corner.

174

Another keyword that is sometimes seen on microcomputer BASICs is USR which is pronounced "user." USR is exactly the same as CALL and has the same format and operation:

```
USR (100)
```

sends the computer to the machine language program starting at address 100 (decimal). Note that in some computers, particularly the 8080 and Z-80 based micros, you may have to have previously defined the address of the machine language programs by using a BASIC command called USRLOC. This is somewhat more limited than the normal CALL but it works just as well in the long run.

CSAVE AND CLOAD

One of the problems with small computers of today (and for that matter all computers that use volatile random-access storage) is that when you turn the power off, your program stored in random-access memory is lost. This is because RAM memory requires electricity to maintain its state—power must constantly be applied to the memory circuits to "hold" up its state. What is really needed is some form of permanent storage media, one that would allow us to put a long BASIC program on it and then take it off at any later time. Historically, the first form of permanent computer storage was paper tapes. These were long delicate ribbons of paper which contained holes punched in a specific order that the computer could understand and convert back to a program. Today most manufacturers use magnetic media for storing computer programs. There are two popular devices that use magnetic storage—cassette tape recorders and floppy disks. The current state of the floppy disk technology is that it is a rather significant expense in the overall computer system. A typical floppy disk drive costs about $500 to $1200 depending on its size and speed, while a "garden variety" cassette tape recorder costs under $40. And cassette tape is also inexpensive and also easy to find. So naturally most small computers for the home come with cassette tape recorders either built in or the computer has connectors for hooking up an external recorder you provide.

In order to use the cassette storage functions, BASIC provides two simple commands: CSAVE and CLOAD. CSAVE works like this:

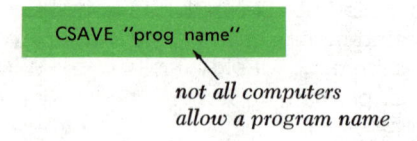

CSAVE "prog name"

not all computers allow a program name

The CSAVE command causes the current program in memory to be stored, or written, on the cassette tape. In some computers the program can be assigned a special name so that it can later be read into the computer memory. A name also allows us to store several programs on a single tape and then have the computer retrieve only the one we specify.

The complementary function of CSAVE is the CLOAD command which looks like this:

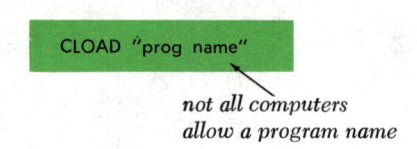

CLOAD "prog name"

not all computers allow a program name

The CLOAD command causes the program called "prog name" to be retrieved from the cassette tape and loaded, or read, into the computer's RAM.

In both cases the user will have to start the tape recorder with the levers and switches in the right state before the command is implemented. Some computers will automatically search for a certain program you have named; others require that you locate the program on the tape and then start the recorder in the proper mode. If you have to locate the program yourself, then it means that you will have trouble storing programs that are long and require using different subprograms. In other words, it is difficult to make programs that have different parts which easily merge together if you do not have the "program name" option available on the recorder commands.

We can visualize the CSAVE and CLOAD commands like this:

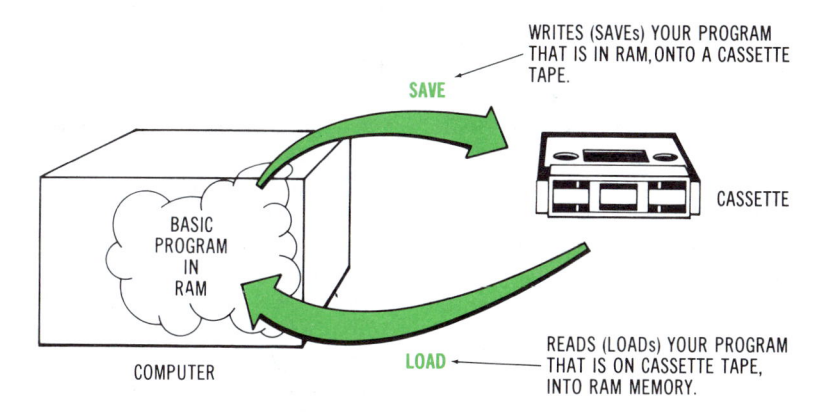

SAVE — WRITES (SAVEs) YOUR PROGRAM THAT IS IN RAM, ONTO A CASSETTE TAPE.

CASSETTE

BASIC PROGRAM IN RAM

COMPUTER

LOAD — READS (LOADs) YOUR PROGRAM THAT IS ON CASSETTE TAPE, INTO RAM MEMORY.

The way CSAVE and CLOAD are used in the development of a BASIC program is like this. First you write your BASIC program and then enter it into the computer from the keyboard. You check that it operates properly and get all the bugs out. Now with the program you want to save in memory, you put a fresh tape in the cassette recorder, then start it in the record mode. At the computer you type the word CSAVE, followed by an optional program name you make up. Now when you press the carriage return key on the computer the circuits will detect what you want done, and begin to convert the program in memory into a series of tiny electrical impulses and send them to the cassette recorder.

The electrical impulses are like the holes punched in a paper tape; they carry information in the way they are ordered on the tape. But instead of being large holes, the impulses create extremely tiny magnetic areas on the cassette to align in certain patterns; therefore, we can store very large programs on very small amounts of tape. In fact, for a reference, typically an 8K byte BASIC program can fit on less than 10 feet of cassette tape.

Because there are thousands and thousands of impulses to store in a typical program, it is easy for a program to miss a bit of code, or pick up noise on the tape itself, which all serves to make the copy of the program wrong. If we try to read it back into the computer it may not run if it has bad information in it. The way around this is that most manufacturers include an error-checking method in the circuits that CSAVE and CLOAD data. The error checking works by adding up in a special manner all the bits that are stored so that when the program is finished, a unique identifying number results. Then the computer takes this number and puts it on the tape at the end of the program area. Now when the program is to be read back into memory with CLOAD, the computer takes all the incoming impulses and adds them up again. It then compares the new sum with the one that was stored on the tape. If they agree then there were no errors when we read or stored the program. If the check sum is different, then an error occurred either when we loaded the program or when it was originally saved. If the error occurred when we originally saved the program, we must save it over again. If the error was a read error, that is something that went wrong when we CLOADed the program, then we must try to CLOAD it again. Usually, you must carefully adjust the volume and tone controls on the tape recorder to make sure the tape is properly read. When you read a program back into memory from tape, it destroys the program currently in memory, so it is important that the program is saved right the first time. One way people usually get around this problem is to make two or three copies of a program in one shot. Since CSAVE is a command that can also be used as a statement, you could type CSAVE:CSAVE:CSAVE and the computer would record the program in memory three times on the tape. Another thing found on a cassette tape circuit is the ability to write a "header" that contains the program name for identification. The computer can search through the tape until it finds the correct program name and then read the program itself into memory.

Some machines place a one or two second "leader" tone on the tape before the actual program data. This leader tone is used to get the circuits in the computer synchronized with the information on the tape itself. The leader tone guarantees that the computer will lock onto the incoming data stream when it occurs.

A drawing of how a BASIC program appears on the cassette tape is shown on the following page.

In the floppy disk we don't have to be concerned about not getting a good copy of our program. This is because most floppies have such good circuits and low error rates. Also, the floppy will store a program very fast and load it back into RAM just as fast. Typical load time for a 8K byte BASIC program from floppy disk is under

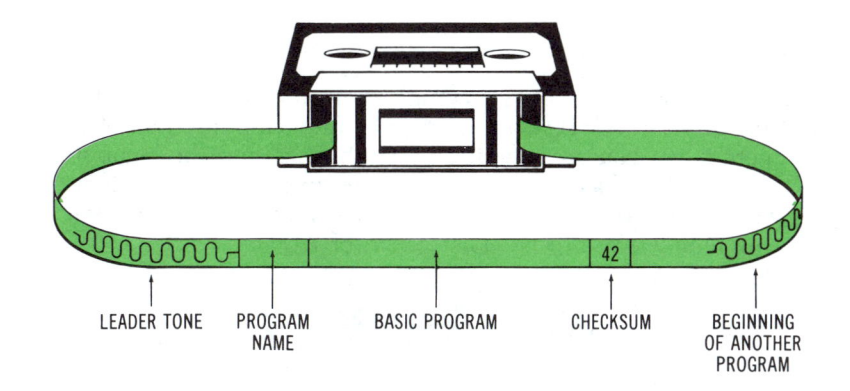

```
         LEADER TONE   PROGRAM    BASIC PROGRAM   CHECKSUM   BEGINNING
                        NAME                                 OF ANOTHER
                                                              PROGRAM
```

one second. The commands SAVE and LOAD are used with floppy disk instead of CSAVE and CLOAD.

BASIC COMMAND AIDS

Perhaps this section should just be called "making life easier on the computer." Given the fact that there is substantial power resting under our finger tips in the way of the internal processing ability of the computer, manufacturers of BASIC have developed several commands for helping in the program development stage. These commands vary from computer to computer, but for the most part they are much alike. Of all of the commands, only NEW is really necessary, so let us begin with it.

NEW or SCRATCH

The purpose of the NEW or SCRATCH command is to completely remove (erase) the current BASIC statements in memory. Recall that you can have only one program in memory at a time (not counting any machine language programs). Therefore there will be times when you need to erase the old program and enter a new program. NEW, when typed in at the command level, causes every statement and line in the computer to be removed or scratched. Some versions of BASIC call the NEW command SCRATCH or just SCR.

Usually you use NEW after you have made a copy of the BASIC program you are working on (remember CSAVE). Once you have a copy CSAVEd you can use NEW to enter and develop a new program.

NEW is also used when you are just trying some simple statements out, perhaps for practice or teaching.

AUTO

Line numbers may be generated automatically by the AUTO command. What AUTO does is provide automatic insertion of line numbers when you are entering program lines into the computer. AUTO saves you having to type a line number manually. It is useful when you have a long program to enter and already know what the line numbers are to be. The format of AUTO is:

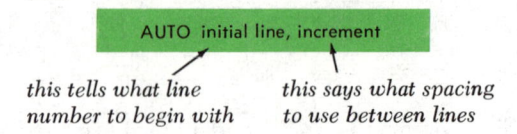

> AUTO initial line, increment
>
> *this tells what line number to begin with*   *this says what spacing to use between lines*

As an example, suppose you want line numbering to begin at 100 and have an increment of 10:

```
AUTO 100,10
100 INPUT X,Y
110 PRINT SQR(X^2 + Y^2)
120 ^C
OK
```

AUTO will continue to number automatically until a Control/C is typed, which will return BASIC to the command level. If the *initial line* is omitted, it is assumed to be 10; and if the *increment* is omitted, it is also assumed to be 10. For example:

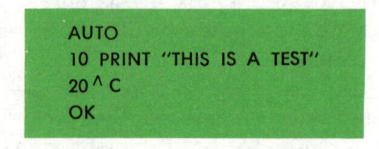

```
AUTO
10 PRINT "THIS IS A TEST"
20 ^C
OK
```

What if AUTO generates a line that already exists in a program currently in memory? Usually the computer will print an asterisk, warning the user that any input will replace the existing line.

CLEAR

CLEAR is the BASIC command that sets all program variables to zero. You would use CLEAR when you are developing a program. After the program is test run, the variables assume certain values that are not what they were when the program started. Now if you want to rerun the program and have all the variables reset to zero, you will have to type CLEAR, before you type RUN. On some computers typing RUN also clears all variables to zero. Of course, it is good programming practice to make all variables start out at their initial values inside the program itself. You can do this before you execute any program statements that use the variables.

For example, if you see statements like this at the beginning of a program you can be almost sure that variables are set by the program:

```
10 LET A=0: LET B1=0: LET Z=9
```

The command CLEAR *expr* is used to set the string space to the value specified by the expression *expr*. The string space is the amount of memory set aside by BASIC to hold the total length of any and all string variables and constants in the program. Usually string space defaults from 50 to 100 bytes when BASIC is first used. Do not confuse setting aside string space with DIMensioning a string array. DIM simply allocates space for string arrays. CLEAR *expr* sets aside string space for undimensioned strings, strings that do not use arrays.

CONT

CONT is a BASIC command that means CONTinue. Its purpose is to continue program execution after a Control/C has been typed, or a STOP or END statement was executed. When CONT is typed execution resumes at the statement where the break occurred.

CONT is useful in debugging, especially where an "infinite loop" is suspected. An infinite loop is a series of statements from which there is no escape. Typing Control/C causes a break in execution and puts BASIC in the command level. Direct mode statements (such as PRINT or LET) can then be used to print out intermediate values, change the value of variables, etc. Execution can then be restarted by typing the CONT command, or by executing a direct mode GOTO, which causes execution to resume at the specified line number.

Some BASICs call the CONT command just CON. The manual with the BASIC language will explain the proper way.

DELETE

DELETE is for eliminating specific lines from your program. We have learned already that you can eliminate any line in a program by simply typing the line number and following it with a carriage return. DELETE allows us to eliminate several successive lines at one time. The most general form of DELETE is:

> DELETE beginning line number-ending line number

This form of DELETE will make the computer eliminate all lines from the specified beginning *line number* to the specified *line number*. You can also type:

> DELETE -line number

This will delete all lines of the current program, from the beginning line of the program to the specified *line number*.

In some computers the DELETE command is just DEL. Whatever the case, be careful when using DELETE so that you do not accidentally delete your entire program.

EDIT

The EDIT command allows editing of a specified line without affecting other lines. The EDIT command usually has a powerful set of subcommands that allows the deleting of only specified items of text in a line, or the insertion of specified text, or the replacement of specified text with other text.

On some computers, instead of EDIT cursor control editing is provided. Instead of using special subcommands, cursor editing allows you to position the cursor with keyboard keys over text you wish to alter and directly type over the old text. You can then copy the old text by moving the cursor through the rest of the statement line. Cursor editing is easier to use, but is not as powerful as command editing.

RENUM or REN

The RENUM command allows all your program lines to be "spread out" so that a new line or lines may be inserted between existing lines. We use RENUM when a program has lines in it which are too close together, or simply do not follow any order. The format of RENUM is:

RENUM start,initial line, increment

Here *start* is the new number of the first line to be resequenced. If *start* is omitted it is assumed to be 10. *Initial* line is the line number at which resequencing will begin. Lines less than the *initial line* will not be renumbered. If the *initial line* is omitted, the whole program will be resequenced. Increment is the value of the increment between lines to be resequenced. If increment is omitted, it is assumed to be 10. Some examples of RENUM are:

RENUM   Renumbers the whole program to start at line 10, with an increment of 10 between line numbers.

RENUM 100,100   Renumbers the whole program to start at line 100 with an increment of 100.

RENUM 6000,5000,1000   Renumbers the lines from 5000 up so they start at 6000 with an increment of 1000.

With RENUM, all line numbers appearing after a GOTO, GOSUB, THEN ON...GOTO, ON...GOSUB will be properly changed to reference the new line number.

Note that RENUM cannot be used to change the order of program lines (for example, RENUM 15,3 when the program has three lines numbered 10, 20, and 30), nor to create line numbers greater than the maximum permitted in your version of BASIC (65529).

Also, if a line number appears after one of the statements above but does not exist in a program, an UNDEFINED LINE XXXX IN YYYYY will usually be printed.

DEBUG COMMANDS

Whenever you write a program you will undoubtedly discover that the program does not work exactly as you planned. This may be discovered when the program runs and produces an error message instead of what you expected. Most of the time the error messages are sufficiently informative to let you find the error and correct it. For example, the message *** REDIMENSIONED ARRAY is fairly self explanatory, and means you have attempted to redimension an array that was previously dimensioned. So all you have to do is find the second DIM statement in the program and eliminate it (unless, of course, it was purposely redimensioned; in which case you have to figure out another way to accomplish the goal). But often we get errors that are not so easy to find and fix. Things like a program that keeps branching to the wrong location, and produces a secondary error because of this. Or, errors due to using several levels of nested loops and having the wrong index on the associated NEXT statements.

To solve these kinds of problems BASIC provides several special commands called the "debugging" commands. The number and type of the debugging commands varies with different computers, but there are several commands that are fairly typical and appear on many of the home computers, including:

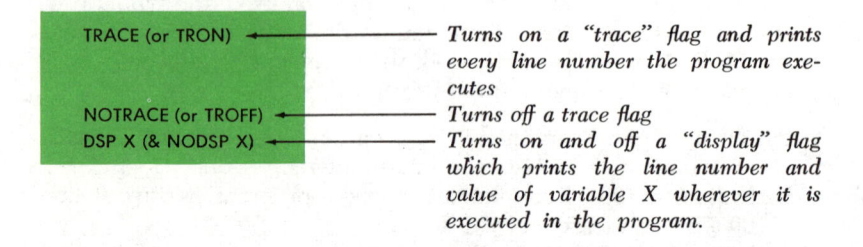

TRACE (or TRON) ⟵——————— *Turns on a "trace" flag and prints every line number the program executes*

NOTRACE (or TROFF) ⟵ *Turns off a trace flag*
DSP X (& NODSP X) ⟵ *Turns on and off a "display" flag which prints the line number and value of variable X wherever it is executed in the program.*

TRACE and NOTRACE (TRON and TROFF)

TRACE (called TRON in some BASICs) is a command that places the computer in the tracing mode. What TRACE does, in effect, is cause the computer to print every line number that is encountered as the program executes. Because the line numbers appear along with all the normal information the program displays, brackets around the line numbers tell us that they are line numbers. So what TRACE does is follow the program flow as it executes, showing you how the branches are made and to where the program is being directed. In essence, the trace is like a running road map of the line numbers the program is following as it cycles along. You can use the line numbers to check that the program is following the course you expect.

For example, suppose you have this program and find that it is hanging up somewhere and not completing its function.. What we do is type TRACE which places the computer in the trace mode and then type RUN to start the program. Here is what happens:

```
TRACE
RUN
[1] [5] [10] [50] [60] [70] [100] [110] [120] [100] [110] [120] [100] [110]
[120] [100] [110] [120] [100] [110] [120] [100] [110] [120] [100] [110]
[120] [100] [110] [120] [100] [110] [120] [100] [110] [120] [100] [110]
[120] . . . . . . . . . . . .
```

What we can tell from this display of trace is that the lines 100, 110, 120 keep repeating over and over. We only showed a portion of the TRACE, but you would eventually see the screen full of the numbers 100, 110, and 120. This obviously points to the fact that the program is caught in an "infinite loop," repeating the same code over and over. TRACE has pointed to the lines at fault, so we can use LIST to examine the code like this:

```
LIST 100-120
100 I=I+2
110 IF I=9 THEN RETURN
120 GOTO 100
```

Take a close look at the program. The variable I is incremented by 2, tested for being equal to 9, and if it is RETURN. If it is not equal to 9, it loops back to line 100 and increments again. That seems fine, but what if the value of the index I was an even number like 0 or 2 when the loop started. The values of I would be 0, 2, 4, 6, 8, 10, 12, 14, etc. Because the index I never equalled exactly 9, the loop repeated way beyond what we wanted. All we have to do to fix things is to change the comparison inside the IF...THEN statement so it causes a branch if we *exceed* the value of 9, like this:

```
110 IF I=>9 THEN RETURN
```

Now we have solved a program "bug" with the aid of the TRACE mode. Since we are done and do not want the line numbers caused by TRACE anymore, we use an associated command called NOTRACE (or TROFF in some BASICs).

NOTRACE simply turns off the TRACE flag and stops the generation of line numbers to appear on the screen.

There are other similar uses for TRACE, but all fall into the area of tracing the path of the program execution as the program runs.

DSP

The DSP command, pronounced DSPlay, is used to print out the actual value of a variable and the line number where it is executed. The format of DSP is:

```
DSP var
```

where *var* is a variable which appears in the program and which is to be displayed. What variable does is cause the line number and the value of *var* to be printed out each time the computer finds it in its execution path. What this does is allow us to see how the values of some variable are changing without using a separate PRINT statement for it *everywhere* it appears in the program.

For example, in our previous "infinite loop" program section we could have typed, DSP I and run the program to cause this effect:

```
DSP I
RUN
100  I=2
100  I=4
100  I=6
100  I=8
100  I=10
100  I=12
    .
    .
    .
```

Here we see how DSP works. The value of I and what it equalled each time it was incremented was printed out in a long column. Note the printing of I would continue until we got an overflow error or stopped the computer with a Control/C.

Now it is obvious that the variable I never equalled the value of 9, and we can fix the program even faster.

We often use DSP as a statement rather than a command. For example:

```
999 DSP X
```

when line 999 is executed the DSPLAY flag will be turned on and all subsequent lines where the variable X appears and actually changes the value of X or redefines it, will be printed out.

When we want to turn the display flag off we use NODSP *var*, where *var* is the same variable that appeared in a previous DSP command or statement. There is no limit to the number of DSP commands or statements you have in effect at the same time. Since the variable is actually printed out with the value, we can tell commands from statements. In the case of several DSP commands the variables following them will be printed in the order in which they are executed. Thus you will get a mix of variables in the display and will have to visually sort them out. Sometimes we forget where the DSP statement appears inside a program, and this makes turning the DSP flag off rather difficult. That is why it is better to keep the DSP as a command rather than a statement. Note also that RUN clears the DSP mode, so to restart a program without turning

BASIC COMMANDS make wonderful programming!

DSP *var* off, use a GOTO or CONT command in the immediate mode to start the program up again.

VIDEO PLOTTING WITH TAB

We can do some pretty neat graphing with TAB and equations. For example suppose we wanted to print out a simple equation such as Y=X. Consider that the X axis is down the screen (0 is at top) and the Y axis is across the screen (0 at the left). Now consider what happens with this program:

Here we have a FOR...NEXT loop which increments through 15 values of X. The variable Y is set to equal the value of X and then we TAB Y spaces to the right and print an asterisk character. Since the equation is Y=X we get a slanted line. Although the slant isn't 45 degrees as would be expected, we still get a straight line. The reason the slant isn't 45 degrees is because the vertical spacing on the terminal doesn't equal the horizontal spacing. Usually there are two to three times as many horizontal column positions as there are vertical positions. The typical terminal or crt screen is 80 columns by 24 lines, as shown by the drawing at the top of page 189.

```
10 FOR X=1 TO 15: Y=X
20 PRINT TAB(Y) "*"
30 NEXT X
RUN
    *
     *
      *
       *
        *
         *
          *
           *
            *
             *
              *
               *
                *
                 *
                  *
```

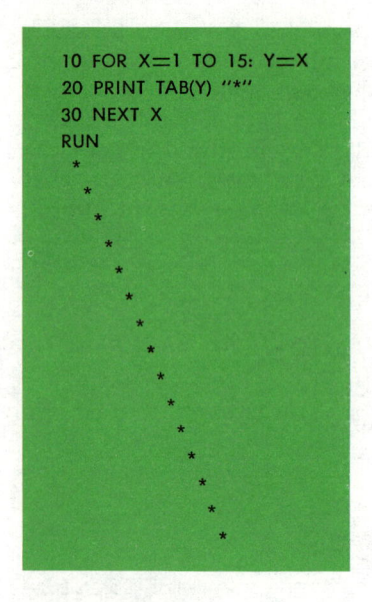

Frequently we see formats of 40 by 40, 64 by 24, and so on. The point is that the spacing is not equal and there will be some distortion in your graphs.

In the example Y=X we have a "linear" equation. Linear equations produce straight lines of different angles and different offsets on the screen. But, we also can print curved-line graphs. Consider the equation Y=X*X/10. Can you tell how the RUN of this program would look?

```
10 FOR X=1 TO 10
20 Y=X*X/10
30 PRINT TAB(Y) "*"
40 NEXT X
```

What happens is that the equation Y=X*X/10 generates decimal fractions between 0 and 10. When X is 1, X*X/10 is 0.1 and because we can only tab an integer number of spaces, TAB(Y) is zero. A table of the values of X, X*X/10, and TAB(Y) are as follows:

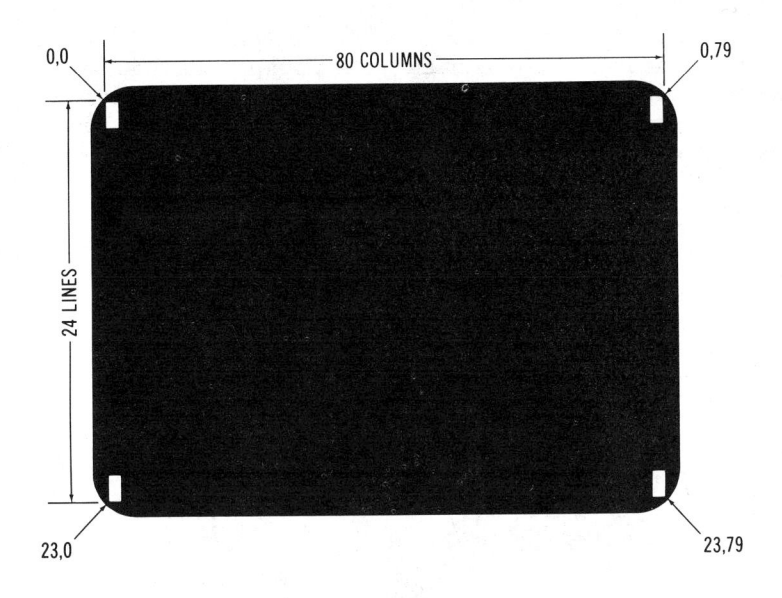

X	Y (X*X/10)	TAB (Y)
1	0.1	0
2	0.4	0
3	0.9	0
4	1.6	1
5	2.5	2
6	3.6	3
7	4.9	4
8	6.4	6
9	8.1	8
10	10.0	10

A RUN of the program produces this graph:

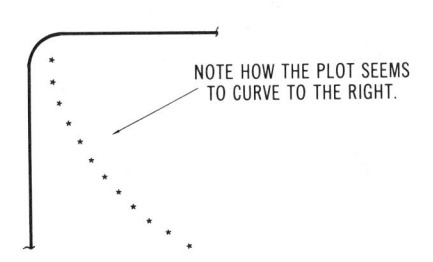

NOTE HOW THE PLOT SEEMS TO CURVE TO THE RIGHT.

What Is Your SIN?

We can take advantage of some of the more powerful BASIC numeric functions in our graphing. For example the trigonometric functions SIN, COS, and ATN may be easily used to create harmonic curves for biorythms, music analysis, modulation studies, and so on. Let us consider the SIN function that we learned earlier produces the trigonometric sine of the angle specified as its argument. So we could use the formula Y=SIN(X) to calculate the value of the Y coordinate we want to TAB out to. Since X is expected to be in radians rather than degrees for the trig functions, we will make X vary from 0 to 6.28 which is one full circle in radians. We will use a FOR...NEXT loop with a variable STEP size to control the number of points of the curve that are displayed.

To make things even more interesting we will make the string that gets PRINTed out a message. Remember this message can be any characters on the keyboard you wish. Here is the program:

```
 0 REM --- SIN CURVE
10 INC=.3
20 FOR X=0 TO 6.28 STEP INC
30 Y=SIN(X)
40 Y=Y*20+20
50 PRINT TAB(Y) "MITCH"
60 NEXT X
```

Note that we changed Y in statement 40 to Y*20+20. This is because Y=SIN(X) produces decimal fractions between −1 and +1 and we cannot TAB a negative number of spaces. So we simply multiply Y by 20 so the numbers are −20 to +20 and then add 20 so the numbers are offset to 0 to 40. Since the screen width varies with different BASICs we could increase the width to 80 by writing Y=40*Y+40.

Here is a RUN of the SIN CURVE program.

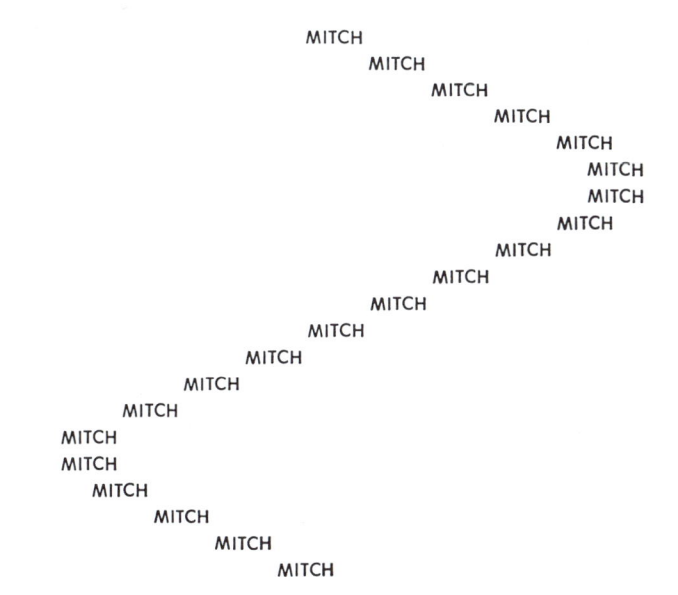

```
                        MITCH
                          MITCH
                            MITCH
                             MITCH
                              MITCH
                               MITCH
                               MITCH
                              MITCH
                             MITCH
                            MITCH
                          MITCH
                        MITCH
                      MITCH
                    MITCH
                  MITCH
                MITCH
              MITCH
            MITCH
          MITCH
         MITCH
        MITCH
         MITCH
           MITCH
             MITCH
               MITCH
```

APPENDIX A

Numbering Systems

"What's one and one and one and one and one and one and one and one and one and one?"
"I don't know," said Alice. "I lost count."
"She can't do addition," said the Red Queen.
(Lewis Carroll, Through the Looking Glass)

No one knows when the first number was recorded, but most likely it dates back to Biblical times. Among the oldest system of numbers was that of the Chinese, which was first based on a system of laying sticks in patterns and later was based on symbols drawn with pen and ink (Fig. A-1).

Calculating in these number systems was exceedingly difficult. This was because each time the basic numerals were exceeded, a new numeral had to be invented. In Roman numerals, when you needed to count above 100, you used a C, and above 1000 an M. The real problem came when these numbers had to be multiplied. The actual process of counting took place on counting boards, such as the Chinese abacus, where answers were converted back to the notation system.

Our current decimal system is much more streamlined than those of the ancient civilizations. We only have to learn the 10 basic symbols and the positional notation system in order to count to any number. For example, what is the meaning of the number 256? In positional notation, the value of each digit is determined by its position. The four in 4000 has a different value than the 4 in 400. Thus, in 256 we have three digits, and each must be "interpreted" in light of where it is in order and relation to the other digits. We learn that the rightmost digit is interpreted as the number of "ones," the next to the left as the number of "tens," and the next digit as "hundreds." The general formula for representing numbers in the decimal system using positional notation is:

$$a_1 10^{n-1} + a_2 10^{n-2} + \ldots + a_n$$

which is expressed as $a_1 a_2 a_3 \ldots a_n$, where n is the number of digits to the left of the decimal point. Therefore,

$$256 = (2 \times 10^2) + (5 \times 10^1) + (6 \times 10^0)$$
$$= 2 \text{ hundreds} + 5 \text{ tens} + 6 \text{ ones}$$

In the decimal system we use 10 as the basic multiplier. We call 10 the *base* or *radix*. Most of recorded history shows mankind counting in the decimal system (base 10). However, it is not difficult to imagine a race of one-armed people who used the quinary system (base 5). We see examples of the duodecimal system in clocks, rulers, the dozen, and so on.

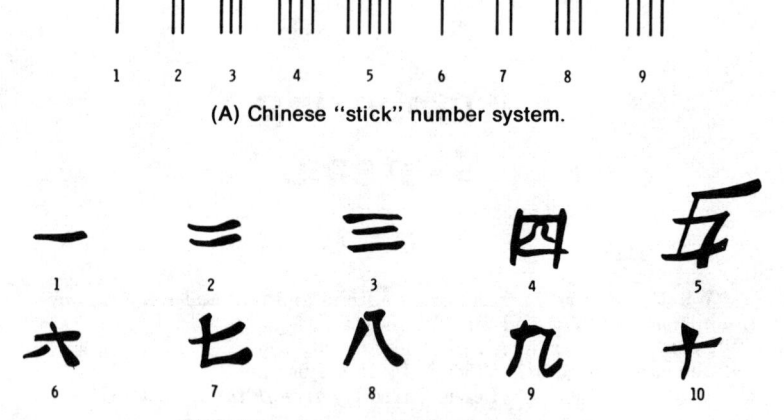

(A) Chinese "stick" number system.

(B) Chinese "pen-and-ink" number system.

Fig. A-1. First number systems.

THE BINARY SYSTEM

Although the seventeenth-century German mathematician Leibnitz was given most of the credit for invention of the binary number system with a base of 2, it was probably the ancient Chinese who realized the simple and natural way of representing numbers as powers of 2.

Early computers used relays and switches as their basic elements. The operation of a switch or a relay is itself binary in nature. A switch can either be on (1) or off (0). Modern computers use transistors like those found in televisions and radios. These components can be arranged to be in one or two "states": on or off. As a matter of fact, the more distinctly different the two states, the more reliable the computer's operation.

The idea is to make the devices work in such a manner that even slight changes in their characteristics will not affect the operation. The best way of doing this is to use a *bistable device*, which has two states.

If a bistable device is in stable state X, an energy pulse will drive it to state Y; and if the bistable component is in stable state Y, an energy pulse will drive it to state X. It is easy for a bistable component to represent the number 0 or 1:

stable state $X = 1$
stable state $Y = 0$

Counting

The same type of positional notation used in the decimal system is used in the binary. Since there are only two possible states for a numeral, either we count the position value or we don't count it. The general rule is: The binary number $a_1a_2a_3 \ldots a_n$ is expressed in decimal as:

$$a_1 2^{n-1} + a_2 2^{n-2} + \ldots + a_n$$

Therefore, the binary number 11010 is converted to decimal as follows:

$$N = a_1 2^{5-1} + a_2 2^{4-1} + a_3 2^{3-1} + a_4 2^{2-1} + a_5 2^{1-1}$$
$$= a_1 16 + a_2 8 + a_3 4 + a_4 2 + a_5 1$$

Substituting the values for a_1, a_2, a_3, a_4, and a_5:

$$11010 = (1 \times 16) + (1 \times 8) + (0 \times 4) + (1 \times 2) + (0 \times 1)$$
$$= 16 + 8 + 0 + 2 + 0$$
$$= 26 \text{ (decimal system)}$$

Table A-1 lists the first 20 binary numbers.

Table A-1. The First 20 Binary Numbers

Decimal	Binary	Decimal	Binary
1	1	11	1011
2	10	12	1100
3	11	13	1101
4	100	14	1110
5	101	15	1111
6	110	16	10000
7	111	17	10001
8	1000	18	10010
9	1001	19	10011
10	1010	20	10100

A simpler way to convert binary numbers to decimal is to use a weighting table (Fig. A-2). This is simply a reduction of the expansion formula just presented. Write down the value of the positions in the binary number over the binary digits, arrange them as an addition, and add them.

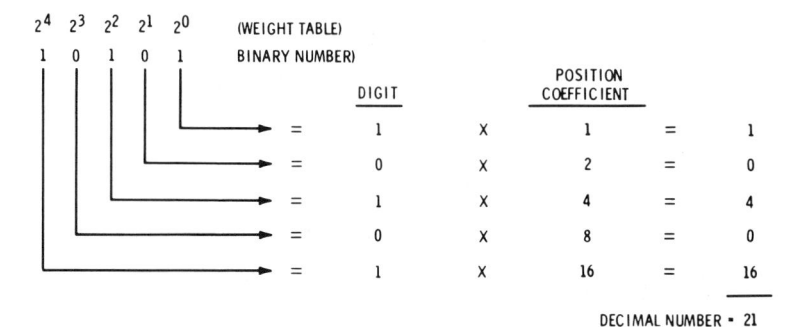

```
2⁴  2³  2²  2¹  2⁰    (WEIGHT TABLE)
1   0   1   0   1     BINARY NUMBER)
                                    POSITION
                        DIGIT       COEFFICIENT
                    =   1       X   1       =   1
                    =   0       X   2       =   0
                    =   1       X   4       =   4
                    =   0       X   8       =   0
                    =   1       X   16      =   16
                                    DECIMAL NUMBER = 21
```

Fig. A-2. Binary-to-decimal conversion using the weighting method.

Frequently we will want to convert in the opposite direction, from decimal to binary. For this method we repeatedly divide the decimal number by 2, and the remainder after each division is used to indicate the coefficients of the binary number to be formed. Fig. A-3 shows the conversion of 47_{10} to binary. Note that decimal 47 is written 47_{10} and that binary numbers are given the subscript 2 if there is danger of confusing the number systems.

47_{10} = ? BINARY

		QUOTIENT	REMAINDER
2 ⟌ 47	=	23	1
2 ⟌ 23	=	11	1
2 ⟌ 11	=	5	1
2 ⟌ 5	=	2	1
2 ⟌ 2	=	1	0
2 ⟌ 1	=	0	1

1 0 1 1 1 1

THEREFORE 47_{10} = 101111_2

Fig. A-3. Decimal-to-binary conversion using the division method.

Fractional numbers are treated in the same manner as in the decimal system. In the decimal system:

$$0.128 = (1 \times 10^{-1}) + (2 \times 10^{-2}) + (8 \times 10^{-3})$$

In the binary system:

$$0.101 = (1 \times 2^{-1}) + (0 \times 2^{-2}) + (1 \times 2^{-3})$$

Binary Addition and Subtraction

Addition in binary is as easy as addition in decimal, and follows the same rules. In adding decimal $1 + 8$, we get a sum of 9. This is the highest-value digit. Adding 1 to 9 requires that we change the digit back to 0 *and carry 1*. Similarly, adding binary $0 + 1$, we reach the highest-value binary digit, 1. Adding 1 to 1 requires that we change the 1 back to a 0 and carry 1, i.e., $1 + 1 = 10$. Thus, for example, add binary 101 to 111:

$$\begin{array}{r} 101_2 = 5_{10} \\ + \ 111_2 = 7_{10} \\ \hline 1100_2 = 12_{10} \end{array}$$

The four rules of binary addition are:

$$0 + 0 = 0$$
$$0 + 1 = 1$$
$$1 + 0 = 1$$
$$1 + 1 = 0, \text{ carry } 1$$

Here are some examples:

$$\begin{array}{rr} 101 & 5 \\ + \ 110 & 6 \\ \hline 1011 & 11 \end{array} \qquad \begin{array}{rr} 11.01 & 3\frac{1}{4} \\ 101.11 & 5\frac{3}{4} \\ \hline 1001.00 & 9 \end{array}$$

Subtraction is just inverted addition. It is necessary to establish a convention for subtracting a large digit from a small digit. This condition occurs in binary math when we subtract a 1 from a 0. The remainder is 1, and we borrow 1 from the column to the left. Just as in decimal subtraction, if the digit on the left is a 1, we make it a zero, and if it's a zero, we make it a 1. The rules for binary subtraction are:

$$0 - 0 = 0$$
$$1 - 0 = 1$$
$$1 - 1 = 0$$
$$0 - 1 = 1, \text{ borrow } 1$$

Here are two examples:

```
  10000        16       110.01      6¼
-    11      -  3      -100.1     -4½
  ─────      ────       ──────      ────
   1101        13         1.11      1¾
```

Binary Multiplication and Division

There are only four basic multiplications to remember in the binary system, instead of the usual 100 we memorize in the decimal system. The binary multiplication table is:

$$0 \times 0 = 0$$
$$1 \times 0 = 0$$
$$0 \times 1 = 0$$
$$1 \times 1 = 1$$

The following examples illustrate how easy binary multiplication is compared with decimal. The rule to remember is: "copy the multiplicand if the multiplier is a 1, and copy all 0's if the multiplier is a 0. Then add down, as in decimal multiplication."

```
 Binary    Decimal      Binary     Decimal
   1100       12         1.01        1.25
 ×1010      ×10        ×10.1        ×2.5
 ─────      ───         ─────        ────
   0000      120          101          625
   1100                  1010          250
  0000                 ──────        ─────
  1100                 11.001        3.125
─────────
1111000
```

Binary division is also very simple. Division by zero is forbidden (meaningless), just as in decimal division. The binary division table is:

$$\frac{0}{1} = 0$$

$$\frac{1}{1} = 1$$

Examples of binary division are:

```
      Binary           Decimal
         101              5
    ───────          ─────
 101)11001           5)25
      101
      ───
        101
        101
```

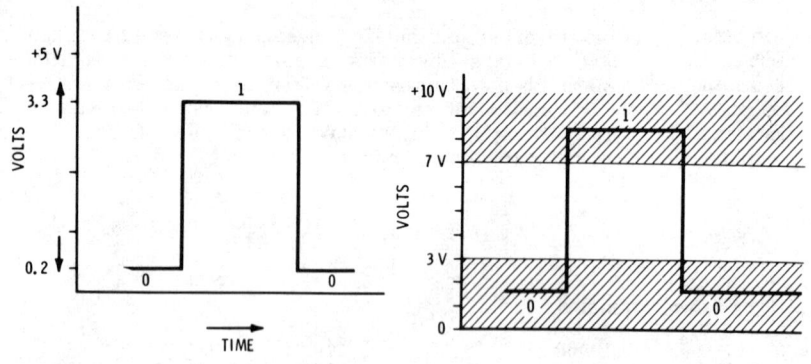

(A) Binary digit representation (TTL).

(B) Binary digit representation (CMOS).

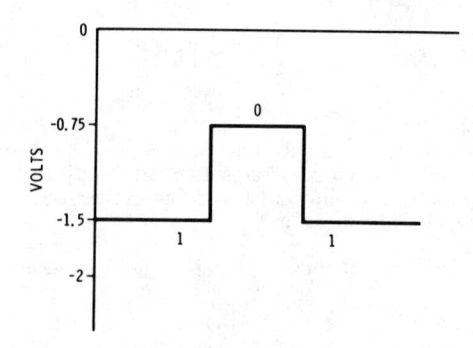

(C) Binary digit representation—negative logic (ECL).

Fig. A-4. Representing binary numbers.

Because of the difficult binary additions and subtractions that result when the numbers are large, octal or hexadecimal notation is often used.

Representing Binary Numbers

Information in digital computers of today is processed by the switching and storing of electrical signals. Computers operating in the binary number system need represent only one of two values (1 and 0) at a time. A single wire can be utilized for this purpose. A method for representing a binary digit on a signal line is shown in Fig. A-4A. In this method a small positive voltage is used to represent a 0, and a larger positive dc voltage is used to represent a 1.

Much importance is placed on the actual voltage values used to represent the binary digit. Usually, the circuitry used to transmit and receive these signals determines the range of voltages. The most ideal circuit is one in which the two logic levels are far apart (Fig. A-4B).

Note that the "1" signal is positive with respect to the "0" signal. This convention could also have been reversed, i.e., the negativemost signal

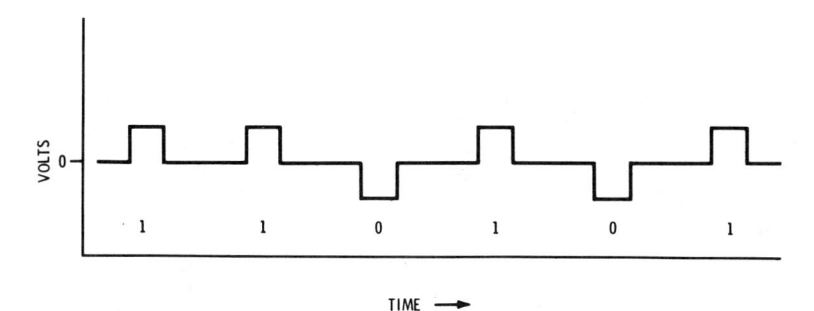

(A) RZ method of representing binary digits.

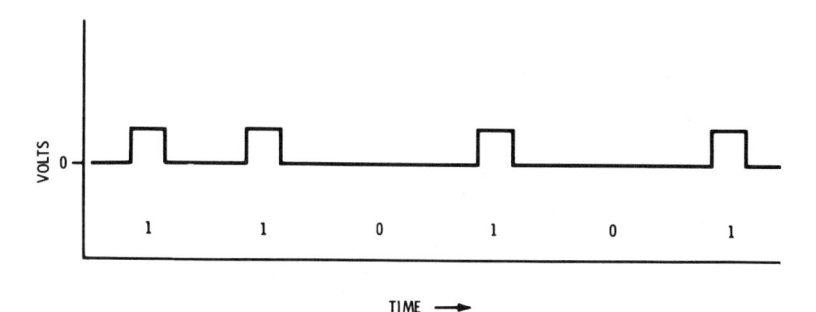

(B) NRZ method of representing binary digits.

Fig. A-5. Pulse representation of binary numbers.

called a "1" and the more positive signal a "0." (See Fig. A-4C.) Usually, one convention is chosen by the designer and then used throughout the computer.

Pulse Representation of Binary Numbers

Binary digits are often transmitted and received as a burst of pulses. Fig. A-5A shows a system in which a positive pulse represents a 1 and a negative pulse a 0. The signal line remains at some in-between value when no pulse is being sent. This technique is used frequently in magnetic recording, and is called *return-to-zero* (RZ) encoding.

A more popular technique is shown in Fig. A-6B. A 1 is represented by a pulse, and a 0 as no pulse. The receive circuitry must keep in synchronization with the incoming signal in order to know when a binary digit is occurring. This technique is called *non-return-to-zero* (NRZ) encoding.

Serial and Parallel Transmission

So far, methods of representing and transmitting a single binary digit have been illustrated. We will find that it is often necessary to transmit complete binary numbers, which is accomplished by transmitting each binary digit over its own wire. Thus, an n-digit binary number would require n wires or signal lines. This is called *parallel transmission*. Fig. A-6A illustrates an 8-bit binary number (10010101) being transmitted over eight parallel lines. In such a system each line is assigned a different weight, based on the positional notation of the binary number system. The leftmost binary digit is assigned the weight of 2^{n-1}, where n is the number of binary digits (8 in this case).

The other method of transmitting binary data is called *serial transmission*. In this method the signals representing the binary digits are transmitted one at a time in sequence, usually starting with the rightmost digit (Fig. A-6B). This method requires some synchronization in order to distinguish several 0's or 1's that follow each other in a sequence.

Negative Numbers

The normal way to express a negative number is to place a minus sign in front of the number. When a negative number is subtracted from a positive number, we *change the sign and add*. For example, $256 - (-128) = 256 + 128 = 384$.

(A) Parallel transmission.

(B) Serial transmission.

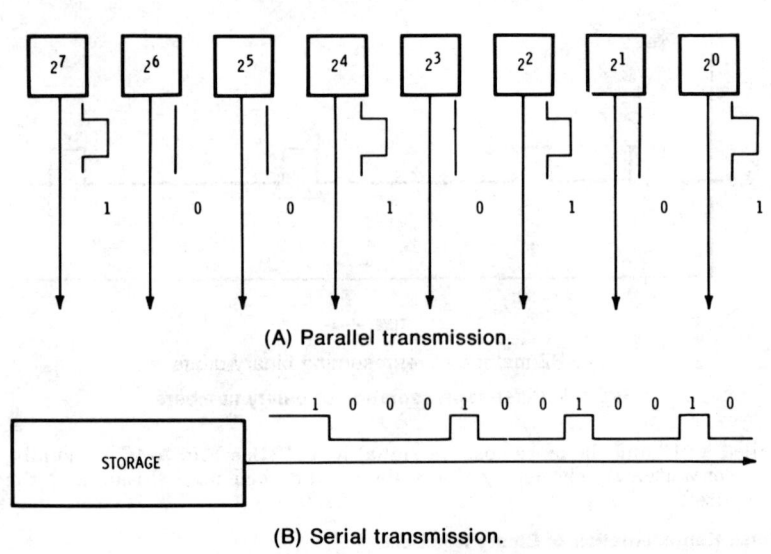

Fig. A-6. Parallel and serial transmission.

Digital computers use binary storage devices to store and represent binary digits. Seven such devices can represent the binary numbers from 0000000 to 1111111 (0 to 127_{10}). However, if we wish to increase the range to include the negative numbers from 0000000 to -1111111, we need another binary digit, or bit. This bit is called the *sign bit* and is placed in front of the most significant digit of the binary number.

The convention for the sign bit is: If the sign bit is 0, the number is positive; and if the sign bit is a 1, the number is negative. The remaining digits form the absolute value of the number. This numerical storage mode is called *signed binary*. Fig. A-7A shows signed binary numbers from $+127$ to -127, and the signed binary number line is shown in Fig. A-7B.

Signed binary, although frequently used, has a few minor flaws that make it less flexible than other codes for negative numbers. Any arithmetic operation requires checking the sign bit and then either adding or subtracting the numerical values, based on the signs.

INTEGER	SIGNED BINARY CODE
	s b_7 b_6 b_5 b_4 b_3 b_2 b_1
+127	0 1 1 1 1 1 1 1
+126	0 1 1 1 1 1 1 0
↓	⋮
↓	⋮
↓	⋮
+3	0 0 0 0 0 0 1 1
+2	0 0 0 0 0 0 1 0
+1	0 0 0 0 0 0 0 1
0	0 0 0 0 0 0 0 0
−1	1 0 0 0 0 0 0 1
−2	1 0 0 0 0 0 1 0
−3	1 0 0 0 0 0 1 1
↓	⋮
↓	⋮
↓	⋮
−126	1 1 1 1 1 1 1 0
−127	1 1 1 1 1 1 1 1

(A) Seven-bit–magnitude table.

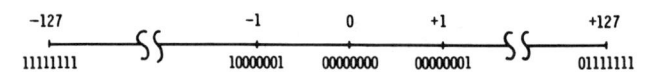

```
  -127            -1      0      +1              +127
├────────⧸⧸───────┼──────┼──────┼──────⧸⧸─────────┤
 11111111       10000001 00000000 00000001      01111111
```
(B) Signed binary number line (seven-bit magnitude).

Fig. A-7. Signed binary code.

The Use of Complements

The use of complemented binary numbers makes it possible to add or subtract binary numbers using only circuitry for addition. To see how negative numbers are used in the computer, consider a mechanical register, such as a car mileage indicator, being rotated backwards. A five-digit register approaching and passing through zero would read as follows:

00005
00004
00003
00002
00001
00000
99999
99998
99997
etc.

It should be clear that the number 99998 corresponds to −2. Furthermore, if we add

$$\begin{array}{r} 00005 \\ +\ 99998 \\ \hline 1\ 00003 \end{array}$$

and ignore the carry to the left, we have effectively formed the operation of subtraction: $5 - 2 = 3$.

The number 99998 is called the *ten's complement* of 2. The ten's complement of any decimal number may be formed by subtracting each digit of the number from 9, and then adding 1 to the least significant digit of the number formed. For example:

normal subtraction	*ten's complement subtraction*
89	89 89
− 23	− 23 + 77
66	┌─ 1 66
	└─ DROP CARRY

Two's Complement

The two's complement is the binary equivalent of the ten's complement in the decimal system. It is defined as that number which, when added to the original number, will result in a sum of zero, ignoring the carry. The following example points this out:

```
      1101   number
      0011   two's complement
┌──── 1 0000 sum
└─IGNORE CARRY
```

The easiest method of finding the two's complement of a binary number is to first find the one's complement, which is formed by setting each bit to the opposite value:

```
11011101   number
00100010   one's complement
```

The two's complement of the number is then obtained by adding 1 to the least significant digit of the one's complement:

```
11011101   number
00100010   one's complement
     +1    add one
00100011   two's complement
```

The complete signed two's complement code is obtained for negative numbers by using a 1 for the sign bit, and two's complement for the magnitude of the number. Fig. A-8A shows the signed two's complement code, and its number line is shown in Fig. A-8B.

In contrast to the signed binary code, in the signed two's complement code, numbers can be added without regard to their signs and the result will always be correct. The following examples should make this clear:

```
    0000101      5        1111011     −5        1111011     −5
   +1111110  + (−2)      +0000010  + (+2)      +1111110  + (−2)
┌── 1 0000011     3        1111101    (−3)┌── 1 1111001    (−7)
└─IGNORE                                   └─IGNORE
```

202

INTEGER	CODE SIGNED 2's COMPLEMENT
	s b_7 b_6 b_5 b_4 b_3 b_2 b_1
+127	0 1 1 1 1 1 1 1
+126	0 1 1 1 1 1 1 0
׀	׀
׀	׀
׀	׀
+3	0 0 0 0 0 0 1 1
+2	0 0 0 0 0 0 1 0
+1	0 0 0 0 0 0 0 1
0	0 0 0 0 0 0 0 0
−1	1 1 1 1 1 1 1 1
−2	1 1 1 1 1 1 1 0
−3	1 1 1 1 1 1 0 1
׀	׀
׀	׀
׀	׀
−126	1 0 0 0 0 0 1 0
−127	1 0 0 0 0 0 0 1
−128	1 0 0 0 0 0 0 0

(A) Seven-bit–magnitude table.

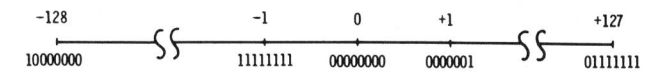

```
  −128              −1        0        +1              +127
 ├────⌇⌇────────────┼────────┼────────┼────⌇⌇──────────┤
10000000          11111111 00000000 00000001          01111111
```

(B) Two's complement number line.

Fig. A-8. Signed two's complement code.

Notice that it is impossible to add +64 to +64 in a 7-bit code and +128 to +128 in an 8-bit code. Also note that in comparing the two systems, signed binary and two's complement, the largest negative two's complement number that can be represented in 8 bits is −128, while in signed binary it's −127. Changing a negative integer from signed binary to two's complement requires simply complementing all bits except the sign bit, and adding 1.

Binary-Coded Number Representation

Since computers operate in the binary number system, while people use the decimal system, it was only natural that some intermediate system be developed. Computers, and some calculators and "intelligent" instruments, use a *binary-coded decimal* system. In such systems, a group of binary bits is used to represent each of the 10 decimal digits.

The binary-coded decimal (bcd) system is called a "weighted binary code" with the weights 8, 4, 2, and 1, as shown in Table A-2. Notice that 4 binary bits are required for each decimal digit, and that each digit is assigned a weight: the leftmost bit has a weight of 8; the rightmost bit a weight of 1.

There's a slight problem with using 4 bits to represent 10 decimal values. Since $2^4 = 16$, the 4 bits could actually represent 16 values. However, the next choice down, 3 bits, allows only 2^3, or 8, possible digits, which is insufficient. To represent the decimal number 127 in bcd, 12 binary bits are required instead of seven if we use pure binary:

$$\begin{array}{ccc} 1 & 2 & 7 \\ 0001 & 0010 & 0111 \end{array}$$

The bcd system has another property that makes it less flexible for binary computation in the computer. The difficulty lies in forming complements of its numbers. As was pointed out, it is common practice to perform subtraction by complementing the subtrahend and adding 1. When the bcd 8-4-2-1 system is used, the complement formed by inverting all the bits may produce an illegal bcd digit. For example, complementing the bcd number 0010 (2_{10}) gives 1101 (13_{10}), which is not a bcd code.

To solve this problem, several other codes have been developed. For example, the *excess-three code* is formed by adding 3 to the decimal number and then forming the bcd code. For example:

$$\begin{array}{rl} 4 & \text{number} \\ +3 & \text{add for excess-three} \\ \hline 7 & \end{array}$$

$7 = 0111$ convert 7 to bcd

Table A-2 also shows the excess-three codes for the 10 decimal digits. Now the complement of the excess-three code doesn't form any illegal bcd digits, i.e., 10_{10} or above.

Table A-2. Binary-Coded Number Representation

Decimal Digit	Binary-Coded Decimal	Excess-3 Coded Binary	2-4-2-1 Coded Binary			
			Weight of Bit			
			2	4	2	1
0	0000	0011	0	0	0	0
1	0001	0100	0	0	0	1
2	0010	0101	0	0	1	0
3	0011	0110	0	0	1	1
4	0100	0111	0	1	0	0
5	0101	1000	1	0	1	1
6	0110	1001	1	1	0	0
7	0111	1010	1	1	0	1
8	1000	1011	1	1	1	0
9	1001	1100	1	1	1	1

The excess-three code is not a weighted code, since the sum of the bits does not equal the number being represented. On the other hand, the bcd 8-4-2-1 code is weighted but forms illegal complements.

A weighted code that does form legal complements is the *2-4-2-1 code* in Table A-2.

OCTAL NUMBER SYSTEM

It is probably quite evident by now that the binary number system, although nice for computers, is a little cumbersome for human usage. For example, communicating binary 11011010 over a telephone would be "one-one-zero-one-one-zero-one-zero," which is quite a mouthful. Also, it is easy to make errors when adding and subtracting large binary numbers. The octal (base 8) number system alleviates most of these problems and is frequently used in the microcomputer literature.

The octal system uses the digits 0 through 7 in forming numbers. Table A-3 shows octal numbers and their decimal equivalents.

Table A-3. First 13 Octal Digits

Decimal	Octal	Binary	Decimal	Octal	Binary
0	0	0	7	7	111
1	1	1	8	10	1000
2	2	10	9	11	1001
3	3	11	10	12	1010
4	4	100	11	13	1011
5	5	101	12	14	1100
6	6	110	13	15	1101

Octal numbers are converted to decimal numbers by using the same expansion formula as that used in binary-to-decimal conversion, except that 8 is used for the base instead of 2.

$$\begin{aligned}
(\text{octal})\ 167 &= (1 \times 8^2) + (6 \times 8^1) + (7 \times 8^0) \\
&= (1 \times 64) + (6 \times 8) + (7 \times 1) \\
&= 64\ \ \ \ +\ \ \ 48\ \ \ +\ \ \ 7 \\
&= 119\ (\text{decimal})
\end{aligned}$$

A *weighting table* (Fig. A-9) is a quick way to convert octal values to decimal.

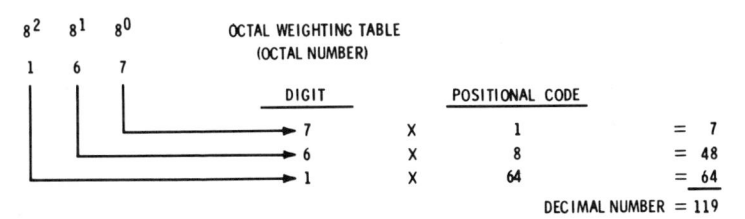

```
 8²   8¹   8⁰       OCTAL WEIGHTING TABLE
 1    6    7           (OCTAL NUMBER)
 │    │    │       DIGIT        POSITIONAL CODE
 │    │    └──►     7       X         1        =   7
 │    └───────►     6       X         8        =  48
 └────────────►     1       X        64        =  64
                                        DECIMAL NUMBER = 119
```

Fig. A-9. Octal-to-decimal conversion.

The primary use of octal is as a convenient way of recording values stored in binary registers. This is accomplished by using a grouping method to convert the binary value to its octal equivalent. The binary number is grouped by threes, starting with the bit corresponding to $2^0 = 1$ and grouping to the left of it. Then each binary group is converted to its octal equivalent. For example, convert 11110101 to octal:

```
       011  110  101    binary number
        3    6    5     octal equivalent
    implied 0
```

The largest 8-bit octal number is 377$_8$, and the largest 7-bit octal number is 177$_8$. Negative octal numbers in 8-bit signed two's complement cover 377$_8$ (-1_{10}) to 200$_8$ (-128_{10}).

Conversion from decimal to octal is performed by repeated division by 8 and using the remainder as a digit in the octal number being formed. Fig. A-10 illustrates this method.

1376_{10} = ? OCTAL

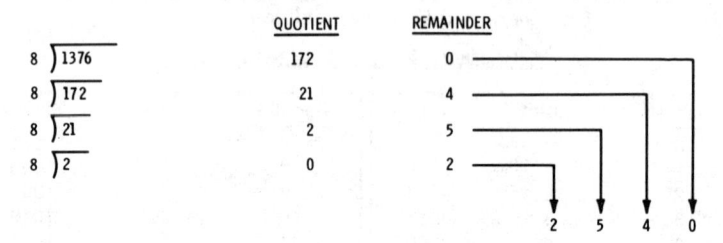

	QUOTIENT	REMAINDER
8) 1376	172	0
8) 172	21	4
8) 21	2	5
8) 2	0	2

THEREFORE 1376_{10} = 2540_8

Fig. A-10. Decimal-to-octal conversion.

Addition in Octal

Octal addition is easy if we remember the following rules (which we will find also apply to hexadecimal):

1. If the sum of any column is equal to or greater than the base of the system being used, the base must be subtracted from the sum to obtain the final result of the column.
2. If the sum of any column is equal to or greater than the base, there will be a carry, equal to the number of times the base was subtracted.
3. If the result of any column is less than the base, the base is not subtracted and no carry will be generated.

Examples:

```
   octal   decimal           octal            decimal
    5  =    5                 35    =           29
   +3  =    3                +63    =          +51
   ──      ──                ────              ────
    8                       1 10  8              80
   -8                        -8 -8
   ──      ──                ────              ────
   10  =    8               1  2  0    =         80
```

Octal Subtraction

Octal subtraction can be performed directly or in the complemented mode by using addition. In direct subtraction, whenever a borrow is needed, an 8 is borrowed and added to the number. For example:

$$2022_8 - 1234_8 = ?$$

$$\begin{array}{r} 2022_8 \\ 1234_8 \\ \hline 566_8 \end{array}$$

Octal subtraction may also be performed by finding the eight's complement and adding. The eight's complement is found by adding 1 to the seven's complement. The seven's complement of the number may be found by subtracting each digit from 7. For example:

$$377_8 - 261_8 = ?$$

a)
```
    777
   -261    (second number)
    516    7's complement
    +1
    517    8's complement
```

b)
```
    377         (first number)
   +517         8's complement of 261
  9 9 14
 -8-8 -8
  1 1  6 = 116₈
```

Octal Multiplication

Octal multiplication is performed by using an octal multiplication table (see Table A-4) in the same manner as a decimal table would be used. All additions are done by using the rules for octal addition. For example:

$17_8 \times 6_8 = ?$

```
octal              decimal
   17     =          15
   ×6     =          ×6
 1 11 2              90
-0 -8 -0
 1  3  2 = 132₈
```

$177_8 \times 27_8 = ?$

```
octal              decimal
   177    =          127
   ×27    =          ×23
  1371               381
   376               254
 5 11 13  1         2921
-0 -8 -8 -0
 5  3  5  1 = 5351₈
```

Numbers are multiplied by looking up the result in the table. The result of any product larger than 7 (the radix or base) is carried and then octally added to the next product. The results are then summed up by using octal addition.

Table A-4. Octal Multiplication Table

×	0	1	2	3	4	5	6	7
0	0	0	0	0	0	0	0	0
1	0	1	2	3	4	5	6	7
2	0	2	4	6	10	12	14	16
3	0	3	6	11	14	17	22	25
4	0	4	10	14	20	24	30	34
5	0	5	12	17	24	31	36	43
6	0	6	14	22	30	36	44	52
7	0	7	16	25	34	43	52	61

Octal Division

Octal division uses the same principles as decimal division. All multiplication and subtraction involved, however, must be done in octal. Refer to the octal multiplication table. Some examples:

$$144_8 \div 2_8 = ?$$
$$\frac{144_8}{2_8} = \frac{100_{10}}{2_{10}} = 50_{10} = 62_8$$

$62_8 \div 2_8 = ?$

$31 = 31_8 = 25_{10}$

```
   31
2)62
   6
   02
    2
    0
```

$1714_8 \div 22_8 = ?$

$66 = 66_8 = 54_{10}$

```
    66
22)1714
   154
   154
   154
```

THE HEXADECIMAL SYSTEM

Hexadecimal is another important and often-used computer number system. "Hex" uses the radix 16 and therefore has 16 digits. The first 10 digits are represented by the decimal digits 0 through 9, and the remaining six are indicated by the letters A, B, C, D, E, and F. There is nothing special about these letters, and any other letters could have been used. Table A-5 shows the first 16 hexadecimal digits.

Table A-5. First 16 Hexadecimal Digits

Binary	Hexadecimal	Decimal
0000	0	0
0001	1	1
0010	2	2
0011	3	3
0100	4	4
0101	5	5
0110	6	6
0111	7	7
1000	8	8
1001	9	9
1010	A	10
1011	B	11
1100	C	12
1101	D	13
1110	E	14
1111	F	15

Binary numbers are easily converted to hex by grouping the bits in groups of four, starting on the right, converting the results to decimal, and then converting to hex. For example:

```
1000  1010  1101   binary
  8    10    13    decimal
  8     A     D    hex = 8AD₁₆
```

As you can probably tell, hex is preferred over octal whenever the binary number to be represented is 16 bits or more. This is because the hex code is more compact than the octal equivalent.

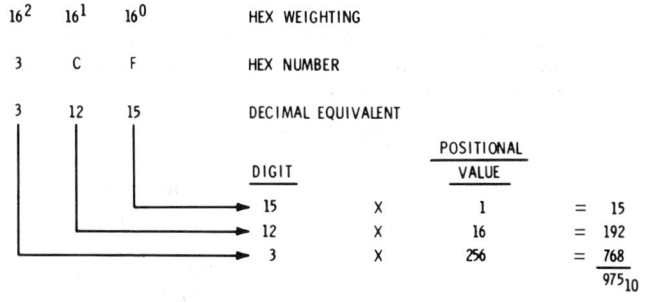

```
16²   16¹   16⁰       HEX WEIGHTING

 3     C     F        HEX NUMBER

 3    12    15        DECIMAL EQUIVALENT
                                        POSITIONAL
                            DIGIT         VALUE
                             15     X       1      =   15
                             12     X      16      =  192
                              3     X     256      =  768
                                                      ─────
                                                      975₁₀
```

Fig. A-11. Hexadecimal-to-decimal conversion.

Conversion from hexadecimal to decimal is straightforward but time-consuming. The expansion formula, or a weighting table with an intermediary hex-to-decimal conversion, is used as shown in Fig. A-11.

Conversion from decimal to hex is performed by repeatedly dividing by 16, and converting the remainder to a hex digit. The quotient becomes the next number to divide. This is shown in Fig. A-12.

975 = ?₁₆

```
                                    REMAINDER        REMAINDER
                       QUOTIENT     IN DECIMAL        IN HEX
         975/16          60             15              F
         60/16            3             12              C
         3/16             0              3              3

                                                      3 C F
```

Fig. A-12. Decimal-to-hexadecimal conversion.

Hexadecimal Addition

Addition in hex is similar to the addition procedure for octal, except the hex digits are first converted to decimal. For example:

$$3CF + 2AD = ?$$

```
  + 2AD = +2  10  13
    3CF =  3  12  15
           ─────────
           6  23  28
          −0 −16 −16
           ─────────
           6   7  12 = 67C
```

Subtraction in Hexadecimal

Subtraction in hex may be accomplished by either the direct or the complement method. In the direct method, the hex digits are converted to decimal. If a borrow is required, 16 is added to the desired number and the digit borrowed from is decreased by 1. In the complement method, the sixteen's complement of the subtrahend is determined and the two numbers are added. The sixteen's complement is found by adding 1 to the fifteen's complement. The fifteen's complement is found by subtracting each of the hex digits from F. For example:

```
                    2BD − 1CE = ?
       FFF =      15   15   15
       −1CE     −  1   12   14      second number
                  14    3    1      15's complement
                            + 1
                  14    3    2      16's complement
       2BD =    + 2   11   13       first number
              1  16   14   15
              −16  − 0  − 0
     ignore carry  0   14   15    = EF (answer)
```

Hexadecimal Multiplication

Direct hex multiplication is rather tedious and time-consuming. This is because there are 256 entries in a hex multiplication table. The best method is to convert to decimal by using the expansion polynomial and then convert back from decimal to hex after computation.

APPENDIX B

ASCII Character Codes

Decimal	Character	Decimal	Character	Decimal	Character
000	NUL	043	+	086	V
001	SCH	044	' (right	087	W
002	STX		apostro-	088	X
003	ETX		phe)	089	Y
004	EOT	045	-	090	Z
005	ENQ	046	.	091	[
006	ACK	047	/	092	\
007	BEL	048	0	093	]
008	BS	049	1	094	^ (or ↑)
009	HT	050	2	095	___ (under-
010	LF	051	3		score)
011	VT	052	4	096	' (left apos-
012	FF	053	5		trophe)
013	CR	054	6	097	a
014	SO	055	7	098	b
015	SI	056	8	099	c
016	DLE	057	9	100	d
017	DC1	058	:	101	e
018	DC2	059	;	102	f
019	DC3	060	<	103	g
020	DC4	061	=	104	h
021	NAK	062	>	105	i
022	SYN	063	?	106	j
023	ETB	064	@	107	k
024	CAN	065	A	108	l
025	EM	066	B	109	m
026	CONTROL	067	C	110	n
027	ESCAPE	068	D	111	o
028	FS	069	E	112	p
029	GS	070	F	113	q
030	RS	071	G	114	r
031	US	072	H	115	s
032	SPACE	073	I	116	t
033	!	074	J	117	u
034	"	075	K	118	v
035	#	076	L	119	w
036	$	077	M	120	x
037	%	078	N	121	y
038	&	079	O	122	z
039	'	080	P	123	{
040	(	081	Q	124	|
041	)	082	R	125	}
042	*	083	S	126	~
		084	T	127	DEL
		085	U		

LF=Line Feed　　FF=Form Feed　　CR=Carriage Return　　DEL=Rubout

APPENDIX
C

When Programs Get Too Big— Space-Slashing Hints

Often when writing a big program you may encounter an error statement in BASIC such as "OUT OF MEMORY." This indicates that your program is too large for the amount of memory space provided by the memory chips in your computer. How large is too large? Well, if your computer has 16K of memory (that is 16K bytes) and the BASIC interpreter itself consumes 12K bytes, then your application program cannot take up more than 16K-12K, or 4K bytes. To determine the number of bytes consumed by your application program you can use the FRE (free) function like this:

```
PRINT FRE(0)
1024
OK
```

The FRE function returns the number of bytes "unused" by the current program. Thus for our 16K machine with a 12K interpreter we have 1024 bytes of our 4096 bytes unused are still available, and our program is then 4096−1024, or 3072 bytes long.

This is all nice, but there is a Murphy's law that states:

FOR EVERY "K" BYTES OF AVAILABLE RAM MEMORY IN A COMPUTER, A PROGRAM WILL EXCEED THIS AMOUNT BY 256 BYTES.

Thus you will eventually be faced with the prospect of either buying more memory chips for your computer (costly at this time), or figuring out how to shorten your program.

Here are 8 "space-slashing" techniques you can apply to help keep the program smaller and save valuable memory space.

213

1. *Use multiple statements per line.* There is a small amount of overhead (5 bytes) associated with each line in the program. Two of these five bytes contain the line number of the line in binary. This means that no matter how many digits you have in your line number (remember minimum line number is 0 or 1 and maximum is usually 65529), it takes the same number of bytes. Putting as many statements as possible on a line will cut down the number of bytes used by your program. A single line can usually contain up to 254 characters.
2. *Delete all rem statements.* This is only a good idea if you *don't* want anyone to understand how your program works. Each REM statement uses at least one byte of memory plus the number of bytes in the text of the REM statement. For example, the statement

```
100 REM PROGRAM WRITTEN BY RAMON PEABODY
```

uses up 5+1+33 or 39 bytes.
In the statement:

```
200 I=I+1: REM INCREMENT INDEX
```

the REM uses 18 bytes of memory including the colon before REM. The "'" symbol used here would consume one less byte because no colon is required.
3. *Use integers instead of single-precision reals.* Integer variables are stored in 5 bytes; single precisions are stored in 7 bytes. Thus, use integer variables in FOR...NEXT loops and whenever large accurate numbers are not needed.

    Particularly, use integer arrays instead of real-single precision arrays to save space consumed by arrays. You can force a variable to be an integer variable using a DEFINT statement at the beginning of your program, or the % sign after the variable name as in A% or A%(I,J). DEFINT I-N would make all variables beginning with the letters I, J, K, L, M, N integer variables.
4. *Use variables instead of constants.* Suppose you use the constant 3.14159 ten times in your program. If you insert a statement

```
10 PI=3.14159
```

in the program, and use PI instead of 3.14159 each time it is needed, you will save 40 bytes. This will also result in a speed improvement, as explained in Appendix G.
5. *A program does not have to end with an END statement.* This will save seven bytes.
6. *Reuse the same variables.* Do not do this if you wish absolute clarity in your programs. If you have a variable "S" that is used to hold a temporary result in one part of the program and you need a temporary variable later

in your program, use "S" again. Or if you have many separate FOR... NEXT loops, the same index may be used over in each loop. Or, if you are asking the terminal user to give a YES or NO answer to two different questions at two different times during the execution of the program, use the same temporary variable A$ to store the reply.
7. *Use GOSUBs.* These can be used to execute sections of program statements that perform identical actions.
8. *Remember to use the zero elements of matrices.* For example X(0), BETA (0), etc. If you have a ten-element array required by a program use DIM ARRAY(9) and call the first element ARRAY(0) and the last element ARRAY(9).

STORAGE ALLOCATION IN MICROSOFT BASIC

In order to fully understand how Microsoft BASIC stores variables in memory, here is a breakdown of the bytes consumed by various BASIC number and string variables.

There are two kinds of numeric variables in BASIC—simple variables such as X, Y, ALPHA and Z9, and array variables such as X(5), ALPHA(199) and BETA(X). The actual numbers in *both* simple and array variables may be one of three types—integer, single precision, or double precision.

Table F-1. Simple Variables

SIMPLE VARIABLES	NUMBER OF BYTES REQUIRED
Integer	5 bytes (2 for name, 3 for value)
Single precision	7 bytes (2 for name, 5 for value)
Double precision	11 bytes (2 for name, 9 for value)
String	6 bytes (2 for name, 2 for length, & 2 for pointer)

Table F-2. Array Variables

ARRAY VARIABLES:	NUMBER OF BYTES REQUIRED
Integer (# of elements)	*2 + 6 + (# of dimensions) *2 bytes
Single precision "	*4 + 6 + " *2 "
Double precision "	*8 + 6 + " *2 "
String "	*3 + 6 + " *2 "

Thus the simple integer variable takes up only 5 bytes per variable, while double-precision variables take up 11 bytes each. Use integers wherever possible to save memory space.

In arrays, very many memory bytes can be used up. From Table F-2 we see that in the case of a single-precision array we consume 12 bytes for each element as follows—two bytes for the variable name, two bytes for the size of the matrix, two bytes for the number of dimensions, and two bytes for each dimension along with four bytes for each matrix element. Thus the array A(9) take up 10*12=120 bytes.

Integer array (XY%(a,b,c...)) variables use only 2 bytes for each matrix element, so only 10 bytes are required for each matrix variable. The integer array A%(9) takes up 10*10=10 bytes.

String variables use one byte of string space for each character in the string, in addition to the numbers computed from Tables F-1 or F-2. This is true whether the string variable is a simple string variable like A$, or an element of string matrix, such as COST$(2,3).

When a new function is defined by a DEF statement, 6 bytes are used for the definition. Reserved words such as FOR, GOTO, or NOT, and the names or the intrinsic functions such as COS, INT, and STR$ take up only one byte of program storage. All other characters in programs use one byte of program storage each.

When a program is being executed, space is dynamically allocated on the stack (the stack is a special area of memory that is used by the BASIC interpreter to keep track of GOSUB and GOTO branches, as well as nested FOR...NEXTs) as follows:

* Each active FOR...NEXT loop uses 17 bytes.
* Each active GOSUB (one that has not returned yet) uses 5 bytes.
* Each parenthesis encountered in an expression uses 6 bytes per set, and each temporary result calculated in an expression uses 12 bytes.

APPENDIX

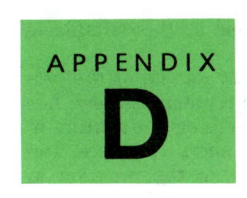

D

When Programs Get Too Slow— Speed Hints

Whenever you create programs that contain long complex mathematical equations and functions, or programs with long FOR...NEXT loops (such as those found in sorting arrays) you are likely to run into a speed problem. Although the computer runs at microsecond rates, the BASIC interpreter takes many steps to "understand" the statement it is to execute, and many more steps to set things up so the statement can be executed.

The following list of hints can be used to improve the execution time of your programs. Notice that some of these hints are the same as those used to decrease the space used by your program (see Appendix F). This means that in many cases you can increase the efficiency of both the speed and the size of your programs at the same time.

1. *Use variables instead of constants.* (This is the most important speed hint of all). It takes more time to convert a constant to its floating point representation than it does to fetch the value of a simple or matrix integer variable. This is especially important within FOR...NEXT loops of other code that is executed repeatedly.
2. *For variables used often, define them at the beginning of a program.* Variables which are encountered first during the execution of a BASIC program are allocated at the start of the "variable table" (a special table BASIC sets up to tell the line number of a variables first definition). This means that a statement such as 10 X=0: Y=4; Z=8, will place X first, Y second, and Z third in the variable symbol table (assuming line 10 is the first statement executed in the program). Later in the program, when BASIC finds a reference to the variable X, it will search only one entry in the symbol table to find X, two entries to find Y, and three entries to find Z.
3. *Use next statements without the index variable when possible.* NEXT is somewhat faster than NEXT I because no check is made to see if the

variable specified in the NEXT statement is the same as the variable in the most recent FOR statement.
4. *Frequently referenced lines should be placed at the beginning of the program.* During program execution when BASIC encounters a new line reference such as GOTO 100 it scans the entire user program starting at the lowest line until it finds the referenced line number. Therefore, frequently referenced lines should be placed as early in the program as possible.
5. *In FOR...NEXT loops use integer variables instead of single precision variables.* It takes much longer to increment a single-precision variable in a loop than an integer variable.

APPENDIX
E

Basic Language Reference

The following list contains all the BASIC keywords, statements, commands, and functions listed in alphabetical order. Each keyword is explained with typical programming notation showing the exact syntax of the keyword, examples of how it appears in a program statement, and a complete description of how the keyword works. All this information is also included on the removable fold-out card inside the back cover.

This listing allows you to easily look up a specific BASIC element and see how it is used correctly. In order to differentiate the commands, statements, functions, etc. we have used the labels below to indicate the type of keyword this is.

```
Commands  . . . . . . . . . . . . C
Statements  . . . . . . . . . . . . S
Numeric Functions  . . . . . . NF
String Functions  . . . . . . . . SF
Logical Operator  . . . . . . . . LO
Numeric Operator  . . . . . . . NO
```

Name	Example	Description
	A	
ABS (expr)	300 PRINT ABS(X) 310 IF ABS(X)>5 THEN 200 320 LET X=ABS(X)	Gives the absolute value of the expression expr. (NF)
AND (expr1 AND expr2)	300 IF A>B AND C<D THEN 200	Expression expr1 AND expr2 must both be "true" for statements to be true. (LO)
ASC (str$)	310 PRINT ASC("BACK") 320 PRINT ASC(B$) 320 PRINT ASC(B$(4,4)) 335 PRINT ASC(B$(Y))	Gives the decimal ASCII value of designated string variable str$. (NF)

Name	Example	Description
ATN (expr)	400 PRINT ATN(X)	Gives the arctangent of the expression expr. Expression must be in radians in the range −PI/2 to +PI/2. (NF)
AUTO num,incr	AUTO 100,10 100 INPUT X,Y 110 PRINT X*Y 120 C OK	Sets automatic line numbering mode. Starts at line number num and increments line numbers by incr. To exit from AUTO type Control/C. (C)

C

Name	Example	Description
CALL expr	100 CALL 4096 110 CALL X+5 120 IF A<B THEN 　　CALL PLOT	Caused BASIC to branch to machine language program starting at memory address specified by expression expr. When machine language program terminates execution continues at statement after CALL statement. (S)
CHR$ (expr)	100 PRINT CHR$(63) 110 PRINT CHR$(1*8) 120 A$=CHR$(34)+ 　　B$+CHR$(34)	Gives a string whose single element has ASCII code given by value of expr. Expr must be in the range of 0 to 255. ASCII codes are given in Appendix D. (SF)
CLEAR expr	CLEAR CLEAR 100	Sets all program variables to zero. Optional expression expr sets string space to value of expr. (C)
CLOAD str$	CLOAD CLOAD "MITCH" CLOAD A$	Reads (loads) a BASIC program from cassette tape. The optional string str$ is the name of the file on the tape. (C)
CSAVE str$	CSAVE CSAVE "STARTREK" CSAVE "MYPROG.BAS"	Causes the current program in memory to be saved (stored) on cassette tape. The string str$ is the name you wish to store the program under. The length of str$ and its format is set by the computer system being used. In some versions str$ is not allowed. The program may be loaded back into memory with the complementary CLOAD command. (C)
CONT	CONT	Continues program execution after a Control/C has been typed or a STOP or END statement has been executed. Does not change values of variables and resumes at statement following where the break occurred. (C)
COS (expr)	300 PRINT COS(X)	Gives the cosine of the expression expr, where expr is in radians. (NF)
CURSOR X,Y	100 CURSOR(20,20)	Places cursor at vertical position Y

Name	Example	Description
		and will TAB out to horizontal position X. (S)

D

Name	Example	Description
DATA <list>	300 DATA 1,2,3,4,5,6 310 DATA 33.33,—2.1 320 DATA "JAN","FEB", "MAR","APR","MAY"	Specifies data to be read with a READ statement. List elements may be constants, variables, or strings. Expressions sometimes allowed. List elements must be separated by commas. (S)
DEF FNV(list) =expr	300 DEF FNAVE(V,W)= (V+W)/2 310 DEF FNRAD(DEG)= 3.14159/180*DEG	Defines a user defined function. Function name is FN followed by a legal variable name (V). The entries in the list are "dummy" variable names. User defined string functions also possible. (NF or SF)
DELETE num1- num2	DELETE 100 DELETE 10-50	Deletes the line in the current program with the specified line number num1 or the range of line numbers num1 to num2. (C)
DIM var1(expr), str$(expr), var2(expr)	100 DIM V(10,10) 110 DIM PAD$(5) 120 DIM A(120),A$(120)	Causes space to be allocated for array variables and DIMensions these arrays. The value of the expression expr sets the number of elements of a dimension. (Maximum subscript value is 255.) Maximum dimensions is as many as can be fitted on one line. Commas separate the dimension subscripts as well as array variables.

E

Name	Example	Description
EDIT num	EDIT 100	Allows editing the specified line without affecting other lines. Not available on all BASICs, EDIT has a powerful set of subcommands. (C)
END	100 END	Stops program execution. Sends carriage return and the BASIC prompt character (if one is used) to screen. (S)
EXP (expr)	100 PRINT EXP(5) 110 PRINT EXP(X MOD 5)	Returns the value of the natural base "e" raised to the power specified by expression expr. Expression expr must be in the range of 0 to 87.3365. (NF)

F

Name	Example	Description
FOR var= expr1 TO expr2 STEP expr3	110 FOR L=0 TO 39 120 FOR X=Y1 TO Y3 130 FOR I=39 to 1 STEP —2 140 FOR C=—2 TO —12	Begins FOR...NEXT loop, initializes variable var to value of expression expr1 then increments it by amount in expression expr3 each time the corresponding "NEXT" statement is

Name	Example	Description
	STEP —1	encountered, until value of expression expr2 is reached, IF STEP expr3 is omitted, a STEP of +1 is assumed. Negative numbers are allowed. (S)

G

Name	Example	Description
GOSUB expr	140 GOSUB 500 150 GOSUB PLOT*3	Causes branch to BASIC subroutine starting at legal line number specified by expression expr. Subroutines may be nested to various levels depending on the version of BASIC, but 16 maximum is typical. In some BASICs expr must be a constant. (S)
GOTO expr	160 GOTO 200 170 GOTO ALPHA+100	Causes immediate jump to legal line number specified by expr. In some BASICs expr must be a constant. (S)

I

Name	Example	Description

IF expr
THEN statement
	220 IF A>B THEN
	    PRINT A
	230 IF X=0 THEN C=1
	240 IF A#10 THEN
	    GOSUB 200
	250 IF A$(1,1)#"Y"
	    THEN 100
		If expression expr is true (nonzero) then execute statement; if false do not execute statement. If statement is an expression, then a GOTO expr type of statement is assumed to be implied. (S)

IF expr
THEN statement
ELSE statement
	400 IF X>Y THEN 100
	    ELSE PRINT A$
	410 IF D=2 AND C<5
	    THEN GOSUB 300
	    ELSE GOTO 111
	420 IF X=2*Y THEN 5
	    ELSE PRINT "ERR"
		Like standard IF...THEN except if expression expr is false the ELSE part of the statement is executed. (S)

INP (expr)	100 PRINT INP (2) 110 PRINT INP(I MOD 2) 120 IF INP(J)=16 THEN PRINT "ON"	Reads a byte from port specified by expression expr which must be an integer between 0 and 255. (NF)
INPUT var1, var2,str$	280 INPUT X,Y,Z(3) 290 INPUT "AMT", DLLR 300 INPUT "Y" OR N",A$	Enters data into memory from the keyboard device and assigns data to variables following INPUT. If number input is expected computer will output a "?"; if string is expected no "?" will be output. Multiple numeric inputs to same statement may be separated by a comma or a carriage return. String inputs must be separated by a carriage return only. One pair of quote marks (" ") may be used immediately after INPUT to output prompting text enclosed within the quotation marks. If data entered in invalid BASIC will print some kind of error message such as 'REDO FROM START?'

Name	Example	Description
		and waits for the correct data to be entered. (S)
INT (expr)	100 PRINT INT(5.9) 110 PRINT INT(.5*X) 120 Z=INT(Z/100)*100	Returns the integer portion of the expression expr that is less than or equal to the expression. (NF)

L

Name	Example	Description
LEFT$(str$, expr)	300 PRINT LEFT$(A$,5) 310 Z$=LEFT$("ABCD",I) 320 C$=LEFT$(W$,8)+ "XYZ"	Returns the leftmost characters based on the value of expression expr of the string str$. (SF)
LEN(str$)	300 PRINT LEN("ABCD") 310 Z=X+LEN(A$) 320 IF LEN(A$)>20 THEN PRINT "TOO LONG"	Returns the length of the string str$. Nonprinting characters and blanks are counted. (NF)
LET var=expr	300 LET A=5 310 LET X=INT(S)*4	Assigns the value of the expression expr to the variable var. LET is optional. (S)
LINE INPUT "prompt str"; str$	100 LINE INPUT A$ 110 LINE INPUT "ENTER YOUR NAME"; N$	Prints out the optional prompt string and assigns all input from keyboard to the string variable str$ until a carriage return is detected. (S)
LIST num1-num2	LIST LIST 100 LIST 1-10 LIST 10- LIST -100	Lists the line numbers of the current program specified by num1 through num2. LIST alone lists the entire program. LIST -num2 lists the entire program up to line num2. LIST num1- lists the entire program from line num1 up. (C)

M

Name	Example	Description
MID$(str$, expr1,expr2)	100 PRINT MID$(A$,5) 110 Z$=MID$(X$,1,5) 120 S$=MID$("ABCDEFG", INT(X),INT(Y))	Without expr2, returns rightmost characters from string str$ beginning with the expr1-th character. If expr1>LEN(str$), MID$ returns the null string Expression expr1 must be >0 and <255. With 3 arguments, MID$ returns a string of length expr2 of characters from str$ beginning with the expr1-th character. If expr2 is greater than the number of characters in str$ to the right of expr1, MID$ returns the rest of the string. 0<=expr2<=255. (SF)
MOD (expr1 MOD expr2)	200 Z=A MOD B 210 PRINT X Y MOD R 220 IF (X MOD 2)=0 THEN 300	The modulus operator gives the remainder of the division of expr1 by expr2. If A=4 and B=2 then A MOD B=0 because there is zero remainder (2 goes evenly into 4). (NO)

Name	Example	Description

N

NEW	NEW	Deletes the current program and clears all variables. Used before entering a new program.
NEXT var1, var2,..	100 NEXT I 200 NEXT A,B,C	Last statement of a FOR loop. Var1 is the variable of the most recent loop, var2 of the next most recent loop and so on. In some BASICs only one variable is allowed. NEXT without variable terminates most recent FOR loop.

O

ON expr GOSUB num1, num2,...	300 ON X GOSUB 10,20,30 310 ON ABS(E) GOSUB 101,102, 103,104,105	Branches to line whose number num is equal to the value of expression expr. When expr=1 GOSUBs to num1, expr=2 GOSUBs to num2, and so on. If expr<0 or >255 error results. If expr=0 or expr> number of elements in list, execution continues at next statement. When subroutine is complete, control resumes at next statement after ON.
ON expr GOTO num1,num2,...	200 ON I GOTO 1,2,3,4 210 ON INT(Z) GOTO 5, 6,7,8,9	Same as ON...GOSUB except branch is absolute.
OR (expr1 OR expr2)	100 Z=A OR B 110 IF A<0 OR B>5 THEN 100 120 IF ALPHA OR BETA +1 THEN 200 130 IF (X OR 32)=0 THEN X=16	If either expression expr1 OR expr2 is true, statement is true. When used numerically performs bit-mapped OR operation on expressions. (LO)
OUT expr1, expr2	100 OUT 1,255 110 OUT PORT,I*8	Sends byte specified by expr2 to port specified by expression expr1. Expr1 and expr2 must be greater than 0 and less than 255. (S)

P

PEEK (expr)	200 PRINT PEEK(2048) 210 IF PEEK(I)=0 THEN PRINT "ZERO" 220 Z=PEEK(I*8/M)	Reads the value of memory byte specified by expression expr, where expr is an integer expression in the range 0 to 65535. The value returned is in the range 0 to 255. Used to pass arguments and results to and from machine language subroutines. In some cases memory locations above 32767, use a negative expr, i.e., HEX location FFF0 is −32751. (NF)
POKE expr1, expr2	100 POKE 2048,0 110 POKE I,J*16	Stores the byte specified by expr2 in the memory location specified by ex-

Name	Example	Description
	120 POKE MEM,INT(X)	pression expr1. Expr1 in the range 0 to 65535, expr2 in the range 0 to 255. Care must be taken not to POKE into a memory location occupied by a BASIC or a program may be POKEd to death. (S)
POP	440 POP	"POPs" nested GOSUB return stack address by 1. Used when a GOSUB is exited from without a return, as in the case of an IF...THEN statement in a FOR...NEXT loop which causes a branch.
POS (expr)	100 COL=POS(0) 110 PRINT POS(X)	Returns the present column position of the terminal's cursor. Leftmost position = 0. Expression expr is a dummy variable and its value is not important. (NF)
PRINT var, expr, str$	450 PRINT L1 460 PRINT L1, X2 470 PRINT "AMT=";DX 480 PRINT A$;B$ 490 PRINT 492 PRINT "HELLO" 494 PRINT 2+3 496 PRINT I*4+ABS(Y)	Outputs data specified by variable var or string variable str$ or expression expr starting at current cursor position. If there is no trailing "," or ";" (Ex 450) a carriage return will be generated. Commas (Ex 460) outputs data in 5-14 left justified columns depending on terminal width and BASIC version. Semicolon (Ex 470) inhibits print of any spaces. Text imbedded in " " will be printed and may appear multiple times. (S)
PRINT @ expr	PRINT @ 540,"CENTER" 110 PRINT @ N+3, X*3	PRINT modifier; begin PRINTing at specified display position expr. (S)
PRINT USING str$, expr	100 PRINT USING A$;X 110 PRINT USING "#.#";Y+Z	PRINT format specifier; output expression expr in form specified by string str$ field. (S)

R

Name	Example	Description
RANDOMIZE	100 RANDOMIZE	Reseeds the pseudorandom number generator. Note that when the RND function is executed it will produce the same series of pseudorandom numbers unless it is reseeded internally with the RANDOMIZE statement. (S) Not used in all BASICs.
READ var1, var2, str$,..	100 READ A,B,C$ 110 READ X,Y,Z,RSET	Assigns values in DATA statements to numeric or string variables. Values are assigned in sequence starting with the first value in the first DATA statement. (S)
RENUM num1,	RENUM	Renumbers the lines in a program so

Name	Example	Description
num2, incr	RENUM 100,,100 RENUM 600,500,100	new lines may be easily inserted or so that the program may be easier to read. Num1 specifies the new number of the first line to be resequenced, and if omitted first line will be 10. Lines less than num2 are not resequenced, and if omitted whole program is renumbered. Incr is the increment between lines, and if omitted the increment is 10. (C)
RESTORE	100 RESTORE	Allows data in DATA statements to be reread. Next READ statement after RESTORE begins with first data of first statement. (S)
RESUME num	RESUME 1000	RESUMES program execution at the line specified after error trapping routine. If number num is omitted, resumes at statement where error occurred. (C)
RETURN	100 RETURN 110 IF X=5 THEN RETURN	Causes branch to statement following last GOSUB; i.e., RETURN ends a subroutine. Not to be confused with the RETURN key on the keyboard. (S)
RIGHT$ (str$, expr)	100 PRINT RIGHT$(A$,5) 110 A$=RIGHT$(A$+B$, I*2) 120 IF RIGHT$(M1$, A(I))="YES" THEN PRINT M1$	Returns the rightmost characters of string str$ specified by the expression expr. Expr is an integer. If expr =>LEN(str$) returns str$. (SF)
RND (expr)	600 X=RND(1) 610 PRINT RND(1)*10 620 IF RND(1)*100<50 THEN 100	RND returns a random number between 0 and 1. If expression expr<0 RND starts a new sequence of random numbers. If expr>0 RND gives next random number in sequence. If expr=0 RND gives the last number returned. Usually sequences started with a negative number will be the same. (NF) Variations: Note in some versions of BASIC that RND(int) returns a random number between 0 and integer int. Also some versions will not produce a new series of random numbers unless the number generator is reseeded with the RANDOMIZE statement.
RUN num	RUN RUN 100 RUN 32767	Starts execution of the program currently in memory at the line specified by num. If the line number is omitted execution begins at the lowest line number. (C)

Name	Example	Description
	S	
SGN (expr)	100 X=SGN(Y) 110 ON SGN(X)+2 GOTO 100,200,300 120 X=INT(X+.5*SGN(X))	Returns the sign of the expression expr. If expr>0 returns 1, if expr=0 returns 0, and if expr<0 returns −1. In Ex 110 program branches to 100 if X is negative, 200 if X is 0, and 300 if X is positive. In Ex 120 SGN does a round off on both negative and positive numbers.
SIN (expr)	700 PRINT SIN(X) 710 X=SIN(3.14159/X) 720 IF SIN(X)=.707 THEN PRINT "45 DEG"	Returns the trigonometric sine of the expression expr, where expr is in radians and result is between 1 and −1. (NF)
SPACE$ (expr)	100 PRINT SPACE$(80) 110 A$=SPACE$(I) 120 A$=X$+SPACE$(F)	Returns a string of spaces of a length specified by expression expr. (NF)
SQR (expr)	300 Z=SQR(X^2+Y^2) 310 IF SQR(X)<8 THEN 300	Returns the square root of expression expr. Expr may not be negative. (NF)
STOP	100 STOP	Stops program execution, prints BREAK IN LINE nnnnn (nnnnn=line number where system stopped), and returns to the command level. In Ex 100 systems prints BREAK IN LINE 100. (S)
STR$ (expr)	500 A$=STR$(4.45) 500 PRINT STR$(X)+A$ 520 IF STR$(I)<>"4" THEN PRINT "NO"	Returns the string representation of the expression expr. (SF)
SWAP var1,var2	100 SWAP A,B 110 SWAP A$,B$ 120 SWAP A(I),B(I)	The value of the second variable var2 is assigned to the first variable var1 and vice-versa. Both variables must be of the same type or a TYPE MISMATCH error will result. (S)
SYSTEM	SYSTEM	Enter the operating system mode (sometimes called the monitor mode), and exit from BASIC.
	T	
TAB (expr)	700 PRINT TAB(20) 710 PRINT TAB(I);A$; TAB(I+10);B$ 720 PRINT TAB(ABS(X))	Spaces to the horizontal position specified by the value of expression expr. 0<=expr<=255. Rightmost position is 0 and leftmost position is usually 71. (NF)
TAN (expr)	400 PRINT TAN(3.14159) 410 X=TAN(R*8) 420 IF TAN(Y)<1 THEN 200	Returns the tangent of the expression expr, where expr is in radians. (NF)
TROFF	TROFF	Turns off the trace flag. The trace flag is turned on by TRON. NEW also

Name	Example	Description
		turns off the trace flag. Also called NOTRACE in some BASICs.
TRON	TRON	Turns on the trace flag. Prints number of each line in square brackets as it is executed. Used for debugging a program. Also called TRACE in some BASICs.

U

Name	Example	Description
USR (expr)	100 USR(2048) 110 USR(X*100) 120 USR(ABS(X))	Calls the machine language subroutine program. Expr is argument for passing values to subroutine. Address is specified by USR LOC. (S)
USRLOC		A special location in memory that contains the starting address of the users machine language program which will be called with USR. USRLOC is a two byte location allowing storage of a 16 bit address. Only used with Microsoft 8080 BASICs.

V

Name	Example	Description
VAL (str$)	200 PRINT VAL("1.3") 210 A=VAL(X$) 220 IF VAL(X$)="YES" THEN PRINT "YES"	Returns the numerical value of the string str$. If the first character of str$ is not $+$, $-$, &, or a digit, then VAL(str$)=0. (SF)
VARPTR (var)	100 PRINT VARPTR(X) 110 X=VARPTR(Y)	Returns the memory address of the variable var given as the argument. The main use of the VARPTR function is to obtain the address of a variable or array so it may be passed to an assembly language subroutine. Arrays are usually passed by specifying VARPTR(A(0)) so that the lowest address element of the array is passed. (NF)
VTAB(expr)	100 VTAB(5)	Causes vertical TAB to line given by expression expr. (S)

W

Name	Example	Description
WAIT (expr1, expr2,expr3)	100 WAIT I,J,K 110 WAIT 111,J 120 WAIT INT(X),255,1	Status of port specified by expression expr1 is ANDed with expr2 and XOR'd with expr3. Program stops and awaits a nonzero result. expr1, expr2, and expr3 are all greater than or equal to zero and less than or equal to 255. (S)
WIDTH var	WIDTH 80 WIDTH 32	Sets the width in characters of the printing terminal line. The variable var must be an integer expression in the range of 15 to 255. (C)

Name	Example	Description
	X	
XOR (expr1 XOR expr2)	100 C=A XOR B 110 IF Z XOR 32 <=0 THEN 200	The exclusive OR operator. If either expr1 and expr2 are true OR expr1 and expr2 are false then the statement is false. If expr1 or expr2 are different the statement is true. (LO)

VARIABLE TYPE DECLARATION CHARACTERS

Character	Example	Typical Values	Definition
$	A$, Z1$	"JOHN Q. DOE" "1 + 2 = ?"	String variable type may contain up to 255 characters.
%	A1%, SUM%	−14, 133, 2001, 1	Integer variable type (whole numbers greater than −32767 and less than +32767).
!	A!, AA!	1, −50, .123, .123456	Single-precision variable type (6 significant figures)
#	A#, ZZ#	−300.12345678, 3.141592653589 1.000000000000001	Double precision variable (14 to 16 significant digits).
D	A#=1.2345 678901 D+12	1.2345678901 X 10 12	Double-precision variable type with scientific notation. For entering constants or during output of large or small numbers.

APPENDIX F

BASIC Graphic Statements

The following statements and functions are presented here as a sampling of what is available in BASIC graphics. The TRS-80 graphic statements are rather elementary, but offer control over a fairly dense 128 × 48 grid. The Apple II graphic statements are quite flexible and allow control over a 40 × 40 color display grid.

GRAPHIC STATEMENTS AND FUNCTIONS: TRS-80 LEVEL II BASIC

Statement	Example	Definition
CLS	100 CLS	Clear-Screen—Turns off all the graphics blocks on the display and moves the cursor to the upper left corner. This wipes out alphanumeric characters as well as graphics blocks.
POINT (expr1, expr2)	100 X=POINT (X,Y) 110 IF POINT (50,28) THEN PRINT "ON" ELSE PRINT "OFF"	Tests whether the specified graphics block is "on" or "off." If the block is "on" (that is if it has been SET), then POINT returns a binary True (−1). If the block is "off," POINT returns a binary False (0). Typically, the POINT test is put inside an IF... THEN statement. (GF)
RESET (expr1, expr2)	200 RESET (X,3)	Turns off a graphics block at the X location specified by expression expr1 and the Y location specified by expr2. This function has the same limits and parameters as SET. (GF)
SET (expr1, expr2)	100 SET (64,24)	Turns on the graphics block at the location specified by the coordinates expr1 (X) and expr2 (Y). For graphics purposes, the display is divided up into a 128 (horizontal) by 48 (vertical)

231

Statement	Example	Definition
		grid. The X-coordinates are numbered from left to right, 0 to 27. The Y-coordinates are numbered from top to bottom, 0 to 47. Therefore the point at (0,0) is the extreme upper left of the display, while the point at (127,47) is in the extreme lower right corner. The arguments expr1 and expr2 need not be integer expressions because SET(X<Y) uses the integer portion of X and Y. SET (X,Y) is valid for: 0<=X<=128 0<=Y<=48

GRAPHIC STATEMENTS AND FUNCTIONS: APPLE II

Statement	Example	Definition
COLOR=expr	30 COLOR=12 25 ORANGE=3: COLOR=ORANGE	In standard resolution color (GR) graphics mode, this command sets screen tv color to value in expression expr in the range 0 to 15 where each value represents a specific color. Actually expr may be in the range 0 to 255 without error message since it is implemented as if it were expression expr MOD 16. (S)
GR	GR 100 GR:CALL-936	Sets mixed color graphics mode. Clears screen to black. Resets scrolling window. Displays 40×40 squares in 15 colors on top of screen and 4 lines of text at bottom. (C)
HLIN expr1, expr2 AT expr3	200 HLIN 0,39 AT 20 210 HLIN Z,Z+6 AT I	In standard resolution color graphics, this statement draws a horizontal line of a predefined color (set by COLOR=) starting at horizontal position defined by expression expr1 and ending at position expr2 at vertical position defined by expression expr3. Expr1 and expr2 must be in the range of 0 to 39 and expr1<=expr2. Expr3 must be in the range 0 to 39 (or 0 to 47 if not in mixed mode). (S)
PLOT expr1, expr2	400 PLOT 15,25 410 PLOT XV,YV 420 PLOT X MOD 2,K*8	In standard resolution color graphics, this statement plots a small square of a predefined color (set by COLOR=) at horizontal location specified by expression expr1 in range 0 to 39 and vertical location specified by expression expr2 in range 0 to 39 (or 0 to

Statement	Example	Definition
		47 if in all graphics mode). NOTE: PLOT 0,0 is upper left and PLOT 39,39 (or PLOT 39,47) is lower right corner. (S)
SCRN (expr1, expr2)	330 PRINT SCRN(X1,Y1)	Gives color (number between 0 and 15) of screen at horizontal location designated by expression expr1 and vertical location designated by expression expr2. Range of expression expr1 is 0 to 39. Range of expression expr2 is 0 to 39 if in standard mixed color graphics display mode as set by GR command or 0 to 47 if in all color mode set by POKE -16304,0: POKE -16302,0. (GF)
TEXT	TEXT 200 TEXT: CALL -936	Sets all text mode. Resets scrolling window to 24 lines by 40 characters. Example 200 also clears screen and homes cursor to upper left corner. TEXT may be used as a command or a statement. (C,S)
VLIN (expr1, expr2 AT expr3	590 VLIN 0,39 AT 15 600 VLIN Z,Z+6 AT Y	Similar to HLIN except draws vertical line starting at expr1 and ending at expr2 at horizontal position expr3. (S)

Index

ABS, absolute value function, 82
ADC, 168
Amortization loan formula, 53
AND, OR, and NOT, 139-143
ANSI, 10
APL, 9
Applications, BASIC, 11-17
  business, 11-12
  educational, 14-16
  entertainment, 12-14
  scientific, 16-17
Arrays and subscripted variables, 103-106
ASC and CHR$, 150-152
ASCII, 150
AUTO, 180

Base e, 146
BASIC
  applications, 11-17
    business, 11-12
    educational, 14-16
    entertainment, 12-14
    scientific, 16-17
  command aids, 179-187
  dialects, 10-11
  figuring in, 35-36
  no-nos's, 51-52
  program on cassette tape, 179
  what it is, 9-11
Bit coding, 140-141
Boolean logic functions, 139
Boxes, variable, 37-41
Byte, 159

CALL or USR, 169-172
CLEAR, 180-181
COBOL, 9
Color graphics, 15
Combining functions, 85-86
Command aids, BASIC, 179-187
Commands, debug, 183-184
Commas, print with, 29-34
Concatenation, 43
CONT, 181
Conditional branches, 64-66
Controlling the external world with PEEK and POKE, 162-164
Crt, 18

CSAVE and CLOAD, 175-179
Customer billing, 12

DAC, 168
Data and read statements, 131-135
Debug commands, 183-184
Debugging, 24
DELETE, 181-182
Decision making statements, 61-72
Dialects, BASIC, 10-11
Dimension with DIM, 106-107
Direct mode, 34-35
Documenting your programs, 58-59
DSP, 185-187

EDIT, 182
Endless loop, 68-69
Enhanced metric conversion program, 135-138
Enhancing the Loan program, 71-76
Error-checking subroutine, 97-101
Expanding a program, 56-57
EXP and LOG, 146-147
Exponentiation, 36-37

Figuring in BASIC, 35-36
Finishing the program, 126-129
  check for a tie, 116-117
  check for a winner, 117-118
  computer move algorithm, 121-125
  displaying the board, 113-114
  input players move, 118-121
  overall flow of the game, 112-113
  representing the board, 111
  representing the men, 112
Flowchart, 112
FOCAL, 9
Formula, amortization loan, 53
FOR...NEXT, the programmed loop, 62-64
FORTRAN, 9
Function(s)
  Boolean logic, 139
  MOD, 149
  numeric, 138-149
  SGN, 148-149
  SQR, 147-148
  statements, simple, 81-87
  string, 150-157

Game BASIC: TIC-TAC-TOE, 110-126
   remember the rules, 111
Games, 12-13
General ledger, 11-12
Getting started, 17-20
GOTO unconditional branch, 67-68
Graphics, 162

Hardware interface, 16

IF...THEN, conditional branches, 64-66
Indexed branching, 69-71
Infinite loop, 185
INP and out, 167-169
Input, 44-48
INT, integerize function, 82
Inventory control, 12
I/O ports, 167

LEFT$, MID$ and RIGHT$, 152-155
LEN function, 156-157
Linear equation, 188
Line numbers, 21-24
   run, 24-25
LISP, 9
List, 23
Little variable boxes, 37-41
Loan program, 52-56
   enhancing, 71-76

Mailing label preparation, 12
Manipulating screen data with PEEK and POKE, 164-166
Metric conversion program and the menu concept, 76-81
   enhanced, 135-138
Mode, direct, 34-35
MOD function, 149
Modulus, 149

Names, variable, 41-42
NEW or SCRATCH, 179
Numbers, 27-29
Numeric
   functions, 138-149
   round-off subroutine, 91-97

OK, 19
ON...GOSUB, indexed subroutine branching, 90-91
ON...GOTO, indexed branching, 69-71
Order processing, 12

PEEK and POKE, 159-169
   controlling the external world with, 162-164
   manipulating screen data with, 164-166
   setting controls and options with, 166-167

PILOT, 9
PL/M, 9
Print
   statement, 21
   with commas, 29-34
Program(s)
   documenting, 58-59
   expanding, 56-57
   loan, 52-56
Programmed loop, 62-64
Pythagorean theorem, 147

Real time applications, 16
REM, 58-59
RENUM or REN, 182-183
Reserved words, 51-52
Reverse video, 166
RND, randomize function, 84
RPG, 9
Run line number, 24-25

Semicolons, 33, 34
Setting controls and options with PEEK and POKE, 166-167
SGN function, 148-149
Simple function statements, 81-87
SIN, COS, and ATN, 143-146
SNOBOL, 9
Sound effects, 14
SQR function, 147-148
Statements, data and read, 131-135
   decision making, 61-72
   print, 21
Stop and end, 25-27
String, 21
String functions, 150-157
String variables, 42-44
STR$ and VAL, 155-156
Subroutine
   concept, 87-91
   error-checking, 97-101
   numeric round-off, 91-97
Syntax error, 19, 20

TAB, 48-50
   video plotting with, 187-191
TRACE and NOTRACE (TRON and TROFF), 184-185
Truth table, 139
Trig functions, 190

Unconditional branch, 67-68

Var, 49
Variable names, 41-42
Variables, string, 42-44
Video plotting with TAB, 187-191

What CALL can do, 172-175
What is BASIC, 9-11
What is your SIN, 190-191

Your first program, 20